Yorkshire Bred

The entire content of this book is copyright

"All Rights Reserved (c) 2018 John Hall"

ISBN 978-0-244-36993-4

The Author

60 years on

YORKSHIRE BRED

Foreword

Memory is a wonderful gift that sadly left my father in his final years and if I'd had the forethought to ask more of his life I would have been all the richer in knowledge of it. Nostalgic thoughts of childhood and teenage years are precious and as the years go by they become even more so.

As we age our outlook on life changes. Throughout our carefree youth and following busy adult years, working, producing, and rearing future generations, our focus is on just that, the here and now. We don't think that our parents are watching and enjoying for the second time what we are seeing as a whole new life experience. I would have loved my mother to have seen more of life and to have asked more of hers but she lost her fight for life 35 years ago at a time when I was thinking only of the here and now.

Now that my youth and working years are done and the whole new life experience of retirement is unfolding before me I have time to reflect. A few years ago I enjoyed writing the memoirs of my early working life in "Bricks and Mortar" and now I have taken to writing some of the precious memories of my youth.

I hope that my jottings of a time in my formative years might also awaken your own memories of a similar era in your own life and if so then that is my gift to you. A time without responsibility or care. When life was all before us, and tomorrow was a world away. We lived for the here and now; days were long, weeks longer, a year a lifetime. Now we wish we were younger, but still able to retain all we have learnt and experienced!! When asked our age we would reply, nearly 8 or nearly 9, always wanting to be older than we actually were. Now as the years race by, we cringe as another birthday passes.

I started out to write about my early years and the many adventures it contains, and of my life at Wallingfield, my family home. What follows is just that but so much more too as along the way I have discovered and realised that life existed before my time in much the same way as it does now with people's dreams and aspirations just the same. People's lives that led to Wallingfield being built, lived in, and enjoyed. To an outsider Wallingfield was little more than bricks and mortar where someone lived but to me and those who have lived there it was so much more, it was part of our lives and of who we are. My extensive research around Wallingfield has taken me in many directions which I hope you will enjoy reading about. Wallingfield had its own life, of how it came about with the people places and events that made it happen. Before I started writing this book my life at Wallingfield was my own and Wallingfield was mine. In my mind that does not change but now I know that Wallingfield has touched many lives over the years and as a result has enriched them all.

I have been a free spirit, a maverick, and a leader of men (and some women) throughout my working life which has given me a unique understanding of the ways of business and how Skinner, Holford, Jennings, Bramley, Yarbrough and others applied their lives. Who are these people I hear you ask? Carry on reading and all will be revealed.

This book is a glimpse into a time and place in my life where I grew up.

I am a 1950's Baby Boomer, born in a time before computers, smart phones, Facebook, and instant News. What follows is a visit to Wales Bar, the village where I was bred though it could be any village, anywhere. It is my recollection of people and places who shaped the area before I arrived and others who continued to do so in my time there, some who are now resigned to history and others not quite yet. A time when the world was changing from the war years of the 40's to the 50's and 60's and a brave, new, and above all free world with challenges to be met. Life was fun growing up, we entertained ourselves, we walked, we explored and got up to all sorts of tricks, scrapes, and adventures that today are frowned upon or considered dangerous, but we survived. What follows is a glimpse into a time and place that will never change for me. Memories are such a powerful and wonderful gift to possess and in a world now dominated by computer technology human memory still remains unsurpassed.

My World

In my world, we walked to school as that was the rule
We hated Sundays and even more so Mondays
We played cards, board games, did puzzles too, and most of us had an outside loo!
We talked to each other face to face and our lives they led a steady pace
Backchat to parents was strictly taboo and if you dared, then woo betide you
Discipline was served by way of a smack which certainly put you back on track
We got clipped round the ear if we were bad, now take that young fellow me lad
Mum gave us teaspoons of cod liver oil, or medicine or malt that tasted like soil
It will do you good was the standard reply so don't even bother to ask me why

Cuts and bruises were common place with lots on our knees and sometimes our face

A cut had to heel without a plaster, let the air too it mum said, it'll heal so much faster

As a special treat we could answer the phone, its grandma and granddad, we might have known

Sweets were a treat, not part of lunch, that's why we were all a really fit bunch

Our parents were thrifty when we were reared; our clothes were darned when holes appeared

Our shoes had insoles from a cornflake packet and the seg's underneath made a right good racket

We had a coal fire in the living room, which took away thoughts of winter gloom

Quick, shut the door, keep the heat in, to leave it ajar was a cardinal sin

Another blanket and coat for my bed please and that thick pair of socks that pull up past my knees

Our breath would freeze in the cold bedroom air, as we huddled in bed in our warm comfy lair

In summer we climbed trees, and were chased by the bees

We played out till dark; it was such a lark

We played games in the street and not a car did we meet

While the old ones would watch us, sat on their bench seat

Reminiscing no doubt of when they were lads, and thinking of good times that they too had had

We had hayp'nys, thrupp'ny bits, tanners and bobs, which we earned from an errand or other odd job

We ate bony fish for Friday school dinners, and in 66 were the world cup winners.

We remember when President Kennedy was shot and we created pictures with dot to dot

A TV programme not to miss was to watch Blue Peter with Val and Chris
Star Trek, Batman, programmes galore, Mr Ed, Bonanza and so many more
All viewed on TV in Black and white, no colour back then but that was all right
Encyclopaedia Britannica if you read it well, would give you the answer for the homework from hell
The teacher when marking gave a tick and a star and her note underneath said, you'll go far
A penny for the guy Mister, no, honest he's not real, go on poke him, have a feel
Christmas carolling from door to door, we walked and walked till our feet were sore
Pressing button A to start a call and then button B when you'd said it all
Or tap the phone if you were skint, that little trick saved us a mint
Lead painted toys for a girl or a boy, toys that gave us so much joy
Fish and chips eaten in the street, wrapped in newspaper, what a treat
Or perhaps just chips and batter bits they all tasted great I must admit
With salt and vinegar and a pickled egg and none of it costing an arm or a leg
No seat belts, No air bags in our old Ford, but that never stopped us from climbing aboard
A ride in the car was a special treat, I baggsy the front seat, cool, that's neat.
We had catapults, penknives, arrows and a bow, how we didn't get hurt, I'll never know

We didn't have allergies and were either clever or thick, we had a school bully whose name was Mick.

We had a school bobby if you were truant from school, and six of the best was a very cruel rule

I remember my school motto was "One and All" but school days were far from being a ball

Hippies, loon pants, flowers in our hair, life was great and we gave not a care

Rockers and Mod's were poles apart, Rockers wore leathers and the Mod's they dressed smart

Rockers rode motorbikes with Mod's on their Scooters, but now everyone prefers to surf their computers

Green Shield stamps were everywhere; we stuck them in books with the greatest of care

When the books were full we would trade them in, for a toaster a kettle or a peddle bin

A Cortina or Mini were our cars of choice, but in our dreams it was a Rolls Royce

We came of age as the 70's arrived, the 60's gone from which we survived

From babes in arms to days at school and then all too soon work was the rule

A whole new decade as yet untouched, but would we like it just as much?

Girlfriends, boyfriends perhaps weddings too, our lives were changing as we grew

Boy meets girl and church bells ring, a new life together, what will it bring

We saved from our wages for the bottom drawer, and filled it with tea towels, bedding and more

A place to live was what we then sought, to fill it with all the things we had bought

To start a new life of adulthood, the future looked bright, the future looked good

In the 70's a must have was a hostess trolley, lets invite some friends round it'll be all so jolly

The trolley we bought with our green shield stamps and another full book bought two table lamps

The Bernie Inn was a good place to eat, when a big juicy steak was a real treat

Prawn cocktail for starters, oh yes please and after the main course we'll have some cheese

Black Forrest Gateau then followed the cheese and we ate every bit though it was a tight squeeze.

These times have now passed but will never be gone as they live in our memory, every last one

We had so much fun and perhaps a few tears but now I know they were the best years

To be seen and not heard I was always told, but that's not so now that I am old.

So here is my story of life as a child, which was sometimes crazy and sometimes wild

I sit back now and watch the youth of today, as they enjoy their work, their rest and their play

I hope you enjoy your lives of today, as us oldies have done in our own special way

When you have read through my book I am sure you will see why my memories are all so precious to me.

To Pamela, our children, grandchildren and those still to come.

YORKSHIRE BRED

Around my Village

I arrived at Wallingfield, Wales Bar in the summer of 1954 as a babe in arms of just 6 months. I confess that I am not Yorkshire born but a Nottinghamshire lad born in Mansfield of a Somerset mum and a Derbyshire dad though I can surely claim that I am YORKSHIRE BRED having spent all my formative years and through to adulthood living in Yorkshire.

People and places change very slowly and this process is often forgotten, or never even seen, or realised, but when reviewed over a period of time it can be significant and in the context of geographical and human evolution, it is permanent. Yet, when a memorable person or place is seen or viewed for the first time it sets an everlasting and permanent memory in the eye of the beholder and only later does it prompt thoughts of remembering how it was at that first memory and how the passing years have made a difference to people and places, be it for better or for worse. What follows is my recollection of growing up in a Yorkshire village, of people and places that were in and around at a very special time in my life. I hope you enjoy meeting these people and visiting the places which were the framework from which formed and surrounded so many unforgettable adventures and experiences in my growing years.

My first view of Wales Bar in the West Riding of Yorkshire (now South Yorkshire) was over 60 years ago and the pictures in my mind of that time were of a village that had always looked that way, of course the same thoughts have rested in the minds of those before me and those to follow but for me my recollections are those which have occurred in my time and I believe are the most significant in the modern history of Wales Bar, perhaps only eclipsed when Wales Bar became a red brick village that evolved from a quiet agricultural rural idle in the latter part of the 19th and early part of the 20th century as a result of the "gold rush" that was coal mining.

The Kiveton Park and Wales History Society have an excellent website which documents the evolution of the area from the doomsday book to date with masses of information, photos and personal accounts of life in and around the parish and I wish to express my sincere thanks for their permission to use some photos from their website.

I have many photos of my time during this fascinating history but more importantly to me is my photographic memory which I hope serves me well as I recount life, people, places and the changes that have occurred through my vision of Wales Bar and places close by, both then, now and the time in between.

Wales Bar in 1954 was a red brick slate roofed village which stood alone, other than the houses that linked it along the left of School Road where Wales Bar hill ascended to its peak to reveal the village of Wales with the Methodist Chapel and Wales Primary School in the distance and giving its name to the road that continued on to Wales Square and beyond.

I am led to believe that Wales Bar developed its name from the toll bar that existed centuries ago at the junction of Mansfield road, School road and Delves Lane where a toll bar and keepers cottage stood on the junction diagonally opposite the site of the Waleswood hotel (now a Chinese restaurant) but I stand corrected if my understanding is wrong.

Obviously my memories from 1954 are rather vague and only really came into focus in the following 4 or 5 years but I am reliably informed that during the time of my evolving memory towards the turn of the decade into the swinging sixties that there was little change to the infrastructure of the village.

My memories of Wales Bar circa late 1950's start from the railway bridge passing over Mansfield Road at Waleswood.

I was always told that this bridge was too low for Sheffield Corporations standard double decker buses to pass under, meaning that they had to use a small fleet of reduced height buses specifically for our no.6 and no.19 route. I often made a point of studying this alleged fact when seeing our 6 and 19 buses alongside others when waiting to board at platform D in Ponds street bus station. This study convinced me that this was in fact true.

(I do recall in later years when the branch line to Brookhouse was removed and as a consequence reduced the railway lines passing over the bridge from 4 to 2, thus allowing the width of the bridge to be reduced resulting in making the headroom higher which I am sure was a great relief for the Sheffield Corporation bus company)

This brings to mind the difference between the no.6 and no.19 routes and how catching the wrong bus could spell disaster and why? The journey from Wales Bar to Sheffield could easily take the best part of an hour on a busy day, especially if the bus stopped at every request and *fare stage* along the route.

Catching a no.19 added at least a further 10 minutes to the journey as, when the bus reached Woodhouse Mill it turned left and trundled its way through Woodhouse and Intake and entered Sheffield via City road instead of the more direct route taken by the no. 6 through Darnell and Attercliffe.

This was ok if you had time on your hands and your final destination was Sheffield's Ponds Street bus station but it was catastrophic if your destination was somewhere in between and you had simply caught the first bus that came along rather than stand in the cold and wet but had failed to notice if it was a 6 or 19!

*A fare stage was a strange phenomenon. Its purpose was to signify the change in cost of a ticket to a greater or lesser amount depending on how many fare stages there were between boarding and alighting the bus. Furthermore it was obligatory for a bus to stop at a fare stage even if there was no one waiting whereas a request stop was just that, you had to request the bus to stop by thrusting your arm out at a right angles to your body which "requested" the bus driver to stop. The only time when this body signal failed was if the bus was full (usually at peak travelling times) and the bus would speed straight past with both upper and lower deck seats fully occupied together with 10 or more passengers stood in the downstairs aisle.

We were fortunate in many ways living at Wallingfield as we had 2 request stops just outside our entrance gate. One on our side of Mansfield road if journeys end was Wales, Kiveton or beyond to Anston and Dinnington and one on the opposite side of the road if the metropolis of Sheffield or its suburbs were our destination.

For the journey to Sheffield Ponds Street the fare was 1/10d (1 shilling and 10 pennies/approx. 9.5 new pence) and the journey the opposite way to Wales or Kiveton was 4d (approx 2 new pence).

The ticket price to Sheffield was not negotiable however, from Wallingfield we had a vantage point of Mansfield Road some 2 miles distant as it passed by Aston Common from where we could see the bus appear on its outward journey from Sheffield before it's decent to the railway bridge at Waleswood. The time and distance required for the bus to arrive and pass by

Wallingfield following a sighting was our signal to walk briskly to Wales Bar corner. Why? Because the bus stop at Wales Bar corner was no ordinary request stop, it was a fare stage which had the effect of reducing our fare to Wales or Kiveton from 4d to 3d. Result!

*Note that prior to February 15, 1971 ("Decimal day," or "D-day"), monetary amounts in the U.K. were expressed as **pounds** (£), shillings (s.) and pence (d.), where £1 = 20s. = 240d. After **1970**, there were 100 pennies in a **pound**, so one (new) penny = 2.4 old pence.*

Anyway, back to the railway bridge.

Emerging from beneath the bridge and to the right were the old pithead baths that had served Waleswood Colliery in its later years until the colliery closure in 1948. The pithead baths now served as a thriving workshop and repairs depot from which the repair and maintenance was masterminded for the housing stock of Wales bar and Kiveton that, almost without exception was in the ownership of the National Coal Board established in 1947 following the nationalisation of the mining industry.

Immediately beyond the pithead baths and running between this building and the adjacent sports field (which I will come too shortly) was a lane running away from the road and into the valley beyond.

This lane led to Waleswood Farm which was tenanted by Mr and Mrs Charlie Coulson and ably assisted by their son Roy. This farm and all the activities on it together with the surrounding land and farms became one of my favourite haunts and to which I shall return later.

Wales wood Colliery was to the left and whilst looking the same as it had prior to its closure in 1948 it now acted as a pumping station to the nearby Kiveton Colliery. There was still plenty going on around the colliery site however with a coking plant still working and providing employment, in part, for those miners no longer needed at the colliery but this too was destined to close in 1956 which prompted the demise of the next landmark on the journey towards Wales Bar.

To the right and just beyond the colliery entrance stretching into the distance was Pigeon Row.

Pigeon Row was , as its name suggested a long row of 48 terraced, 2 up 2 down houses which in its heyday had provided accommodation for the miners of Waleswood Colliery and there is no doubt in my mind that every man and boy eligible for work would have done so at the colliery.

Away to the rear of Pigeon Row and beyond the colliery and running alongside the railway was a small stream that meandered gently along a wooded valley called Rookery Bottom, a small bridge passed over the stream on Mansfield road to the north west of the railway bridge which was called Pigeon Bridge. This bridge gave its name to this residential hotspot of Waleswood that was Pigeon Row.

Pigeon Row in the early 1900's

I recall that somewhere towards the middle of Pigeon Row was a shop which looked barely different from all the houses other than having an enamel sign projecting from the red brickwork advertising Hovis Bread and other staple dietary needs. The shop was entered via the front door where you would then pass through the front parlour and beneath the stairs to enter the rear room where a long counter and shelving stretched out ahead. These were not massively stocked shelves but there were always sweets on display which was the sole reason for me and my siblings to visit.

Facing Pigeon Row and to the right side of Mansfield road was Waleswood sports ground. The sports ground had it all. Alongside and running parallel to the road was the football pitch with changing rooms on a high banking to the Southern end of the pitch. The changing rooms (or room) were clad with corrugated iron sheeting and consisted of a bench running the entire length of the interior, there was no home and away segregation! To the rear was a 3 sided enclosure, presumably the urinal?

Beyond the football pitch was the cricket field with the cricket pavilion commanding the perfect view of proceedings on the field of play.

The pavilion was typical of its type but no less grand for that. A front covered terrace sporting benches for the players to sit expectantly waiting for their turn to bat and behind them a centrally positioned door leading to a large room used for everything that happened off the field of play. Beyond the large room was a storeroom to the left and an internal toilet to the right. These palatial facilities certainly put the football accommodation in the second division.

Even further back from the road and to the left of the pavilion was a bowling green which, in its heyday must have been a magnificent site. It was totally surrounded by a tall privet hedges and the bowling green had a dwarf wall around its perimeter with the ground beyond gently rising to the surrounding privets which not only provided protection from the elements but also created the impression of an arena of which the crown green was the centre piece. By this time the Bowling Green had already become overgrown through lack of use but I have no doubt that beneath the long grass there still lurked a perfectly shaped crown green.

To the right and rear of the pavilion was a large area of perfectly flat grass which although now equally overgrown had the size and shape that must have been perhaps tennis courts.

To the front of this area were the remains of a structure that were most certainly the cricket practice nets.

Travelling on towards Wales Bar there were mainly fields to the left and right of Mansfield road save for a few allotment gardens and 4 landmarks that I can recall quite vividly.

Past Pigeon row and on the same side of the road had been allotments where the residents of Pigeon row had grown their own in a bid to be self sufficient as far as their leisure time would allow. No wonder we were always told to "eat yer greens" as they were our staple diet. To the rear of the allotments was an area of wetland which often became flooded after heavy rain but obviously ensured that the earth beneath the allotments was rich and fertile. Overlooking this wetland and at right angles to the road was a brick built mission hall or Chapel. This chapel had long since seen its last service of worship and I recall that the wooden floor that had been the assembly hall was already worse for wear as the holes in the roof above had allowed the weather to slowly but surely destroy the structure. The pilfering of various building materials from the structure, which had no doubt been reused in nearby allotments, had also contributed to the buildings demise.

To the side of the fast deteriorating chapel was a lane giving access to the fields beyond which were farmed by the Coulsons. These fields stretched out into the distance and from this point you could walk unhindered to Wales meeting up with the bottom of Manor road and the splendid buildings of Wales Court.

(For more on Wales Court read chapter 2 'The Routine of Work' in my first book "Bricks and Mortar")

I must recall at this point an incident that allegedly took place circa late 1960's on a cold and dark winters evening along the lane that passed by the crumbling mission hall.

It was a daily evening pilgrimage for my father to walk the fields with our family pet who at that time was a beautiful yellow Labrador called Mandy. Come rain or shine and following my father's strict regime of home by 5.30pm, tea on the table and finished by 6 (now generally referred to as evening meal) followed by 30 minutes with his beloved Manchester Guardian after which he would put on his coat and beret, much to the delight of the patiently waiting Mandy, and head for the back door. Mandy's lead hung by the kitchen door along with my father's walking stick, with both of these items being of equal important to both master and his dog. Mandy knew that her lead meant a walk and the walking stick too as a walk was the only time that the stick ever left its resting place.

My father didn't need a walking stick for himself or for any other reason; it was simply his weapon of choice! Within minutes of starting his walk he would burst into song, not tuneful song or indeed anything that actually resembled a song or tune. What burst forth were " la la,s de dee's and arrhh arh's" in no particular order but at very high volume whilst at the same time lashing the walking stick from side to side, up and down and round and round like a frenzied conductor reaching the climax of Tchaikovsky's 1812 overture. Anything that stood before him was in danger of total destruction, be it an innocent clump of grass, an overhanging branch or even an insect in mid flight. Nothing was safe save for Mandy who had seen this ritual so many times and knew to keep her distance.

The evening in question was cold, dark and wet and not one which anyone less than an avid dog walker would venture out in, but this was my dad and nothing and no one stood in the way of his daily ritual. His evening walk could be an hour or more in the summer months which gradually shortened as the nights drew in. It was now mid winter and 'walkies' time was nearer to 30 minutes.

This night he left by 6.30pm and was still out by well past 7. It was always easy to estimate the time of his return as his 'singing' would get louder and louder as he approached home but tonight the first sound we heard was the kitchen door opening as both Mandy and master made their entrance.

The master's face was white and he looked shaken.

What on earth has happened to you we asked and why have you been so long?

It took several minutes for my father to compose himself and then he began to tell of his experience by the chapel.

It seems that he had been making his way along the lane from the open fields towards the chapel and Mansfield Road when he had heard, then felt, an exceptionally cold rush of wind spiralling along the lane and coming directly at him. Leaves and branches were carried by the rush which had forced both man and dog to take cover in the ditch that ran alongside the lane.

Then, just as he thought that this strange happening was over, in the distance, and this time coming from the direction of the Mansfield Road and the chapel were the distinct sound of horses, galloping horses, and metal on stone like a speeding cartwheel over cobbles.

By this time he had scrambled out of the ditch and was stood on the lane but as this new cacophony of sound approached him he knew that if he didn't take cover once again that he would be run down by the fast approaching coach and horses.

We all stood listening intently to our father's resume of events and then laughed.

Our father was not a big story teller, indeed he was a man of very few words and the fact that, on regaining our composure following fits of laughter that he simply stood there with ashen face and a distinctly ill at ease look did make us think.

Perhaps something strange really did happen that night?

Without doubt the most outstanding and dominating landmark when looking out over the fields beyond the Mission Hall was the pit tip. A red shale, conical shaped towering pile of waste material created from the many years of mining at Waleswood Colliery and work at the coking plant. A special railway track ran up the side of the pit tip, where, in the past small dump trucks had been ferried from the coking plant to the top of the towering tip via a system of wires and pulleys to deposit their load of spoil, cascading down all sides of the tip thus forming its iconic shape.

I recall that on some days there would be a column of smoke rising from the summit like a volcano ready to blow and as we grew older and dared to climb the tip you could feel the heat of the ground beneath your feet.

On the opposite side of the lane to the chapel was a smaller brick building that housed a number of pipes, tubes and valves which formed some sort of gas substation, or at least that is what it smelt like and judging from the "keep out" notices and high barbed wire fences that surrounded it then it was most certainly intended as no go area. Of course for young explorers such notices and fences are always a clear enticement to see what is beyond them; hence I know what was inside the building! The large fenced area to the rear of the gas station was a mystery and only after researching old cine camera footage was this mystery solved.

*This cine camera footage has provided me with invaluable information particularly to the history of Wallingfield which I have written about extensively later *

On the horizon is the mission room/chapel which hides the gas station building beyond. To the left is a gasometer that stood within the fenced area. To the right of the mission room/chapel is Mansfield Road ascending towards Wales Bar. In the foreground and looking like gun turrets are pipes spraying water over the steaming coke, heaped in great piles fresh from the coke ovens.

The landmarks of the chapel, pit tip and gas substation may have been uninspiring to some but are now long gone epitaphs to the history of the area save for the last of the 4 landmarks being perhaps less prolific but most definitely the most historic.

To the right of the roadside and equidistance from the chapel and houses that denoted the start of Wales Bar proper was a milestone. This milestone was quite a piece of architecture, standing about 3 feet tall with 2 faces to the front with each face inclined so to be seen when approaching from up or down Mansfield Road.

The inscriptions I can recall were Mansfield 20 miles, Clowne 5 and 3/4 miles and Rotherham 7 miles. Miraculously this milestone still stands in the same place to this day and what a story it could tell! Interestingly the inscription at the top of the stone says Rotherham and Pleasley Road, Wales, rather than Mansfield Road as it is known today. This milestone would have been erected sometime in the 1700 or early 1800's so is probably in the region of 250 years old so truly is a miracle that it still stands today.

Arriving at Wales Bar the houses start on each side of Mansfield road simultaneously.

To the left is Waleswood Villas, a row of large houses, the first is Wallingfield, a large detached house set well back from the road in its own grounds and following along the road towards "Bar Corner" are 3 further large semi detached houses. These houses are known as Waleswood Villas.

Waleswood villas were typical of houses of such size and grandeur built close to collieries where the owners and management of the establishments would live.

Immediately to the left of Wallingfield was an access lane leading to a kitchen garden belonging to Wallingfield, then to the fields beyond that were farmed by the Coulsons.

This lane also gave access to the rear of the 3 semi detached houses collectively forming Waleswood villas and in the field immediately to the rear of these houses was a large semi submerged concrete air raid shelter specifically for their use. Wallingfield had its own attached air raid shelter while the rest of the village probably had to make do with their own Anderson shelter or other DIY protection (read more later)

They were impressive houses built by Waleswood colliery owners Skinner and Holford with Wallingfield being by far the largest detached house set in its own grounds and built as the residence for the colliery manager, while the following six semi-detached villas were homes for the lower colliery management. These 7 villas stood in isolation from the other houses in the village which in itself clearly defined the hierarchy from management and downwards to the mass workforce who lived on the right of Mansfield road in terraced houses stretching into the distance as far as "Bar Corner", this was East Terrace, a row of terraced houses comprising of 5 blocks of 6 and 2 blocks of 4 houses. They were houses were for the rank and file who toiled daily below ground to mine the coal that was their bread and butter and their employer's fortune.

While I don't know the date that these terraces were built it is safe to say that they were built sometime later than Pigeon Row and though still not having modern sanitation as we know it today they certainly were far better equipped than their near neighbours in Pigeon Row as the outside toilet was now situated within the enclosed rear yard of each terraced house and much closer to the actual house. It was during the next decade of the 60's when government legislation decreed that all houses should have internal sanitary accommodation which sparked off a massive building programme by the National Coal Board to construct single storey attached accommodation to each of the East and South Terrace houses. This building programme transformed the terraces with a bathroom and toilet added on the space where the outside toilets had once occupied.

Beyond the last villa was an area of grassland that extended to the boundary walls of the Mansfield and district Cooperative Shop that stood on the crossroads of Wales Bar. This was a large shop typical of the cooperative society's dominance of all things retail at that time and had a captive audience of customers in Wales Bar as travel to shops further afield was unheard of and predominantly precluded due to the lack of transport. The vast majority of its customers were stay at home miner's wives who would shop maybe 2 or 3 times daily. It was a regular sight watching them "nip to shop" with purse clutched in one hand and a pre-school "nipper" being dragged along in the other. On entering the shop there was an enormous customer area which was flanked on 3 sides by long serving counters. The 4th side was the shop front which displayed various goods and provisions. The counter to the right was the hardware section; the middle counter for general groceries and fresh produce while the marble counter to the left was the butchery department.

The rear yard that serviced the co-op had numerous outbuildings within it, ranging from stables with accommodation above to garages and butchery come slaughter house.

This yard also afforded access to the rear entrance of the Waleswood Hotel and the landlord's accommodation above the licensed rooms.

The Waleswood Hotel was built integrally with the cooperative building as both stood as one large building which dominated the crossroads that was Wales Bar or " Bar Corner " as it was known locally.

The customer entrance to the Waleswood Hotel was on School road and typical of many public house entrances. It was not grand, consisting of a double door entrance which, if only one door was open meant that you had to enter sideways.

Passing through these doors didn't give immediate access to the licensed areas but to an inner entrance flanked with doors to the left and right and a serving hatch in the wall immediately opposite the double entrance doors.

The left door was the tap room entrance and the right door took you into the lounge or best room.

And the serving hatch? This was the off license, a license granted to the landlord to allow him to sell alcohol for consumption off the premises; this facility was often referred to as "the offie". A knock on the hatch door would attract the landlord's attention and purchases could be made to take out or take home.

In the taproom there was a rather grand set of stairs that led to the accommodation on the floors above as, it was a Hotel after all, though I would guess that circa 1955 to 1960 this was a less well used service along with the stable accommodation in the rear yard.

Waleswood hotel with the Co-op shop on the left although at the time this photo was taken it was pre Co-op shop and the hotel occupied the entire building.

Attached to the end of The Waleswood Hotel and extending along School Road were 6 Terraced houses. These terraces were 2 up 2 down with a very small yard to the rear that linked them all.. The only access to this yard was via a gate at the top end of the block so little privacy was afforded to the 6 families except perhaps for the innermost terrace, but that was considered to be quite normal living.

A rough stone road at the end of the 6 terraces led to two further rows of terraced houses to the rear. They were also 2 up 2 down and at the time of my description were already being gradually vacated as plans were afoot to demolish one of the rows. The second row, which was bigger and sat overlooking Mansfield Road was fully occupied at that time but soon to go the same way as its near neighbours with a continuing programme of re-housing and demolition. I remember walking past these terraces along a brick pathway that ran their entire length and seeing the occupants sat on their front steps and generally spending as much time outside the house as they did in, such was the size of the houses. The mind can play tricks but it truly resembled scenes from Dickensian times which were long gone even then. I distinctly remember the road sign that denoted the start of Wales being positioned just after the last 2 houses that I will describe as the accent up Wales Bar hill commenced. Each day while making my way to school I would run past this sign and take a giant leap in the hope of touching the horizontal sign high above me that read "Wales". Gradually I got nearer and nearer until eventually my fingertips made contact. I was in junior school by then!

To the right of the rough stone road was a bungalow. It was owned by Mr and Mrs Pashley. They seemed to be a secretive couple and this was compounded by the intense growth of buses and trees all around the bungalow which seemed to add mystery and secrecy to what lay within. Of course this was all in my mind and probably created by my vivid imagination, however I recall glancing old Mr Pashley in his garden on a number of occasions when passing to and from my journey to school.

He was best described a looking like Harold Steptoe Senior of Steptoe and son which was quite a scary site, and probably the reason for my vivid impression of him.

The house above the Pashley bungalow belonged to the Radford Family and the head of the family Des Radford was the local family butcher. The front room of the house was given over to the butchers shop and large walk in cool room. Mr Radford was a fine butcher and in addition to his shop he ran a van that was his mobile shop. Mrs Radford would attend to the shop when Mr Radford was doing his rounds, which seemed to most of the time.

I particularly recall that he was the current day equivalent of 'cash back ' as, on his rounds he would be paid in cash for his meat and when he delivered to us on a Friday my mother would hand over a cheque for our meat "plus some" and he would hand back the" plus some" in cash "which saved a trip to the bank and provided the cash required for the week.

Beyond Radford's Family Butchers was a field and then 4 bungalows, the last of these signified the summit of Wales Bar Hill with the view of Wales beyond. Only when turning back for the descent to the cross a road at Wales Bar was there the realisation of just how far you could see from this vantage point. On the horizon beyond was Norton and Gleadless in Sheffield, and not many years later 3 blocks of high rise flats were built at Gleadless which became a prominent landmark on the Sheffield skyline and clearly visible from the brow of this hill. On the right of the road and opposite the bungalows and butchers was a large hedge which denoted the boundary between the wide grass verge and the open fields beyond. Looking back it becomes clear that what had already started as a new housing development midway between the summit of Wales Bar hill and Wales Junior School beyond was to extend into what was locally called the New Tree Estate. This estate eventually took over the open fields to the right of Wales Bar hill and made a permanent urban connection between Wales Bar and Wales. The estate was so called as all the roads were named after trees. Perhaps the developers should have been a little more creative with the road names? (See page 15)
Arriving back at the crossroads and looking straight forward towards Norton and Gleadless was Delves Lane which stretched off into the distance, eventually arriving at Waleswood hamlet, or by turning sharp left some way along the lane it led to Pithouses Farm tenanted by the Brabb's family and on the right to Wraggs Farm tenanted by the Pinders family or, by continuing

even further the lane to Bedgreave Farm down in the valley by the River Rother.

Where East Terrace ended South Terrace began. South Terrace faced on to Delves lane and ran at right angles to East terrace. South Terrace was not as long, consisting of just 3 blocks of 6 houses and one block of 4. It was identical in design to East terrace but had the advantage of commanding a wonderful view looking out onto open fields to Norwood and Killamarsh in the distance with the only blot on the landscape being the Yorkshire Tar Distillery Company whose works were in the valley below. The fumes and smoke produced by the works could often be carried on a Southerly wind up the valley towards South Terrace which was quite unpleasant when that happened.

I am not quite sure if the Yorkshire Tar Distillery Company's county title was strictly correct as the works sat on both sides of the Norwood railway branch line and took up a considerable amount of land on both. On the Wales and Yorkshire side were large square ponds that from a distance looked to be full of dirty water but a closer inspection revealed that they were holding ponds of creosote. I know this for sure as a school friend's father worked as a tanker driver for the company and was a source of supply for creosote used on many sheds and fences in the area for the buildings protection. It was extremely potent stuff and not surprisingly is now a long since banned substance. The actual works for the distillery were to the Norwood and Derbyshire side of the railway and consisted of a mass of buildings from which protruded a mass of pipes chimneys and towers.

This Norwood railway branch line passed over the A618 Mansfield Road on a high bridge to the left of the works, taking the line on towards Norwood tunnel and beyond to Kiveton Colliery. Travelling along Mansfield Road towards Norwood and immediately after passing under the bridge following the steep descent from Wale Bar was a road sign on the right. The sign announced that you were crossing the county border into Derbyshire in which Norwood and its neighbouring Killamarsh were situated. Maps from the late 1800's describe the company as The Derbyshire Chemical Works so surely this meant that the works were actually in Derbyshire? But perhaps the company's owners chose to change the title at some point to give the company its Yorkshire identity with this county being more associated with industry while Derbyshire was its polar opposite as a rural enclave?

So there we have it, my minds picture of Wales bar as it was when I arrived and to me how it had always been, but, as I mentioned earlier, those who have gone before would have seen Wales Bar very differently just as much as those still to come. Before I chart the progress of Wales Bar with its residents, buildings, changes and most importantly my adventures, experiences and memories of my life in and around Wales Bar following my arrival I am going to look back over a similar number of years to the Victorian age which undoubtedly signalled the start of what we see today.

***

Victorian & Edwardian Waleswood

Looking at Maps of the late 19th century Wales Bar was very different. It was still called Wales Bar
(note my earlier reference to it being a toll bar) but all that existed was the Waleswood Hotel and the cluster of 3 rows of terraced houses around it, one row attached and 2 further rows to the rear. I cannot even confirm if the hotel was the same building that we see today.

Nothing else existed between Wales Bar and Wales with the first building in Wales being the Methodist Chapel on the left and the School on the right. Interestingly this road, now called School Road was then called Woodhill Road. Wales Bar was part of the parish of Wales and although geographically it was in the centre of the parish it was by far the smallest settlement and very probably also the least important.

The parish boundaries were generally defined by the railways that had already been established and surrounded the parish, an intricate network of tracks leading to and from every point of manufacture and
production that needed its goods transporting and of course to bring the coal to power the machinery of theses manufacturing bases. The railways had long taken over the role that canals had previously played and dominated the landscape. To the north was the Great Central Railway line that came from Retford in the East and passed on to Sheffield in the West. To the Eastern parish boundary was the Waleswood Curve line and to the South boundary was the Norwood Branch line.

From records I have of land transactions it suggests that the dominant owners of Wales Parish were the Right Honourable Charles Alfred Worsley Earl of Yarborough and his wife, the

Right Honourable Marcia Amelia Mary Countess of Yarborough.
Sales of land and buildings are documented throughout the first half of the 20th century both by the above and by their descendants to a point where in December 1944 the mining company of Skinner and Holford ultimately own most of the land, farms, and scattered housing that form Wales Bar and Waleswood. This ownership then passed to The National Coal Board in 1947 when coal mining was nationalised.
I have studied these land and property transactions in great detail but have no intention to bore you with the finer points though permit me to share some interesting snippets.
The purchase in 1944 has a very interesting twist of which I will return too later. It included a number of farms including Pithouses Farm, Waleswood Farm, Waleswood Hall Farm, Wraggs Farm, Brookhouse Farm and Bedgreave Farm, all of which are long gone in a sacrifice to opencast mining and ultimately the Rother Valley Leisure Park.

The deeds describe each area of land in great detail and are taken from the ancient deeds of the Earl of Yarborough. The named parcels of land would surely whet the appetite of today's housing developers when naming roads in a new development, Nicholas Croft, Wilson Close, Great Close, Short Butts, Lower Ladies Mead, Upper Ladies Mead, Far Spring Long Close, Near Nether Pasture, High Warren Close, Sheepcote Well Close, Cawtree Platt, Garner Meadow, Upper Barn Platt and Mill Pasture to name just a few.
There are many more with names just as delightful, all of which should have been perhaps considered when the road names of the New Tree estate were created!!

Before I recount memories of my childhood and times past the
following is a very interesting description made by a traveller in
1900 when passing from under the same bridge where my
journey starts and on to Wales Bar which I feel gives a full
flavour of that time.

In making a detour from Woodhouse to Shireoaks, I passed
through three of the most interesting and least known
villages in South Yorkshire - Wales, Harthill and Thorpe
Salvin. But as far as Wales, the most exasperating feature of
this countryside consists of scattered collieries with domestic
colonies to match. Collected together with three
appurtenances - grimy, red brick, jerry-built terraces of
cottages - and forced into one town with authorities at the
head, all well and good from every point of view except the
hygiene. From Aston you may take the by-roads, and go
farther and fare worse than if you kept to the highways.
Plodding eastwards from Sheffield, for a goodly distance of
the way to Worksop, one no sooner seems to gain on a little
rural ground sweet in its primitive or cultivated state, where
swallows, thrushes and blue tits make their abode, then one
comes to the most depressing lines of cottages tenanted by
collier families, the women often twice their bread-winners
girth and weight - for pitmen are necessarily "slippery little
fellows". In an evening the children play about on the door-
stones, and the portly dames stand there in dishabille, with
arms akimbo, to stare at anybody who happens to go by,
finding in gossip the very salt of their existence. Waleswood
is such a place today, taking its inspiration from the
Waleswood Colliery, not far away, and there is still another
separate settlement of the same stamp between bucolic Aston
and bucolic Wales. Thirty years ago old men who had neither

garth nor stray rights tended their cattle unmolested upon these roads and their ample swards, the track itself being so green over that cart-traffic threatened to become circumstance of the past. Waleswood appears to have taken its name from an ancient hall, from which some respectable family may have driven away to quieter scenes, indeed, I am not sure that the hall any longer exists, though the colliery flourishes, as you may judge by the many inscribed railway trucks on the South Yorkshire lines. At the cross-roads there appears to have been a toll-bar, but that has been swept away too, and a somewhat villainous-looking hotel for colliers substituted, one of its glaring announcements being billiards. A long terrace stretches away from this house, and in front is a football field, where I found the younger men "roughing it" at dusk. True, these isolated settlements have pure air, fresh spring water, beautiful environment, and many other advantages that Barnsley colliers have not. Despite the fact that in wintertime they are much benighted, still they are not congested in their breathing area, they are not choked and blinded with smoke, or deafened with traffic. The laws of good friendship unite every member of the colony, and the misfortunes of one household effect the rest. Now, I am strongly of the opinion the the vast majority of these rural pitmen are confirmed native stock, sons, may be, of the old agricultural labourers, who discovered that coal-hewing commanded better wages than working the land. The credit due to them I will not withhold, for everywhere during the course of my peregrinations in this part I heard that a soberer, kinder hearted lot of men never walked. Respect for their childish gentleness is compelled, and they have a special inaptitude for any kind of sharp practice, and an untiring readiness to condole with and help one another, deserving throughout their walk through life a generous allowance for the little foibles so incidental to character which has to be developed in great measure underground.

***

Railway Children

The now aging and redundant industrial and associated residential infrastructure together with the farming activities in and Around Wales Bar provided me and my friends with endless enjoyment in equal measures throughout our youth and childhood. The railways, tunnels, ponds, farms, fields, redundant buildings, trees and hedgerows and the arrival of the M1 motorway were our playground. I consider that I was extremely lucky and privileged to witness and experience those exciting times of so much change and progress.

Let me take you back to the railway bridge below the Waleswood colliery entrance and the pithead baths and start my journey charting memories recalled of these cherished years. Around the time of my arrival in 1954 the railway system that circumnavigated the boundaries of Wales parish were all working lines, though the Norwood branch line linking Killamarsh with Kiveton was nearing the end of its life with it finally closing in 1961. The closure of the Wales wood Curve followed in 1967 though hardly any trains used either of the lines so the system became our playground. Of course as young explorers we were totally unaware of these impending closures and this simply added to the excitement that, at any time there may be a speeding train passing, we were the railway children! All our adventures seemed to take place under blue skies and lush green surroundings due to the fact that most took place in the long hot days of the 6 week school holiday or Whitsuntide and perhaps Easter or potato picking week too, it never seemed to rain and was always hot and sunny, surely a true reflection of a happy childhood.

To scramble up the railway embankment beyond the bridge we took the lane between the pithead baths and the cricket field which led us towards Coulsons farm. There always seemed to be trains coming and going on the main line by the bridge and we believed that if the train driver happened to spot us then he might stop the train and chase us!

By taking the lane we could then cross the fields to the railway line somewhere between the main line and Coulsons farm.

Our point of entry was via the steep embankment and when reaching the twin tracks at the top we were free to walk, out of sight from both the farm and the main line. It wasn't long before the embankment became a cutting as we walked the line towards the tunnel ahead. This tunnel was just beyond the village of Waleswood and allowed Delves Lane high above it at the point where it changed its name Waleswood Road to continue its way towards Brookhouse and Brookhouse as the lane descended into the valley. The tenant farmer of Brookhouse farm was Clarence Smith whom I will return later.

From Waleswood and Delves lane it was impossible to know that the tunnel beneath existed.

Research has told me that this tunnel was a mere 66 yards long but to us at the time it seemed a mile or more from one end to the other.

Looking into the dark depths of the tunnel we pretended to be fearless, daring each other to walk through (or rather run) until we entered back into daylight through the Arch topped floodlit window far in the distance that was the opposite end tunnel entrance.

Looking, listening and smelling the air of the tunnel told us that the tunnels interior was a cold, dark, wet and sinister place.

There was the repetitive sound of dripping water as it fell from the vaulted roof of the tunnel onto the tracks below and a constant wind that whistled through and brought the dank tunnel smell to our nostrils.

It was not just the thought of actually making this terrifying journey through the tunnel but also what might lie ahead at the opposite end. Would there be someone there to chase us away or capture us as trespassers or, and this was the most terrifying of all, would we meet with a train when half way through?

Whether or not we had been told or seen it on a Wild West film I don't recall but, we thought that if we put our ear to the track and listen then we could hear if there was a train coming anytime soon.

We would lie there, each listening intently and convincing ourselves that we could hear a train coming which meant that our dare to run the tunnel was too risky. In reality we all heard nothing but it served to heighten the fear within us.

Then we hit on a brainwave.

If one of us were to climb the steep embankment that surrounded the tunnel entrance and go overland to the opposite end of the tunnel we could then be sure that once we had run the tunnel and entered into sunshine once more, we would not come to a sticky end. Our lookout could check for people and trains and any other disaster that might befall us.

A great idea and we would all volunteer in the hope that the subterranean sprint could be avoided so we would draw straws to see who was for under and who was for over.

My memory only recalls the tunnel run.

Looking into the tunnel, a distant silhouette in the arch topped window beyond would shout the all clear and we were at the point of no return, but, should we run between the 2 sets of tracks or between the rails of the left or right track? To run between the track and the tunnel wall was a non starter due to the ground falling away steeply from the track towards the tunnel wall and creating a ditch where the water gathered from the dripping roof and who knew how deep that would be?

To run between the two sets of tracks was almost as dangerous as the sleepers that sat beneath the tracks were not in line with those on the opposite track and the sleeper ends protruded above the ground creating the perfect trip hazard.

The best and only way was to run between the 2 tracks of one or other of the lines and providing that your stride matched the distance for one sleeper to the next it was easy!

It probably took no more than a minute or two to make this intrepid journey from one end to the other but it seemed a whole lot longer. As we journeyed towards the centre of the tunnel it got blacker, the water from above became a torrent and the arch topped window that was our goal in front of us didn't seem to get any bigger.

We made it through the tunnel on a number of occasions but it never got any easier and neither did our heart rate.

I took this photo in 1965 of one of the last trains to run along the Waleswood curve. The line was closed in 1967.

Beyond the tunnel we were into open countryside and although the railway lines gradually became more prominent as the cutting to the tunnel gave way to a steep embankment, again it didn't really bother us as we had a good vantage point of any oncoming trains or railway employees and, if spotted we could quick make our escape.

We never actually knew where the tracks would eventually lead us and it was of no concern.

Intrepid explorers we might have been but we knew our boundaries and our train track exploits never took us any further than the next landmark along the line. I suppose looking back there was a very simple explanation for this as some distance along the tracks the embankments gave way once more to a cutting over which was a bridge. This bridge was our way home as the road above us led back to Wales Bar via Delves Lane in one direction while the other way led to Bedgreave Farm in the valley beyond. Once back on the road the tracks could be seen disappearing into the distance over a magnificent bridge supported by numerous pillars. This was the Rother valley viaduct which took the trains high above the River Rother and on to Killamarsh while the River Rother continued its journey downstream towards Rotherham where it merged with the much larger River Don in the Don valley where Sheffield lay. This viaduct was a natural boundary for us as we always preferred the dare of a subterranean dash rather than an over the bridge splash. The viaduct and the area around it was the scene of three memorable events which happened some years apart but were undeniably linked and I will recall them both here so as not to forget later.

The first memorable event was one summer which took place around the same time as our railway adventures and probably was a spin off from one of them.

Following the track from the bridge that I have just mentioned it descended down to the valley of the River Rother where, away to the left we had full view of the now towering viaduct above us. To the right was Bedgreave farm, formally Bedgreave Mill. On this adventure our destination was not the farm but some way before reaching the River Rother there was a pond in the field which we always referred to as the cow pond which was no surprise really as it sat in the middle of a field full of cows!

My mother was a keen swimmer and although my father preferred to paddle with trousers rolled up to the knee, it was without doubt my mother who had insisted that my siblings and I should learn to swim. There was no facility or opportunity to do this at our school although I know that some schools did arrange lessons at the local swimming baths but our school was not one of them.

Lessons were arranged and every Friday night we would clamber into the family car and travel to Creswell where there were public swimming baths. I am sure that all children attending school in Creswell could swim as the swimming baths were actually part of the school complex!

I hated the smell of chlorine and the hot damp atmosphere in and around the swimming pool and I hated even more the swimming instructor whose name was Mr Woods. I can visualise him vividly even now, stood by the side of the pool in his dark purple trunks shouting gruff instructions and when we failed to succeed in the instructed task he would leap into the pool and proceed to demonstrate how it should be done, usually by grabbing one of us as his demo model. Mrs Woods was far less fearsome and would occasionally take the lessons which were almost an enjoyable experience as she was kind and gentle but it still had little effect on my ability to learn to swim.

Without doubt the highlight of this miserable Friday night outing was the journey home. Doom and gloom suddenly disappeared as my father pulled up outside the fish and chip shop at Hard Lane on the outskirts of Kiveton where fish and chips were bought and then wrapped in local editions of the Sheffield Star or Morning Telegraph to keep them warm on the journey home for our Friday night supper. It was almost worth the trial and torture of those terrifying swimming lessons.

Returning to the cow pond, it was of reasonable size with an extremely muddy shore line. Stinging nettles, cow pats, large stones and numerous broken twigs and branches from the single large tree that overhung the pond also made their contribution. The water was surprisingly quite clear and the reeds that grew from beneath the surface at one end were visible from both beneath and above the water's surface.

Swimming attire was however much clothing you chose to leave on and discarded clothing was then used to get dry later together with the warmth of the summer sunshine.

My swimming lessons had at least taught me the principle of swimming and how to stay afloat so when it came to my turn to enter the waters of the cow pond I did so with some bravado but deep down I was terrified. I had no idea how deep the water was as I moved further from the shore but thankfully I was somehow able to disguise the fact that I had one foot on the floor while giving the impression that I was actually swimming, leaving street credibility intact for another day.

The second memorable event was much later.

On the 25th of November 1977 work was well underway to open cast the entire Rother Valley basin to retrieve coal that previous local mines had failed to do due to the shallow depth of the coal seams and that modern technology and practices now permitted.

This work sadly destroyed many farmsteads, railways, tunnels, bridges and so much more that were my childhood haunts, wiping them off the face of the local map forever but fortunately such progress cannot destroy memories and these places are always there to revisit at will as they live on in the minds of those who remember them.

The Rother valley viaduct was one of many key structures that were an integral part of the transport network that kept the wheels of industry turning during the Second World War and as a consequence was an obvious target for German bombers to destroy. Their efforts to do just that thankfully failed but it was not until THE 25th of November 1977 that the realisation of just how close they came to taking out the viaduct was actually realised.

As the gigantic opencast machinery dug deep into the ground around the viaduct a massive 4000 pound unexploded German bomb was unearthed.

The Royal Engineers bomb disposal team were immediately dispatched from Caterham in Surrey to deal with the five foot long "Herman" type bomb. Records suggest that the bomb disposal team were only able to safely remove less than half of the explosive material contained within the deadly device and the following day at 4.45 pm they carried out a controlled explosion. Controlled it may have been but the blast was felt as far away as Sheffield and Chesterfield and many windows in nearby Killamarsh that faced onto the bombsite were left cracked or broken.

I was in the warehouse of McClure timber Supplies that afternoon where I helped out on Saturdays (read Bricks & Mortar chapter 19 A Lucky Break) where we had closed just 45 minutes before the bomb was detonated. The warehouse was empty but for the staff. The whole building shook when the bomb went off and it was not until later that evening did we realise why.

Looking back now to our visits to the cow pond, could this pond actually have been the hole that was created when the German bomb fell but missed the viaduct? My one foot on the ground swimming antic's may well have been within inches of this deadly weapon, we shall never know but it is a very interesting thought.

The bomb disposal engineers with the Rother Valley bomb

I mentioned that the viaduct was one of three memorable events and I have alluded to two so what was the third?

On the 12th and 15th of December 1940 the German Luftwaffe carried out the bombing of Sheffield now known as the "Sheffield Blitz". In total over 660 people were killed, 1,500 injured and 40,000 made homeless. 3,000 homes were demolished with a further 3,000 badly damage with a total of 78,000 homes receiving some damage. Around 355 tons of high explosive bombs were dropped on Sheffield on those 2 nights together with some 16000 incendiary canisters. The Luftwaffe's primary targets were the Steel works to the East of the city but as history has proved not all bombs hit their intended targets. We will never know if the Rother Valley bomb fell short of the steel works or if its aim was to take out the Rother Valley viaduct but thankfully it did neither.

A train on the viaduct heading for Killamarsh and the world beyond!

Staying with the Railways, there was one more landmark that always attracted our attention. This was Norwood tunnel. As I mentioned earlier we never ventured along the railway beyond the viaduct or in the direction of the Killamarsh branch line where it met with the Waleswood Curve.
It was unchartered territory.
In our exploration days of the 1960's the Branch line from Kiveton Colliery running down towards Killamarsh had seen the last train run in 1960 and was officially closed in 1961 and this section included 300 yard long Norwood tunnel.

The railway tunnel was not the only tunnel at Norwood, there was also the Chesterfield canal tunnel which was almost 2 miles long and built and built around 1775! The entrance to the canal tunnel at Norwood was still visible with just a wire mesh preventing entry which in later years was replaced by a brick wall and this entrance is still visible to this day! Ironically while it was used to transport coal from the mines as late as 1907 it was the mines that ultimately brought an end to this transport link as the deep mining of coal nearby caused the ground to subside which in turn broke the canal tunnel in two. It was also possible to trace the root of the Chesterfield canal tunnel from above the ground under which it passed as in a number of places over the open fields there were fenced areas surrounding holes in the ground where the canal tunnel had previously collapsed. We never ventured too close to these potentially bottomless pits as they surely led to a watery grave.

Norwood Canal Tunnel entrance still visible 250 years after it was first built

To get to the railway tunnel our route was to walk to the village square in neighbouring Wales and then up Church Street to the very top where the road ended by the cemetery gates. At this point we would then follow the lane down into the fields that eventually brought us to the tunnel top on the Kiveton side.
The tunnel entrance was in a deep cutting and as this was a single track railway and the width of the cutting minimal it served to increase the feeling of claustrophobia as we cast our gaze skywards after sliding down the steep embankment to the tunnel entrance below. The grand stone archway that was the tunnel entrance had turned black from years of smoke from passing steam engines and unlike the much wider tunnel entrance of the Waleswood Curve, Norwood was taller narrower darker and all together more sinister looking.
The same smell of dampness was there, as was the whistling wind and the running water from the roof above. The main difference however was that there was no light at the other end of the tunnel.
As little light as there was deep down in the railway cutting, this light fast faded away to nothing as we took tentative steps into the mouth of the tunnel until all that was before us was darkness. 300 yards is no distance when walking in the great outdoors but to attempt the same distance through a pitch black tunnel, not knowing how long before the window of light from the entrance behind us would disappear and the window of light somewhere ahead would start to appear from the blackness that increasingly surrounded us was a step too far.
 Give me the Waleswood curve tunnel any day.

Norwood Tunnel entrance from the Norwood end which is no longer visible

*Unlike the bridges, tunnels and other spectacular structures of civil engineering from an age gone by that disappeared for ever when the Rother Valley Country Park was created from the enormous hole left when open cast mining enveloped the entire Rother Valley, both the railway and canal tunnels at Norwood still in exist in part today, albeit buried deep beneath the M1 motorway that now passes high above them. The canal tunnel, a tribute to 18th century civil engineering excellence and the railway tunnel honouring the 19th century, both built almost totally by hand and now the M1 leaving its lasting legacy to 20th century modern engineering.

Ironically the UK Government have now approved plans for the High Speed 2 rail link (HS2) to be constructed alongside the M1 as it passes through Wales meaning that it will also pass above the old canal and railway tunnels of Norwood making this new rail link an engineering spectacle of the 21st century. Surely a

plaque should be commissioned and erected to 4 engineering structures from 4 consecutive centuries and all in one place; undoubtedly this must be a unique coincidence? amazing.
It should also be noted that just one farm survived in part following the creation of the country park. Bedgreave Farm that stood only yards from where the WW11 bomb was unearthed is now the country parks craft centre.*

***

Pigeons

So, let's now return to the where we started at the railway bridge spanning Mansfield Road just below the Waleswood Colliery entrance.

The bridge has changed very little over the last 60 years and indeed little since it was first built to carry the railway in the 1840,s as a superior mode of transport to the nearby Chesterfield canal that was constructed in the 1770,s

The bridge has the same stone walls and probably much the same steelwork structure that spans the walls to carry the tracks, though the bridge only carries 2 sets of tracks instead of the original 4 following the demise of the Waleswood Curve.

Travelling from the bridge and up the sharp incline to the brow of the hill where Wales bar comes into view in the distance, the pithead baths stood on the right and the colliery entrance on the left. From this point on, changes over the last 60 years is beyond all recognition.

My memories start in earnest in the earlier 1960's. Waleswood pit had ceased coal production in 1948 as the coal seams of the smaller pits became interlinked as Waleswood pit became a pumping station for the larger colliery at Kiveton. From Kiveton colliery coal continued to be mined and brought to the surface until the 1980's when the infamous programme of pit closures spelt the end of deep mine coal production in the area.

Before my time there had also been a railway station at Waleswood! Which was first opened in 1907 to serve the expanding local population as coal production increased and there were demands for a growing workforce.

The station booking office caught fire in 1953 which quite probably was as a result of sparks created from passing steam trains as the station buildings and platform were built almost entirely of timber. This proved to be the final blow for the station which closed just 2 years later in 1955.

I don't recall the remnants that may have survived from the station or the detail of the red brick buildings that clustered around the pit head winding gear that dominated the landscape, however clear in my memory are the two enormous spindled wheels that were the key to raising and lowering the cage to give access to the warren of tunnels deep underground.

There was always the threat of being caught by grownups so we preferred to explore the wider area of the old coke ovens, marshalling yard, ponds and pit tip where we knew that, should we be chased then we could quickly make our getaway to the many hiding places we had, or into the fields and hedgerows beyond which were our domain and not theirs.

I do recall on the right just beyond the entrance was a large sunken structure that was surrounded by tall concrete walls which had probably been some sort of storage for water, but for some reason it was no longer watertight and had become a nature reserve with plants, undergrowth and saplings that were fast becoming young trees. The walls were incredibly high, or so it seemed to us, yet the urge was irresistible in wanting to get in there and explore even though there was the ever present risk of being captured by grownups.

Our way in was via the branches of an elderberry bush which was fast maturing into a tree and had branches that were strong enough to support us. We would scale down through the greenery and arrive into our own secret jungle. It was an incredible place as the walls shielded the sights and sounds of the world beyond and we were the only ones in this very private space.

In later years as industry expanded and numerous companies took over the disused colliery buildings a wall to our jungle was breached and it became a lorry park!

I recalled earlier our visits to the sweet shop in Pigeon row which by the 60's had become no more that a ghost terrace with almost every house empty. The last 2 families to leave were the occupants of the end terrace and their immediate neighbour, situated at the opposite end to the colliery.

I remember my father saying at the time that these two families had refused to move but they, along with all the families of a once thriving pigeon row were the victims of progress and had to eventually move on.

Following their departure it was not long before the houses were reduced to rubble yet it was

a while later before the area was totally cleared meaning that for a short time it provided yet another place to explore.

Pigeon Row was just that, a very long row of terraced houses without a break from one end to the other. The front doors opened directly onto the pavement which was probably 20 feet wide from the doorstep to the road side kerb.

The back doors to each house opened directly on to steps leading down to a wide cobbled lane serving as an access road stretching the entire length of Pigeon Row. This rear access was considerably lower that the front pavement making Pigeon Row look so much taller when viewed from the "backs", a term we used when referring to the rear of a row of terraces. The only access to this rear street was via an entrance that past close by our private jungle. The height difference from front to rear was a significant, each house had a cellar or "coal hole" and in front of each house was a grid that gave access to a chute allowing coal to be sent tumbling down into the cellar where it was stored until required, then easily accessed from a "coal hole" in the back yard beneath the house floors. Coal was a part of the miners wage and there was plenty of it. It was used every day of the year as it was the only source of heat for cooking and hot water. We can only imagine now how unhealthy it must have been with every single house on the row belching smoke from their chimneys and then mixing with the dirt, grime, smoke and fumes that the nearby pit and coke ovens were producing.

When Pigeon row had first been built the age of the motor vehicle was still some way off and this access road would have catered for a horse and cart and a social meeting place and play area for its occupants. In fact even up to the time of its demise I doubt that car ownership was high on the agenda of the Pigeon Row families as their needs were few. The bread winner's employment was literally on the doorstep, they had a transport link at Waleswood station and a shop within the row for anything that they could not grow and milk delivered or collected from the many local farms. There was no pub but a walk up the road to the Waleswood Hotel at Wales Bar would quench the thirst of every single miner and worship was catered for by a chapel just up the road.

The sanitary arrangements were unacceptable, or certainly by today's standards but did exist in a more primitive form. Beyond the rear lane was a row of single storey buildings that were the outside toilets. Between these buildings there were gates that gave access to a long stripe of garden beyond.

Each house had its own garden which was used to grow and rear virtually everything that was required to feed the family, be it Chickens, rabbits, pigs or vegetables. The gardens may have offered an escape from the daily toil of work but a reminder was always present of that fact as immediately behind the gardens were the cooling beds for the coke ovens giving off hot, smelly and probably toxic fumes most times of the day and night.

Pigeon row and pit head gear viewed from the Sports field during a rare day of fun and games

Looking to the rear of Pigeon Row with the outside toilets and gardens and the cooling beds for the coke ovens clearly visible in the foreground.

Our exploits in and around the ruins of Pigeon Row were few and mainly consisted of clambering in and around the ruins of the houses. It all seemed rather strange as although the houses had been reduced to rubble, for some strange reason, the lane, outside toilets and gardens beyond remained almost untouched for a long while before the whole area was finally cleared.

Perhaps the demolition of the houses ensured that no one would return?

Pigeon row was now resigned to history of a bygone era and rapid change had begun.

Today there is almost nothing that remains from the playground of my youth. All the buildings have gradually been replaced with utilitarian industrial buildings built specifically for their purpose. To the northern end of where Pigeon Row once stood there is now a large access road leading to an industrial estate. Most of the site of Pigeon Row and its gardens are now managed grassland with trees forming a pleasant swath of green in front of the Luk complex of factory and offices which now stands on the site of the coke ovens cooling beds and stock yard.

Just our secret jungle remains! Not our secret garden anymore but now a warehouse and open storage exists inside its walls with a neat hole cut through the high concrete wall to the rear providing the entrance.

The real secret jungle remains forever in my mind.

***

Money Mountains and Motorways

Beyond the colliery buildings and pit yard were the coke ovens and a large flat area between the ovens and the main railway line where there were still a number of railway lines although no longer connected to the main line. These lines were where wagons would have been shunted from the main line allowing the processed coke to be loaded and ready for delivery.

There was also a small building of typical railway design which stood unused and unloved but inside held it held a treasure-trove of railway memorabilia. This had been the control centre for changing the points on the now disused railway sidings. We had great fun turning the 3 large wheels that had once slowly repositioned the connecting points from one track to another. The wheels spun freely now but would have taken considerable strength to turn when connected to the complex wires, rods and pulleys that transferred the physical instruction from the control room to the track.

The left photo is from the 1930's with William Bramley (more of him later) posing on a shunting train at the colliery and on the right is train from the 1950's with all the train tracks in the foreground and Pigeon Row in the distance.

Also, passing through this area and on to the towering red shale pit tip beyond was the track that took small wagons of burnt waste from the coke ovens on their journey to the top of the tip. The track ascended the tip not unlike a funicular railway and on reaching the summit deposited its load to cascade down the surface of the conical shaped mound.

This intricate miniature railway had long since lay redundant by the time we had taken ownership of this vast unexplored industrial wasteland save for the track that still remained leading all the way to the summit of the tip.

We were constantly warned by our parents not to venture on or around the tip as there were numerous unforeseen dangers but, as young explorers this was like a red rag to a bull, we could not keep away.

I often wonder how we actually survived to tell the tale.

Many pit tips or "slag heaps" were familiar landmarks in the area but Wales pit tip was different.

Most of the material that made up this man made mountain was waste produced from converting coal to coke and the tip was ruddy brown in colour rather than the dirty black colour of its near neighbours. The waste material must have been red hot when first tipped as many years after the coke production had ceased wisps' of smoke still floated in the air around the summit. The material that made up the tip was loose, like small beads of solid ash mixed with dust and other small particles and this made scaling the sides of the tip almost impossible, however, the disused tracks were still in place and provided a perfect aid to attempt the skyward climb.

Even this was not easy as the tip fell away steeply to each side of the track but undeterred we would dare each other to make the assent.

As the safety of flat ground lay far below us each step was a tentative one, clinging to the rails we would move forward, our feet disturbing the ground beneath them which sent mini avalanches of stone and ash rolling down the tip.

Beneath, where the rails had once firmly laid on the tips surface were now craters and holes as years of rain had washed away the surface and at some points along our journey the tracks were suspended in mid air between one solid point to the next. This undoubtedly served to heighten our fears that the entire structure might come crashing down around us at any moment.

Nevertheless our desire to reach the top remained. It may have been the long hot days of summer but, as we climbed the metal of the tracks seemed to get warmer and warmer and this thought was further compounded by the acrid smell of burning and the sight of smoke rising from the summit beyond.

We may have been reckless in the adventures of our youth yet a strong feeling of self preservation always prevailed. I think it is referred too today as Health and Safety but I like to think of it as good old fashioned common sense.

We never did reach the summit.

Between the tip and the main railway line were 2 large ponds. I think they were manmade and were probably accidentally created as the valley of Rookery Bottom and the stream that ran in it was gradually filled in with spoil from the pit and coke ovens. In the time that had elapsed between these industries ceasing and my arrival on the scene nature had taken over. This was now the habitat of trees shrubs and an abundance of wildlife both in and around the water. The water was deep and clear and revealed the steepness of the banks were not only above but also below the waterline too. We kept our distance and chose to throw everything and anything that we could find into the water from the relative safety of the tracks that ran alongside the steep banks, simply to see who could throw the greatest distance and create the biggest splash. A childish game but it provided hours of entertainment.

There were a few smaller ponds from which we would extract sticklebacks and tadpoles and carry them home in any watertight container we could find.

Once back home we would transfer our catch into a large stone sink together with plants and greenery taken from the same pond thinking that this would be the food that guaranteed their continuing existence but, without the life supporting microscopic content of the pond and the addition of chemically tinged tap water there days were numbered.

The main railway line passed alongside these ponds immediately to the north. In addition to lots of coal laden trains passing back and forth it was also the link from Sheffield Victoria station to Retford and on to Kings Cross in London via the East Coast Line which was the route taken by the Master Cutler, a high speed passenger train that ran daily, passing by in the morning and returning in the early evening. There were other passenger trains too making more local journeys.

We kept clear of the tracks if a passenger train was due as they travelled much faster than the coal trains and we believed that they were also not heavy enough for our little game.

Occasionally today the news might report an incident where children have been playing "chicken" on the tracks which is a crazy practice and one that invariably ends in tears. We would not have dreamt of such madness and always applied common sense and self preservation to our antics!

The trains passed along open land between the Mansfield railway bridge and the ponds before passing through a cutting which provided the perfect spot for our game.

Being pre 1967 the money in our pockets was real and heavy too.

12 pennies made a shilling and there were 20 shillings in a pound, we also used thrupp'ny bits, tanners , bobs, florins, half crowns and ten bob notes just to name a few !

 We didn't have much nmoney nor did we need it as our days were spent on adventures which needed no currency. All we required for our game was a penny, a pre decimal penny, which was so much bigger and heavier than its decimalised successor. We would make sure that the railway line was clear and the best way to be certain of this was to play our game immediately after a train had past as the likelihood of another one following soon after was slim.

As soon as the train had passed we would run down to the track side and place our penny on the top of the shiny rail and quickly retreat to our hiding place in the undergrowth of the embankment. We then lay in wait for the next train. It seemed to take ages to arrive during which time we would fantasise over what great catastrophe may unfold just because our penny was on the line.

When a train finally made its way towards us our spirits were heightened if it was a heavy train, a coal train which would produce the effect that we were hoping for.

There was just one potential major drawback with a coal train in that the last piece of rolling stock was not a coal filled wagon but the guards van. The guards van was a small house on wheels where the guard would spend his time during the entire length of the journey. The guards van had an open balcony at each end so that the guard had a good vantage point both in front and behind.

There was no communication link between the train driver and his guard in his guards van other than by semaphore and it was also extremely unlikely that the train driver would spot our penny on the track and therefore feel the need to alert his guardsman to look out for the likes of us. Even so we had to be sure that the train was long gone before we re-emerged from the undergrowth to search the trackside for our prize for fear of being spotted by the guardsman from his vantage point.

We would hear the "ping" of the penny as the wheel of the train passed over it and it could often fly quite a distance so we didn't always find our modified coinage, but when we did the result was very satisfying. Our penny was now much thinner and at least twice the size. Result.

A major development in the surrounding landscape happened in the mid 1960,s with the coming of the M1 motorway. The first real sign that the motorway was arriving, which would eventually provide a direct link from London to Leeds, was the erection of a fence to the extremity of each side of the motorway that the road and general infrastructure would swallow up. The fencing looked strange as it was not in a straight line but meandered in and out to take account of the embankments and cuttings that would soon become reality. Before work commenced in earnest the area of land that was to be swallowed up was mind blowing. Not only that, but the motorway was to divide two communities forever. No longer would it be possible to walk over the fields from Waleswood to Wales as we often did, our rural idle was about to be destroyed forever. From memory the section of motorway between junction 30 and 31 took around 2 years to complete, during which time we were interested bystanders of its progress. There was so much heavy machinery going back and forth and generally too many workers to risk tangling with. Our time was at the weekend when work stopped, although I do remember that at one point there was an announcement that working was to be extended to 7 days as the project was behind. This was at the time when the earthmoving was at its height as the "cut and fill" operation of removing the hills and placing them in the valleys was carried out, a practice that has continued from as far back as Roman times. I remember standing by the new fences on many occasions watching the giant Euclid excavators racing back and forth with their tons of earth on board. There was no protective cab around the driver as he sat sit perched high on his seat with controls around him at the front of the giant machine bouncing along the rough terrain. Occasionally the driver would wave as he past and caught a glimpse of our frantic arm waving. One driver we all looked out for and who was guaranteed to give us a cheery wave was an Indian driver. He was quite a celebrity and easily spotted as he wore a turban and his wide and happy smile always beamed through his dusty face and beard, he was a very happy chap. The company doing the work had their name emblazoned on each Euclid, "Dick Hampton"was the name but I doubt that our Indian friend was a family member.

Giant Euclid in action

The motorway crossed the railway line just a few yards from where we had previously played our penny game and at this point a bridge was constructed for the motorway to eventually cross high above the tracks. By the side of the railway and much lower was the valley of Rookery bottom and the stream over which the motorway also had to cross. This crossing was achieved by constructing a culvert of circular concrete interlocking pipes along the path of the stream and when the railway bridge was complete hundreds of tonnes of earth were replaced around the structures.

The culvert was probably 100 Yards in length and for us was an irresistible place to explore. During the motorway construction lots of thick sheets of polystyrene was used, mainly in association with the shuttering and formwork used to shape the wet concrete until set to create the various structures associated with such a massive civil engineering undertaking. This polystyrene was cast aside after a single use and could be found scattered and discarded everywhere.

Not only was this stuff very light but more importantly for us it also floated!

We must have had a thing about tunnels, they were there to explore and the culvert needed exploring and conquering.

Come the weekend when all was quiet and long before traffic took over the completed motorway we would walk along the swathe of mud and dust that had been cut across our land to take in the progress of that week. Our destination was the culvert.

Each end of the culvert was wide open although soon after the motorway was complete steel grills were fitted to prevent human access.

Thinking back to the Norwood tunnel and our cowardliness of not daring the subterranean crossing then the culvert was certainly on a par, even worse the culvert had a stream running though it but, we were older now and braver or, at least we thought we were.

Firstly we had to find a piece of polystyrene that was big enough for one or two of us to sit on but also small enough to fit in the culvert. The culvert must have been at least 6 feet in diameter as when we stood in the stream at its entrance the top of the tube was a good foot above us. The stream filled barely a quarter of the culvert and flowed from the Wales side towards Waleswood at a steady pace.

Looking into the culvert was a chilling sight; it was extremely long, very straight, and almost dark in the middle with a very small circle of light signalling the exit at the other end.

We decided to use a variation of the "pooh sticks" method to test out our planned journey.

Made famous by AA Milne in "The House at Pooh Corner" first published in 1928.

Much later in 1996 the then owner of the cottage that had previously been AA Milne's inspiration for his Pooh books wrote the following rules to commemorate the 70th anniversary of the publication of Winnie-the-Pooh.
I must say that we were not aware of Winnie-the-Pooh and his stick method at the time but it must have been a game played for centuries by children across the world long before AA Milne used it with great success in his Pooh books.

1. First, you each select a stick and show it to your fellow competitors. You must agree which stick is which – or whose, as it were.
2. Check which way the stream is flowing. Competitors need to face the stream on the side where it runs in, under the bridge (upstream). Note: If the stream runs out, from under the bridge you are standing on the wrong side! (downstream).
3. Choose someone to be a Starter. This can be either the oldest or the youngest competitor.
4. All the competitors stand side by side facing upstream.
5. Each competitor holds their stick at arms length over the stream. The tall competitors should lower their arms to bring all the sticks to the same height over the stream as the shortest competitor's stick.
6. The starter calls, 'Ready – Steady – Go!" and all the competitors drop their sticks. Note: the stick must not be thrown into the water.
7. At this point in the game all the players must cross to the downstream side of the bridge. Please take

care – young players like to race across.
Remember, other people use bridges and some of
them have vehicles or horses.

8. Look over the edge of the bridge for the sticks to
emerge. The owner of the first Stick to float from
under the bridge, is the winner.
Remember: Falling into the water is SAD (Silly
And Daft)

Our first tests were based on Pooh Sticks but polystyrene was
our choice of weapon! As soon as our pieces of polystyrene hit
the water we were off, clambering over the rough earth and mud,
leaping over the enormous ruts left by the wheels of the Euclid's
until we reached the downstream end of the culvert. The stream
had a steady flow but we would arrive in good time to see the
white pieces of foam emerge back into the sunshine. After
successful tests it was our turn.

Returning to the upstream end we prepared our boat. The large
white slab was big enough for two of us to ride and after each
finding a sturdy stick to propel ourselves forward by pushing
hard on the smooth concrete sides of the culvert, we were ready.
We knelt, one in front and one behind and we were off. There
was no turning back now, although we each had in the back of
our minds the thought that we could still abandon ship without
serious consequences as the water level barely reached our
knees. Of course this was our individual thoughts which we dare
not divulge to each other for fear of been labelled a chicken and
a coward!

Deeper into the darkening tube we floated with the streams
current carrying us at a good pace without the need for our
sticks. Surprisingly as we reached the middle we could still see
as the equal circles of light from both the Wales and Waleswood

ends were penetrating the tunnels dark depths. Our thoughts of any disaster that might befall us quickly subsided as the circle of light at the Waleswood end grew ever larger and then we were out into the bright sunshine, our maiden voyage complete.
Were you scared we asked each other? No, were you? No was the reply.
 Our real thoughts remained a secret!

The pit tip on the left where so many of our adventures were played out and in the foreground early work is underway on the motorway construction where unexpected coal deposits were found.

As work commenced on the MI project a base was set up on the old shunting yard by Waleswood Colliery consisting of numerous offices and storage buildings where the staff could administer the daily operations.

I remember the company being called "French" and their company colours were black and white.

The complex was very distinctive with each building sporting the two colours, like a field of Zebras.

Such a temporary site settlement today would be fully fenced with steel shutters to every cabin and a 24 hour surveillance system in place but this was the 1960's and no such security was needed.

The company were civil engineers and were the contactors responsible for constructing the bridges and of course our culvert.

When the motorway was complete their temporary black and white village was abandoned and remained for many months after. We gradually realised this fact and our attention quickly focused on exploration in and around the site. The doors and windows had been left open so we saw this as our invitation to enter. The offices were like the Mary Celeste with desks, chairs, filing cabinets, plans, telephones and every kind of equipment that you
would expect in such a place. We felt that someone might appear at any time but they didn't. We played in and around the village on many occasions until gradually the buildings were emptied of their contents, by who knows who?

Eventually the buildings were dismantled and either taken away or simply burnt where they stood.

Looking back now I think it is reasonable to assume that Motorway building was quite a lucrative business.

School Road a short time before the M1 sliced through and changed the landscape forever.

The New Tree estate was by this time established which can be seen on the right of the photo of School Road. Although the estate was not structurally affected by the coming of the motorway it has been blighted ever since with its physical presence and by every increasing noise from the swelling volumes of traffic that now passes by in the deep cutting below the new road bridge.

To the left of school road were fine semi detached and detached houses together with two bungalows. The bungalows and the four houses immediately beyond were demolished to make way for the new motorway.

Out of sight and just beyond the large tree on the right was the Cricket field.

I have many recollections of the coming of the motorway but my memories of this area are most vivid prior to its arrival as every school day I would walk this road from our home at Wales Bar to the Primary School at Wales, the school being opposite Wales Chapel that can be seen just to the left of the large tree.

1 of 6 houses demolished to make way for the motorway.

Wales Cricket field on the right is now 6 lanes of the M1.

The changing rooms and Cricket pavilion had already seen better days.

***

School Days

We walked to school, yes that's right, we walked and what's more we walked alone, no parents with us but just other school friends that happened to appear from their homes as we passed by.

The trek to school was just in excess of 1000 yards but for little people with small strides it seemed much further. The walk from our house to Wales Bar corner was flat and straight but as we rounded the corner we were faced with 2 challenges. It always seemed to be windy on the corner and the wind direction was always from the direction of Wales and gusting down the hill that now loomed before us. The hill was probably no more distance to what we had already walked but it was steep, very steep, and our legs ached by the time we reached the top where the view of School Road stretched out before us with the school in the far distance, now we had a long and welcome steady decent towards the school.

Coming back home after a long day at school this particular part of our morning walk was not as pleasant as it seemed to stretch out endlessly before us. The treat that awaited us at the top of this steady incline was to run down from the top of Wales Bar hill with the wind now behind us, spreading our arms wide so that our coats acted as wings, we were flying.

School was a necessary evil for most of us of that I am sure, although perhaps others must have drawn a pleasure from it. I was in the former group. I have heard tell that schooldays are supposed to be the best years of your life but at the time it rarely seems so and only looking back many years later do you see that there was perhaps some truth in it after all.

Of course, these words of wisdom always come from the lips of adults, never from school children.

 I rest my case.

I'm not going to dwell on my school days at Wales Junior mixed and infant's school for long (1959 to 1965) but there were a few highs and lows worthy of mention.

I wore short trousers throughout my time at the school, not by choice I should note.

All ready for school pictured here with my Granddad, my all time hero

The winter of 1962/63 was one of the coldest on record. Snow fell and reached window ledges and higher, the wind whipped up the snow into enormous snow drifts as high as houses and then the temperatures plummeted. I recall a snow drift at Wales Bar corner that stretched from the Co-op on one side of the crossroads to South Terrace on the other. It was so large and still kept growing due to the ever present wind that blew down Wales Bar hill whipping up the snow and drifting it ever higher. Nothing could pass and school was closed for a least a week.

We played out in the snow, blissfully happy that there was no school and with the pleasures that snow provides all around us in abundance. Of course, we were made to wrap up warm with hats, scarves, coats and long trousers tucked into our wellies. We had no objections to these layers upon layer of clothing as without them we would have been forbidden to play outside in the winter wonderland that had settled around us. The memory that stays with me vividly is that while our home knitted winter woollies were very warm, if they came in contact with the snow then it would stick like glue to the fabric in small white balls and with the heat of our bodies would quickly melt resulting in very wet woollies.

School reopened after a few days and all was back to normal save for the fact that there was still so much lying snow around that our walk to school was more like an arctic expedition.

I was back in short trousers of course, why are parents so cruel? I was given just one concession however and that was that I could wear my jeans over my short trousers just for the journey to and from school but I had to remove them once at school and leave them in the cloakroom to dry.

The cloakrooms consisted of back to back rows of coat hangers above long wooden benches and running between the benches were red hot pipes that served to dry all the wet clothing hanging above them. This system was very efficient but the side effect was a hot steam filled room mixed with the odour of drying socks boots and coats, some of which were not as well washed as others, a memorable smell indeed.

At last I had been able to wear long trousers to school and I fully intended to keep them on so that just for once I would feel and look grown up like my friends.

I was out of sight from my parents, they would never know.

Our parents were the kind who made sure that we attended school every day come hell or high water. There were few children that lived further away from the school than us. We were always there while those living much closer could often not make it for some reason or another.

The disastrous winter weather had drastically reduced school attendance leaving much smaller class sizes and unbeknown to me it was decided that on this particular afternoon our class would join with the one above us.

I was sat comfortably in class with my long trousers on when the mixed class arrangement was announced and to my horror and disbelief the older class entered, including my older sister!

That same morning my sister had witnessed my protest against having to remove my long trousers on arrival at school and here I was sat in class wearing them.

It must have been the fear that my sister would tell on me when we got home as, throughout the lesson I conducted a Houdini style escape from my long trousers while all the time still seated at my desk!

When the lesson ended I was able to stand up, sporting my short trousers and file out of the room as if nothing had happened. Whether or not the teacher or my sister even noticed my contortions, I don't know.

I recall at a similar time that my classes hand writing skills were under scrutiny and the promise was that as soon as our teacher was happy that we had reached a certain standard she would then allow us to discard our pencils and write with a pen. Gradually my fellow classmates changed from pencil to pen until it was obvious to me that I was in the minority yet still I waited for her instruction for promotion to the elite band of pen pushers. Half term arrived without progression and still I was sharpening my pencil with the large handle driven pencil sharpener that was fixed securely to teacher's desk.

I can hear her now saying "Don't turn it too much or you will have no pencil left", which brings to mind another pencil rule that she had.

We were all issued with a brand new pencil at the beginning of term with the promise that if we looked after it and were able to return a similar sized pencil to her at the end of term them we would be issued with a new one for the following term. Those who failed in this quest had to make do with a choice from the box containing the longest of the second hand pencils that these "goodie two shoes" had discarded.

During that first half term I had little thought of school except for the pencil to pen promotion.

By the end of the half term promotion had eluded me but that didn't stop me telling my parents that when we returned to school I had been given permission to write in pen so could I have a biro for my pencil case?

We returned to school and my pen got to work. A few days later while in class we were busy writing when I felt the presence of the teacher from behind looking over my shoulder as I wrote. This is it I thought, I am in for it now. There was silence as I continued to write until the silence was broken by my teacher complimenting me on my writing. The loss of my teacher's memory during the half term break was a great relief to me.

A similar experience happened some years later at Dinnington Comprehensive School. I hated games lessons with a passion although somehow I did make into the school basket ball team and actually won a medal at a tournament where our team were the victors. At every opportunity I would ask my mum to write an excuse note which was always easier said than done. The few occasions that I managed to get a note was enough though as providing the games teacher didn't actually take the note from you it was good for another time. In the early years at Dinnington Comp the games staff were pretty keen in making sure that unless you only had one leg or a missing head then you had to take part and they would even try on occasions to override the instruction that any off games letter carried. In the later years they seemed to lose interest to the point where, having produced so many "excuse me" letters in the past, I had become an unknown on the sports field and when the games teacher asked at the beginning of a lesson for those who were permanently excused to stand to one side I could confidently join them without fear of reprisal. Result.

Back at Wales infants school, when I was in class 3 we had a student teacher who worked alongside our real teacher. Our proper teacher was Mrs Waite and I really liked her. Our student teacher was called Miss Molyneux and I liked her even more. She is quite probably still around now, enjoying her retirement as she must only have been in her late teens or early 20's at that time.

She was a breath of fresh air and so enthusiastic. She took us on a school trip which included a boat trip on the Manchester ship canal but what I remember most is the school project that we did with her. It was around 1963 and we knew that the M1 motorway was coming so we spent the summer term putting together a project that recorded every landmark that was soon to change or disappear forever. The school at that time didn't have a school playing field but close by was Wales Cricket Field that lay between the school and the fast developing New Tree housing estate. We would all file along the pavement between the school and the cricket field in a neat two by two formation with Miss Molyneux in the lead and Mrs Waite at the rear. On arrival at the

cricket field we would first have a project lesson and then
afterwards play games on the short mown grass.
I often wonder if our project still exists somewhere in the school
archives and what a great teacher
Miss Molyneux must have made.

***

The Crying Game

Having meandered from Waleswood pit entrance, through the railway sidings, scaled almost to the top of the pit tip, rafted under the MI and then on to School road and the school, let me now take you back to Mansfield Road by the old colliery entrance where opposite was the towering building that started its life as the pit head baths. The building was unusual in shape but identical to most buildings that served its purpose for miners to bathe following a long gruelling shift, deep underground, often on their hands and knees and in unimaginable conditions of dust and grime where their bodies would become thick with coal deposits and dirt.

Their return to the surface following an 8 hour shift was signalled by the two giant spoke wheels of the pit head winding gear spinning rapidly as they brought the cage full of miners back up the pit shaft from the depths of the earth. They would then walk the short distance to the baths where they could wash away what they could of the dust and grime that their strained and tired bodies had collected.

Even after this welcome cleansing it was easy to recognise a freshly washed coal face worker as around their eye sockets it was much cleaner than their face and gave the look of "Panda Eyes".

Beneath their shirts the scars of work in a confined space remained, impossible to wash away as the cuts inflicted by the roof of the coal seam on their torso as they crawled along, striped to the waist, hacking coal from the coal face with no more than a hand held pick, left deep scars on their backs where, during the course of the shift these cuts had ingested particles of black dust into the wound where it stayed sealed into the healing skin forever.

The unusual design of this building was due to it incorporating a large, high, square tower at one end with long vertical vented openings to each side and all crowned with a flat roof, not unlike a Norman church tower. In the tower was a large water storage tank held aloft to provide the water pressure for the showers below.

At the time of my recollections the pit head baths had long since ceased their original function but had been adopted and adapted to serve as the headquarters of the building maintenance team that were employed to maintain the mass of housing and other National Coal Board property that was owned by them in Wales Bar and neighbouring Kiveton Park.

One particular middle aged bricklayer employed on the team became quite a celebrity to many young ladies and went by the name of Mr Grundy. Mr Grundy was a good bricklayer and as I remember quite a reserved man. At that time the "swinging sixties" pop scene was well underway and young girls were keen to follow all the latest pop singers.

Mr Grundy had an apprentice called Stuart and it was Stuart who could see the benefit of disclosing his mentor's secret. In doing so Stuart hoped that he would also become attractive to the girls by association.

Mr Grundy lived in nearby Woodhouse with his family, one of which was his son David.

David was into the pop scene working in the Sheffield pups and clubs; he called himself Dave Berry and became famous in the early 60's for his songs "The Crying Game" and "Little Things". For the teenage girls to be able to get close to any connection with their locally born pop idol was a dream come true and Stuart would always have a wad of signed photos tucked in his pocket of the local idol ready to hand out to Dave Berry's adoring fans.

I think that secretly Stuart actually thought that he was Dave Berry or at least his agent.

***

Farming Days and Bygone Ways

As I described earlier in our adventures on Waleswood Curve, to get there we took the lane between the pithead baths and the cricket field which also led us towards Coulsons farm. This was called New Lane but taking a walk down New Lane now would be impossible as both it and the lands beyond have been swallowed up by opencast mining activities which have changed the landscape forever. New Lane was the gateway to my farming exploits and adventures of which there were many.

Agriculture has seen many advances in technology over hundreds of years and perhaps the industrial revolution of the Victorian era heralded the biggest changes. While this may be so I feel privileged to have seen working and also worked on pieces of machinery that were ancient even in the 1960,s yet for the farmers that used them they still provided a living.

Coulsons, Staniforth's, Clarence Smiths and Reg Smiths were all farms that I worked on for pleasure or occasionally money and all hold so many memories that I now want to share.

Coulsons Farm or Waleswood Farm as it was officially called lay in the valley beyond the sports field and at the end of New Lane.

The farm was run by the Coulson family and extended to around 125 acres, not a big farm by today's standards but typical of its day.

I became connected to the farm as much of this land surrounded Wallingfield; our family home in Wales Bar and the comings and goings of the Coulsons was a familiar sight long before I became old enough to get involved with their farming activities.

Old Mr Coulson (or Charlie as he would have us call him) and his wife lived on the farm while their son Roy worked the farm with them but treated his employment as a 9 to 5 job, if such a job exists in farming! He lived in nearby Kiveton Park and travelled to Waleswood farm daily in his rather scruffy and beaten up old Austin car. Charlie was always around the farm while his wife spent most of her time in the farmhouse. Roy, or Mr Coulson as we always addressed him, did most of the work on the farm and at peak times of harvesting or potato picking Roy's brother Bernard would also lend as hand.

In my formative years I would watch avidly from the safety of our garden as the land around us was farmed season by season. Autumn was ploughing time, allowing the large turned furrows of earth left by the plough at least a chance of being broken down by winter frosts so that come the spring the heavy clay soil would react more favourably to preparation for sowing spring barley.

Mr Coulson would arrive early in the morning with his big orange Nuffield tractor and 3 furrow plough. There was no cab to the tractor and come rain or shine the job had to be done. He always wore a full length brown leather coat and flat cap and if it was exceptionally cold perhaps a scarf too, pulled over his face allowing just his eyes to see the task before him.

It was essential clothing for the time yet now the same style of clothing is seen as trendy with the country set of today but perhaps instead with the scarf slung loosely over the shoulder as a fashion item!

Each field would take two or 3 days to plough as Mr Coulson relentlessly travelled up and down the field. As each furrow turned and formed, gulls would descend from the sky as if from nowhere, looking for rich pickings in the cold damp soil and although we were many miles from the coast as the crow flies the gulls seemed to know when the time was right for them to appear.

Sometimes winter wheat was sown which was far more work intensive as, after ploughing the ground had to be prepared immediately but not as it is done today in one operation with a multifunctional machine. Following the arduous task of ploughing the disc harrow followed and then the chain harrow before finally the seed drill could be employed. Each process was a separate operation and each field would take days to prepare.

The arrival of the seed drill was my first chance to get up close and personal to the action.

Mr Coulson always had a friendly wave but was too busy to get involved with my questions however Charlie was different. He obviously loved children and always had time to talk and entertain.

With the arrival of the seed drill Charlie would arrive too. Charlie would bring a second tractor, a large blue Fordson Major pulling a long 4 wheeled dray (trailer) full of sacks of seed corn. The seed drill was extremely wide and was supported at each side by a very large spoke wheel looking not dissimilar to the stage coach wheels of old.

Between each wheel and along the entire length of the drill was a series of tines that did the final preparation of the earth while at the same time seeds from a hopper above fed into the groove made by the tine while a second tine would complete the process of covering the seed.

All very technical but this was not the focus of my interest.

Along the entire width of the seed drill and to the rear of the hopper was a platform or step, not very wide but enough to stand on.

As I watched, father and son Coulson would raise the lid to the hopper and fill it with seed corn while standing on the platform. So that's what the step is for I thought.

Imagine my surprise as, when the seed drill was ready for action not only did Mr Coulson climb on board his Nuffield but simultaneously Charlie mounted the rear platform of the seed drill and off they went, up and down the field with Charlie bobbing up and down as the two metal brackets holding the step at each end literally put a spring into the step!

Well, I was hooked; I had to get on that step with Charlie.

Come lunchtime father and son Coulson returned to Waleswood farm on the Fordson while leaving the Nuffield, drill and dray in the field awaiting their return.

Note: - Back in the day lunch was not a word in our vocabulary.
Breakfast was breakfast
Lunchtime was dinnertime
Dinner time was teatime
Supper time was Horlicks time, Bovril time or a glass of warm milk time and a digestive biscuit.
However, just to confuse the issue even more:-

We had school dinners paid for with dinner money (1shilling per day or 5 pence in today's money) and a lunch box was a snap tin which contained your snap or lunch, now I'm confused!!
I almost feel a traitor to my upbringing using such posh words as evening meal or afternoon tea (a 4pm cuppa and a slice of cake) but, there we are that's progress I suppose.

With father and son "at lunch" it was my opportunity to explore the Nuffield and seed drill at close quarters. I climbed onto the step of the seed drill and imagined myself riding shotgun while Charlie tended to the seeds of corn in the hopper so on their return I made my presence felt.
 Charlie greeted me in his usual welcoming way and I was soon busying myself helping to drag the tough, seed filled hessian sacks from the dray to the seed drill where Charlie and Mr Coulson hoisted them onto the platform and spilled their contents into the hopper. Once full, father and son were off again drilling the seed in long straight rows across the field. During the course of the afternoon the seed drill was refilled once or twice and each time I made sure I did what I could to help. My persistence paid off as the last sack of seed corn was placed in the hopper of the drill, Charlie beckoned to me to climb aboard the step and signalled for me to hold tight to a metal handle that was fixed on the wooden face of the seed hopper, I didn't need asking twice! Charlie was an old hand at riding the seed drill. As we bounced along he kept both hands free while watching the drill do its work and moved effortlessly from one end of the platform to the other with perfect balance. There was no safety guard between the platform and the hoppers where the tines were in full view and to slip into that space would have spelt disaster. I made sure to hang on for dear life without hopefully showing the fear of self preservation that was just beneath the surface. I survived my

first white knuckle ride without incident and must have portrayed confidence to Charlie as this was the first of many rides that I was to experience.

This is an old photo I came across of Charlie (on the left) and his brother Joe some years before I was born. They are harvesting with a binder near the farm and in the far background a train can be seen on the Waleswood Curve.

Thinking back it must have been autumn time and probably half term at school. This half term holiday was always referred as Spud Bashing Week or Potato Picking Week and as the school holidays adopted name suggests it was when we got involved in the potato harvest. Of course it was impossible to guarantee that the harvest would be ready to pick during this one week but generally the potato harvest was in full flow at that time of the year and without the aid of the machinery used in today's harvesting it was an extremely labour intensive affair.

The Coulsons were not big potato growers but I remember that one year the field immediately behind Wallingfield was planted with a potato crop.

Potato picking paid good money, one pound per day, which was an amount of money that we could only dream of as youngsters and with the crop being literally just outside our back door we could see that easy money was for the taking.

Harvesting a potato crop was nothing like today's modern methods where one intricate machine plucks them from the ground and then passes them to another machine and then another machine before eventually arriving at the factory for yet another machine to process them without them once being touched by human hand.

The clue to our way of harvesting is in the description "potato picking". Word would go out that a farmer wanted pickers on a certain day and miraculously at around 9am on the given day a group of chatty women, often with young children, would descend on the chosen field having previously sent their school age offspring to school unless of course it was our holiday week. They would have their youngsters and babes in arms with them as, up to the age of five, life was spent at home, no nursery schools existed, but simply a baptism of fire when reaching the age of five when you were packed off to school on the first week in September following your 5th birthday and dumped in a playground of boys and girls, most of which were complete strangers to each other. The chorus of tears at the school gate on that first day was deafening and only slowly dissipated as the week progressed. Of course if the harvest happened to fall at half term (potato picking week) then there would also be school age children arriving to pick. It was this category that me and my sister fitted the year that potatoes were grown behind Wallingfield.

The field of potatoes was planted in long rows of ridges and hollows and the potatoes were lurking beneath the ridges. To break open the ridge and expose the golden nuggets of potato the tractor would drive down each ridge pulling an implement on which was a single tool in the shape of a ship's bow. As this implement tore through the ridge the crop of potatoes was laid bare appearing through the soil totally undamaged. Now it was our turn. Most hardened pickers would bring their own bucket but just in case the farmer always had a plentiful supply. We would descend on the opened ridge and start picking and as our bucket became full the contents were then transferred into a nearby hessian sack. Not all the crop was exposed by the ship's bow tool and it was necessary to turn the loosened earth with bare hands to be sure that all the potatoes were found. The expert pickers were quick to tell you if you had missed some and only when the farmer was satisfied that all the potatoes had been lifted would he then repeat the process on the next ridge.

Picking was hard back breaking work and it took all of 3 days to completely pick the field. The women stuck to the task in hand as the reward was a healthy boost to the household budget.

 My sister and I lasted just one day. On day two we were so stiff that we just could not face another day's work, let alone two. We watched the picking continue from the safety of our garden.

To us our earnings were pure spending money but to the women it was their bread and butter. The women must have ached just as we did but their incentives to see the job through were different. Throughout the 3 days Charlie was nowhere to be seen as with all the pickers there many hands were making light work and the boss took a back seat.

Not long after the last potatoes had been lifted in the afternoon of day 3 a shiny black Morris Oxford car arrived at the head of the field from which Charlie and his wife emerged. The gaggle of women swarmed around the both of them, eager to get rewarded for their hard work.

Charlie took a cotton money bag from the glove box in the front dashboard and proceeded to pay his tired workers. When it came to me and my sister he gave us a wry smile and placed a pound note in our hands and suggesting that perhaps next year we might do better!

The most exciting time of the farming year for me was the summer. I was free from School and it was harvest time.

Today the processing of cutting the corn, baling the straw and collecting the large round bales all happens in the wink of an eye as massive pieces of machinery descend on a field and follow each other round and round completing their tasks in quick succession.

Not so with Coulsons farm and many others like it.

During the 1960's there were still some local farms clinging on to the outdated practice of cutting, binding and threshing the harvest which I had the privilege to be part of and will recall shortly.

On Coulsons farm they had moved into the modern era of combined harvesting although looking back now their combined harvester was one of the early designs that required 2 men to operate which was the fun part for me.

Most combined harvesters of the day would have only the driver and the grain was collected in a large hopper on the machine and then discharged into a waiting trailer via a large auger pipe. The pipe would swing out from the combine harvester and rest high above the trailer a continuous stream of golden grain would cascade into the trailer below from the open ended pipe.

Of course this process necessitated a suitable silo storage system for the loose grain back on the farm which the Coulsons didn't have.

The Coulsons was a modern machine in every sense of the word or at least to look at but it lacked the storage hopper and discharge pipe. Instead on the side of the combine there was a large square wooden platform on which Charlie would stand. There were three inline chutes above the platform with a sliding shutter above each to open or close the chute entrance from which the grain would fall. From two of the chutes the harvested grain would tumble into large hessian sacks securely tied to a purpose made framework allowing the neck of the sack to be kept wide open. From the third chute the chaff (grass seed and other plant seeds) would discharge into another hessian sack. This system meant that Charlie was fully occupied swapping and changing the sacks as they became full and then each brimming sack would be stacked to the side of the platform until the combine came around the field to a point where the tractor and trailer was parked.

Here the sacks were unceremoniously dumped off the platform and left ready for loading.

These sacks of grain were extremely heavy and awkward to handle as, although the sacks were securely fastened the only firm grip to be had was from the gathered neck of the sack. By grasping this neck and then hugging the bottom of the sack simultaneously with your arm it was just possible to manhandle it from the ground to the bed of the trailer.

A chance photo shoot on the Coulsons combine harvester and on the right is the same type of machine in action where the ride on platform can be seen.

As with the seed drill it wasn't long before Charlie invited me to ride on the platform and what a treat that was. I would help him change each sack as it became full and delighted in pushing the sacks from the platform to the floor each time we passed the tractor and trailer.

Once the corn had been cut and the sacks of grain safely stored at Waleswood Farm there was the straw to think about. Large round bales were just starting to appear in the 60's but they too required a different type of equipment to collect and carry them, not to mention farm buildings and practices that were user friendly towards them. They would weigh perhaps half a ton or more which only a tractor could handle.

Waleswood Farm and its many buildings were a relic from farming of old and could not accommodate such modern farming practices.

First of all Mr Coulson would turn the straw with the straw turner into long heaped rows of straw and then arrive with his baler. The baler was pulled by the Nuffield tractor over the heaped rows while the baler would swallow up the straw before finally discharging a neat oblong bale of straw from the rear of the machine to the field below and once the baling was complete the field was strewn with neat packages of straw as far as the eye could see.

I had watched this process long before actually taking part and when it came to collecting the bales and loading them onto the dray for the journey back to the farm, Mr Coulson would walk back and forth numerous times to collect and load the bales by tossing each one individually with his pitchfork onto the slow moving platform of the dray while the tractor pulled it slowly around the field with Charlie at the wheel. As the dray filled with bales and got higher and higher the effort to raise these compact packages of straw high above Mr Coulsons head was immense until he finally made one last effort to reach the topmost layer.

As children, my siblings and I had spent long summer holidays at our grandparents in Somerset. Our summers were spent roaming the countryside in idyllic surroundings and while watching Mr Coulson walking back and forth I remembered that in Somerset the bales in the fields had been placed in piles of 8 or 10 by the farm labourer before the tractor and dray arrived to collect them, very sensible I thought.

By now I felt that I was really starting to make a contribution to the Coulson farming activities and looking out onto the field full of scattered bales behind our house where the baler had been left for collection the following day I knew what I had to do. The long hot summer evening afforded me the opportunity to pile the bales just as I had seen in Somerset and without a thought of what Mr Coulson might think I set too and worked my way through the entire field of bales. Straw certainly provides a soft bed for animals to lie on but it is not as soft to human skin, particularly to bear arms when wearing a tee shirt! By the time my work was done my arms were heavily scratched and I was hot, sweaty, and itchy but inwardly extremely satisfied with my evening's effort.

Bath and bed followed and by the time I was up and around the following morning I could see from the dining room window that Mr Coulson was already hard at work loading the dray with bales.

Should I put in an appearance or lay low and blame my work on the bale fairy?

After breakfast I went for broke. I walked up the field to where the tractor and dray stood, now almost half full with bales and climbed onto the dray to help stack the cargo.

 You will remember I mentioned earlier that Mr Coulson was a man of few words so the smile and thanks that I received from him meant everything to me and I felt my effort had been rewarded, however, my real reward was to come later that day. In the afternoon Mr Coulson returned for another load of straw and I was there in the field waiting.

He stopped the tractor and beckoned me to climb onto the dray. Once aboard he signalled me to hold tight to the large wooden framework that allowed bales to be securely loaded and we were off. The dray jumped and bumped across the field as I hung on for dear life.

Straw had to be kept dry and if there was chance of rain or, even worse a thunderstorm, which are not uncommon in the August heat, then it was essential for the straw to be gathered and stacked under the dry barn at Waleswood Farm. The Coulsons had 3 large drays to carry the hay or straw yet to my knowledge had only two tractors to pull them, or so I thought.

The Nuffield and the Fordson I knew well and as time went by I even got the chance of driving them in the fields on a number of occasions. What I was not aware of was that Charlie had a girlfriend at Waleswood Farm. She lived behind closed doors at the end of the long low implement shed that was the first building that greeted you on arrival at the farm entrance.

Her name was Alice or to give her full name, Alice Chalmers. Alice was smaller than her 2 tractor workmates and had bright orange bodywork. She was older than Nuffield and Fordson who both definitely sounded and looked male while Alice's more slender lines definitely confirmed her as female. Alice also sounded different with her 2 cylinder engine being less powerful then the 4 cylinder engines of her workmates but she was perfectly capable of completing any task that Charlie chose to give her.

Rain was promised the following day so Alice was put into service.

 Mr Coulsons brother Bernard was also summoned and all 3 tractors with their drays in tow arrived to do a clean sweep of the field so to be sure that all was safely gathered in.

I spent the afternoon helping to load the drays and eventually the job was done with the long journey back to the farm beckoning.

Charlie asked me if I wanted to ride with him and he didn't have to ask me twice, but, Alice only had one seat, where was I to go? Up top was Charlie's reply. Up top? I replied, yes up there on top of the loaded dray. It seemed as tall as a double Decker bus as I pulled myself up to the topmost layer of bales using the ropes that Mr Coulson had meticulously strapped around to secure them and once up there it was as high as I had imagined. All 3 tractors pulled out of the field and on to Mansfield road with Alice bringing up the rear. On our slow downward journey to Waleswood Farm we began holding up the traffic. Alice was not very fast and she had an enormous load to pull. At the head of the queue of traffic that formed behind us was the number 6 bus on its journey back to Sheffield and from my vantage point I was looking straight down the aisle of the upper deck!

The journey to the farm was a good 20 minutes and every minute was magical and while the bus driver was probably more concerned at keeping to his timetable his top deck passengers were more than happy to give me a wave.

 I wonder what health and safety would say today?

I knew that once at the farm that I would have to walk all the way back home but thankfully there was a shortcut over the fields which helped reduce the journey time but even so it was a good forty minute walk but worth every step.

When there was work to be done in the fields it always seemed to be between the hours of 9 am and 4 pm. Mr Coulson was never seen outside these hours. Farmers kept short hours, or so I thought.

Mr Coulsons working day actually started long before I awoke and was not complete until evening had arrived. Not only did he have all the tasks to do that I have already touched on but at Waleswood Farm there was a herd of dairy cows that needed milking twice a day.

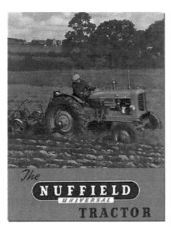 

**Here they are Nuffield, Fordson and Alice
The best of Farm Friends**

In order to keep the milk yield to a profitable level each dairy cow had to produce a calf every year to be sure the milk flow continued and this need meant even more jobs for Mr Coulson to do.

The calves would stay with their mother for no more than a week which was just long enough for them to suckle the lifesaving colostrums from their mother's teats. Following these few precious days the calf and mother were parted and mum would return to the herd to continue her twice daily milk production while the calf was kept with numerous other in the briars within the farm complex to be reared to what would be eventually an addition to the dairy herd, gender permitting. For this reason The Coulsons were always hopeful that their dairy cows would produce a female offspring but at that time the control of this eventuality was not as it is today. AI (artificial insemination) was available but required a vet to carry out the procedure and of course was at a cost although it did create the possibility of a calf with the preferred gender whereas keeping a bull with the herd "cost nowt" but left the gender choice to mother nature.

Of course the male calf was good for beef but they required an awful lot of food and time to get to the point when they were ready for the market and for this reason heifers that would go on to produce milk were the preference for the Coulsons.

As I became aware of the milking activities I wanted to be involved and that meant spending time at the farm. This was not a possibility in school term time but when the holidays arrived there was nothing that would keep me away.

Mum would make me sandwiches neatly packed in my snap box with hopefully a slice of fruitcake too. I would put the box in my duffle bag together with a bottle of diluted Robinsons lemon barley water and would joyfully set of down Mansfield road, turning left by the old chapel mission hall and then over the fields to Waleswood farm. It was downhill all the way and took less than 30 minutes but as I mentioned earlier the return journey was closer to 40 minutes, principally due to the uphill climb and a hard day's work!

The morning milking started early and it was my aim to arrive at the start, but that never happened. One day I made a determined effort to arrive at the milking parlour before the morning session and I was extremely pleased with myself when I arrived at the farm a few minutes before 8 am. I entered the milking parlour with great anticipation of being the first one there but already some of the herd had been milked. What time do farmers start their day?

I have watched many episodes of "Country File "and other such programmes and seen the methods of modern milking practices which bear no resemblance to the method that the Coulsons used yet their method was state of the art compared to that of a milkmaid perched on a three-legged stool !

*Why a three legged stool?
The reason is that due to the unevenness of the diary floor in years of old which would have been of cobbled stone or similar this meant that three legs were much more likely to settle on solid ground than 4 resulting in the three legged stool being much more stable to sit on.*

The milking parlour had five stalls, each having space for two cows that were separated by a shoulder height division made of concrete sporting a highly polished surface due to decades of contact with cow hide where each dairy cow had brushed along the surface while arriving or leaving on their twice daily visit. The stalls ran the full length of the parlour along one wall and at the head of each stall was a continuous stone trough where the cows were fed cow cake (small pellets of concentrated food) to keep them happy during the milking operation.

The row of stalls took up around two thirds of the parlours internal width with an open drainage channel running along the floor and a cobbled walkway beyond.

Each cow was tethered in position while being milked but that didn't stop them throwing out their back legs to the rear if they got agitated. Walking along the cobbled walkway was not without danger and it was always necessary to keep one eye out for a flying hoof while the other eye kept watch on the cobbled floor to make sure that you didn't place your foot in a hot and steaming cowpat that Daisy or Tulip had deposited on their way to the stalls.

Connecting with either could easily result in a bruise or worse, be it from a flying hoof or slipping on a steaming cowpat and landing on your back with limbs spread-eagled.

The Coulsons milking system was like that pictured over the page which consisted of purpose made stainless steel buckets on which clamped a lid that had tubes and four teat holders. These were placed on each of the cows teats. A final tube was connected to an overhead pipework system that provided the pulsating air sucking action required to stimulate the cow to release its milk.

Walking past the rear of a milking cow was not without risk!

This action was created by a large petrol generator that was
housed in a lean-to, tin clad, ramshackle building attached to the
milking parlour at the opposite end to the diary where the milk
was stored prior to collection. Protruding through the tin side
wall of the lean-to was the exhaust from the generator which
emitted a continual sky blue plume of smoke whenever the
generator was doing its job. The sucking action created by the
generator drew the milk from the cow's udder and into the
bucket. All highly mechanised you might think? Well not really.
As the cows were let into the milking parlour there was no need
to guide them. Each knew their place and would slowly and
purposefully pick their way along the cobbled walkway, then
turn in to the same vacant stall day in and day out and stand
patiently until Mr Coulson arrived to start the milking process.
I recall on more than one occasion as he made his way between
the two cows in their double stall, both cows would decide to
move towards each other and create a sandwich with Mr Coulson
as its filling! He would quickly brace himself against each cow
and smack their rump with the flat of his hand while shouting out
an order and simultaneously pushing them apart.

The two ladies were very obliging and would respond to his command immediately by moving left and right and in doing so would brush there enormous frames along the concrete dividers and apply a bit more shine to the concrete surface.

Hygiene, together with health and safety was more a case of common sense rather than the written rule back in the 1960's and with millions of us having survived till now then it's questionable that such practices 'back in the day' were not really that bad.

We didn't have allergies that seem to be fashionable today, yes we would get the occasional stomach ache or bout of diarrhoea (I think that's referred to as food poisoning today) but as soon as the nasty bug had been conquered by our immune system it never came back !

We drank from streams in the woods; we ate all manner of fruits from the hedgerows and sandwiches that had curled at the edges with the summer heat, let alone the hot sweaty cheese or meat that was their filling.

And best of all was the fresh milk straight from the cow, still warm or, better still was an hour or so later with the absolute delight of spooning the thick layer of cream that had settled on top of the milk, heaven.

Mr Coulson was conscious of hygiene and played his part.

As he placed the milking pale alongside the cow, with one hand he would connect the sucking pipe to the overhead pipework while simultaneously taking a cloth from the bucket of water that he had carried in his other hand and skilfully squeeze out the excess moisture from the cloth back into the bucket, then clean around each of the cows four teats and matching teat holders of the milking machine which, by now were gently pulsating via the air from the connected overhead pipe work.

No sooner was this contribution to hygienic practice complete that the teat holders were placed on the cow's teats and milk flowed gently into the stainless steel bucket of this ingenious piece of milking apparatus while the 'hygienic' cloth returned to the murky depths of the water filled bucket.

This task was worked over and over again until all the milking was complete.

So what became of the bucket of water and wiping cloth I hear you ask?

Both were rinsed out at the end of the session and the bucket left upturned to dry out internally while the cloth was laid on top of the bucket to dry in readiness for the next milking! Now that's health and hygiene at its very best!

Through all this it was my job to take the stainless steel bucket when full of milk to the diary and pour the contents into a milk churn.

Pouring the milk into the churn was a delicate operation, the weight of the milk and the height of the churn together with the additional height created by the funnel and filter fixed over the churns rim made it hard to hold the bucket steady while the milk entered the open top of the funnel, but knowing how precious the milk was I can assure you that not a drop was spilt.

An Ariel view of Coulsons Farm, the milking parlour is the long low building in the centre of the picture and Alice lived in the low building on the right by the stack yard.

Coulsons Waleswood Farm in the valley with Wraggs Farm on the horizon where the Pinders lived.

By the time the milking was nearing the end there would be quite a congregation of farmyard cats gathering outside the dairy door. When the churn was full the funnel and filter were removed and the paper filter discarded and this proved to be the reason for the congregation of cats. The filter, being paper had swollen considerably in size and was full of cream. Mr Coulson would toss the used filter through the open door to the waiting pride and the law of the jungle ensued. The cats would pounce on the congealed lump of cream and fight and eat simultaneously and in no time the entire filter was devoured. As quickly as they had arrived then the cats were gone, to sleep off their feast and look forward to the next milking.

The twice daily milking produced three ten Gallon churns of milk which were collected each day from the farm entrance. Here they were placed on a raised stone platform set at just the height of the flat bed lorry that collected them. Sometime between the hours of dusk and dawn they would be gone and in their place would be three empty churns waiting for the process to start all over again. The churns were extremely heavy when full and took great effort to move around requiring enormous strength, as did so many tasks on a farm of the 1960's and although there was plenty of mechanisation on some farms it had not all yet reached a rural farm such as that at Waleswood. Over time we became friendly with other neighbouring farms. All the farms in and around Waleswood were tenant farms, owned by the Coal Board following

Nationisation in 1947, however their tenants had been in residence long before that. Many of the tenants were senior citizens who, in any other walk of life would have taken retirement long ago together with the less strenuous activities associated with their aging bones but, farming was their life and

they could see no need, nor had any desire to change their
farming days and ways but farming modernisation was catching
up with their stayed ways and great changes were afoot.
The growing realisation that opencast mining of coal that lay in
shallow seams beneath their idyllic countryside farms was
slowly but surely becoming a reality.
They knew that told in the not too distant future the farms and
land that had provided them and their forefathers their
livelihoods would soon disappear forever. Their enthusiasm and
need to change was not there. Consequently it gave us the
opportunity to experience farms and farm practices that had all
but disappeared with an age gone by but was still alive and well
in our here and now of the 1960,s in the Waleswood farming
year which was our countryside playground.
The access to Coulsons Waleswood Farm was along New Road
and as I mentioned earlier, on arrival at Waleswood farm you
could go no further which very much dictated the land farmed by
the Coulsons. This land was to the left and right of New Road
and similarly along Mansfield Road towards Wales Bar.
Waleswood Hall farm was barely 300 yards as the crow flies
from the Coulsons but in terms of access was very much
different. Waleswood Hall Farm was in old Waleswood Hamlet
and reached via Wales Bar and along Delves Lane. Delves Lane
was a long and leafy byway and even with our young and willing
legs it seemed a very long walk from Wales Bar Corner to
Waleswood. It was some distance along Delves Lane before the
lane took a right fork at which point the road straight ahead
changed to Bedgreave Lane, continuing down into the Rother
valley and the scene of exploits I took you on earlier. To the left
was a short Road that led to Brabb's Farm but this farm never
featured in our adventures.

Continuing right along Delves Lane as Waleswood came into view it was Waleswood Hall Farm on the right that signified the start of the hamlet. I remember the Farm as being set back from Delves lane and only partially visible due to a large orchard between the farm and the Lane. As Delves Lane passed on through the hamlet and into open countryside, again the vista opened up towards Brookhouse in the valley beyond and it was at this point that the lane changed its name to Waleswood Road which, for those travelling in the opposite direction from Brookhouse, told them where the lane would take them!

At this point where the names changed was the place some yards beneath where we had played our games of 'Tunnel dashing' a few pages earlier!

Brookhouse Farm lay in the valley where Waleswood Road began its assent to Waleswood hamlet and the tenant farmer of Brookhouse Farm was Clarence Smith.

The road link between Brookhouse Farm and Waleswood Hall Farm meant that the land of each farm met and as a consequence they often shared both their farm workers and farm implements.

Comparing harvest time at these two farms to the practices that the Coulsons adopted was like comparing chalk with cheese as by comparison Both Brookhouse and Waleswood Hall farms were still in the dark ages while Coulsons was at the cutting edge of farming, so to speak!

I had seen pictures of harvesting of old and through that was aware of old farming words such as binder, binding, sheaves, stooks, threshing, wheat and chaff and such like but assumed that all this was now resigned to the history books but nothing could have been further from the truth to the reality of day to day life at Brookhouse Farm and Waleswood Hall Farm.

Earlier that Spring when wandering the fields and lanes around Waleswood in search of adventure we had met and befriended

Clarence Smith's farmhand. He introduced himself to us as Owd Ned as we came across him busying himself repairing one of many fences and hedgerows that divided the landscape into a mixed pattern of interlocking shapes and sizes. Owd Ned hailed from Brookhouse which to us was the other side of the world to our happy hunting ground and we never considered going there. Owd Ned told us that he had worked for Clarence Smith as both man and boy and the rare sightings we had made of Clarence Smith told us that they were of a similar age.

The stories that Owd Ned told of Clarence made us keep our distance. He told us that Clarence was something of an eccentric and a bit wacky to boot so; being impressionable young lads we had no reason to think otherwise.

Owd Ned told us of the need on the farm for many hands come summer harvest time and that we should keep an eye out for a start to the harvest activities.

We learnt that harvesting was to begin the following week, weather permitting.

For us this meant that the weather would be fine (surely like me your memories of childhood was of sunshine every day?) so with a spring in our step we arrived in the fields on the following Monday morning expecting to enjoy a similar harvest experience to that at the Coulsons.

 Wrong, we were about to relive a harvest of yesteryear.

The tractor was just about the only piece of agricultural machinery that we recognised during the whole harvest although that was extremely old and older still was the threshing machine and the Steam engine but that I will come to later. I suppose at least some modern practices had been embraced as there were no harnessed horses, oxen or donkeys in sight, instead it was us who had to do the donkey work!

The first thing we noticed was the absence of a combine harvester. Instead an ancient contraption arrived, towed by an equally ancient tractor. We were informed that this was the Binder.

A harvest Binder towed by a Nuffield like the Coulsons owned but the tractor that pulled Clarence's Binder was much older

This was a 2 man operation as the picture suggests so where did we come in?

It soon became clear as, following a circuit of the field and laying in the wake of the binder were many bundles of corn, all bound together in the middle (hence the 'binding' machine) and these bundles were called sheaves.

Owd Ned explained that all the sheaves had to be collected by hand and put into stooks. This instantly produced blank faces from us which prompted Owd Ned to give us a quick demonstration on the creation of a stook and the rest was then down to us.

By now, the tractor, binder and its two operators were away in the distance on another circuit of the field and Owd Ned was already on his 3rd stook.

The demonstration had looked easy enough and practice does make perfect I am told. Through the whole of the next week our practicing did improve and our efforts were suitably rewarded by a smile and thanks from our mentor. I should say that money was not our reason for participation but the five shillings per day that came our way at the end of the week was most welcome.

The idea of forming a stook was to allow the grain to dry to a point where it could be collected and returned to the farmyard to be threshed.

One distinct advantage, and probably the only advantage, was that the wheat could be cut irrespective of how much moisture was in the ripened grain as the sun would dry the grain while stacked in the stook, but of course while ever the grain was drying out in the field it could also get wet again and the longer it remained in sheaves in the stook then the grain would gradually part from the ears, fall to the floor and so reduce the yield.

Modern day harvesting may have the restrictions of having to be done in the right weather conditions but when these conditions are right the machinery employed to do the harvest ensure quick work and a maximum yield.

Whilst there were many willing farmhands for the harvest it still took two weeks and more to harvest the fields of cereal with the binder. Towards the end of the first week an equally ancient tractor as that which had pulled the binder arrived, towing behind it a dray ready to collect the sheaves and take them to Waleswood Hall Farm where we were told the threshing operation would take place. Once again we did our bit and helped toss the sheaves onto the dray as it slowly wound its way up and down the field behind the ancient tractor.

The fumes from the tractors exhaust had a distinctive smell and have stayed with me in much the same way as the aroma of roast beef on a Sunday! This distinctive smell was created from TVO, or tractor vapour oil, which was a mix of petrol and paraffin. It is a while now since I have savoured the smell but if you happen to be near a Mr Softee ice cream van of a certain age then the smell from the rear engine that cools the on board freezers is exactly the smell that Clarence's old tractor emitted.

The process of firstly cutting the crop, then placing in stooks, followed by the loading of the dray in the field and unloading in the stack yard at the farm invariably resulted in a gradual loss of the precious grain from the harvested crop and the final stage from stack yard to threshing machine would have been the last straw, in more ways than one!

In earlier times when threshing of the harvest was commonplace the entire threshing machine ensemble would be owned by a contractor who in turn was employed by local farms to process the harvest. The contractor would travel to each farm or to a common point to do the work. Many hands were required in the threshing process and we were enlisted as part of the team.

We were told that the threshing machine was due to arrive at Waleswood Hall farm imminently and not really knowing what to expect we eagerly awaited its arrival.

As we sat on the warm grass in front of the orchard alongside the entrance to Waleswood Hall Farm we noticed in the distance a thin plume of dark smoke rising above the hawthorn hedgerows that adorned both sides of Delves Lane together with the familiar sound of a steam train? Surely not, we thought, how could that be?

A few minutes later the most spectacular sight unfolded before us as into view came a steam powered traction engine towing behind it the largest piece of complicated equipment we had ever seen.

This was the mid 1960,s yet before us was a scene that could have been from the last century. Looking back I feel extremely privileged to have been there that day. It proved to be the very last time that commercial threshing took place at Waleswood Hall Farm and quite probably in the whole area as times were indeed changing. The entire existence of life as we knew it was soon to be confined to memory and the history books but for me the memories of that day are still as fresh and clear as if it were just yesterday.

It took the rest of the day to set up the Threshing machine and all the paraphernalia around it in readiness for the task ahead.

Owd Ned told us to turn up the following morning by 8am and be ready for some hard graft.

The threshing machine had been positioned on the stone track which ran alongside the stone barn. a The entire threshing ensemble covered almost the total length of the barn. On the other side of the track and running parallel to the barn and was the stack yard with a Dutch barn almost as long as the stone barn opposite. The stone barn formed one side of a large covered quadrangle housing the many pens where cattle lived in the winter months but this day they were empty as all its bovine residents were out in the fields enjoying the delights of summer grazing.

The barn was typical of thousands built on farms catering for agricultural practices that were now fast becoming uneconomical and being replaced with large metal hangers built to house equally large modern day machinery and up to date animal husbandry practices.

The barn doors were central to the long building and mirrored each other on opposite elevations. The two pairs of large wooden arch topped doors opened outwards and were now swung open and neatly hooked back against the external stone walls of the barn.

Beneath the Dutch barn all the sheaves had been neatly stacked and almost reached the barns curved roof which, when the Dutch barn was empty looked very strange supported only by a slender steel structure beneath the distinctively shaped roof.

Beyond the threshing machine and on the same stone track was the steam engine positioned perfectly in line with the mass of machinery that it was to provide the power too.

Linking the two beasts of yesteryear were two large, flat, thick material belts made from finely woven hemp, suspended from the ground and wrapped around two flywheels, one on the traction engine and one on the threshing machine. Smoke was billowing gently from the funnel of the traction engine which by now had built up steam and was ready for the day's work.

In addition to Owd Ned there were a number of farmhands stood around and Ned assured us that they all had a job to do. Also looking eager for work were two Jack Russell Terriers,running back and forth showing shear excitement with the prospect of what the day would bring.

Bloody good ratters them are said Ned, just watch um when thee see one, them vermin don't stand a chance.

The signal came to start work via a shrill whistle as the traction engine let off steam and slowly the flywheels on the engine started to spin which in turn rotated the long flat belts fastened to the pulleys of the threshing machine.

The thresher came to life and the noise was deafening as the whole machine was shaking with belts, pulleys, rods and all manner of technical wizardry moving back and forth, up and down and side to side, this surely was an engineering miracle at work.

By the time the thresher was up to speed two of the farmhands had climbed up into the Dutch barn.

The two farmhands did their work with great speed and dexterity. With one hand they would cut the string that bound the sheaf and swiftly tucked this under their trouser belt for safe keeping while the other hand held a pitch fork that was already firmly attached to the sheaf. With pinpoint accuracy they tossed the individual sheaf on to the top of the thresher where moving belts carried the sheaf along until it disappeared deep into the mass of moving parts to be processed by parting the wheat from the chaff and straw.

At the back of the machine were a series of hoppers under which was hung a hessian sack and it was these sacks that collected the golden grain. Two more farmhands were busy here filling the sacks and when full tied the neck of the sack tightly with the string that their workmates, still high up in the Dutch barn, had collected for them and thrown down at the sack men's feet when their trouser belt had reached string storage capacity.

As each sack was completed it was dropped to the floor and with a flick of a powerful foot it was kicked, rolling away from the hopper men's feet to be collected and then picked up by a third team of two farmhands.

Without doubt these two brawny fellows were the strongest and toughest of the entire threshing crew. Each would stoop to pick up a brimming sack of corn and with one hand around the neck of the sack would then swing the sack a full half circle into the air where it would land perfectly across their shoulders to be carried some 20 yards along the stone track to a building just beyond the stone barn. Here a wooden ladder leant against the building leading to a doorway on the first floor that was the entrance to the loft where the grain was to be stored. Without missing a step the farmhand scaled the ladder and with a slight movement of his shoulders the sack and its contents were launched through the doorway. Inside in the darkness of the loft was yet another farmhand methodically stacking each sack in long straight rows.

So where did we come into all this activity?

The front of the machine was where the straw appeared and the machine had been perfectly placed so that the ever increasing pile of straw mounted up just outside the stone barn doors. Owd Ned explained that it was our job to take the straw and pile it in the stone barn. Using his pitchfork Ned folded and turned the straw until almost the entire pile that had collected under the machine was loaded onto his fork. He then turned his back on the captured pile and as he did so he lifted the pitchfork to rest on his shoulder while the staff of the fork neatly tucked under the crook of his elbow and with the enormous ball of straw now suspended behind him he walked through the barn entrance to the far end of the barn and neatly replayed his previous actions in reverse and deposited the straw in a pile.

He turned to us and with a broad smile saying, there tha are, nice steady job for's yer naw geron wi it.

We stuck at it but for each single load that Ned carried we must have carried ten and still his output was greater than ours.

The threshing took three whole days to complete and during all of that time the two Jack Russell's ran back and forth having the time of their lives, searching, chasing and sometimes even catching a mouse or rat that had lost its hiding somewhere in the sheaves.

With two men in the Dutch barn, two bagging up, two carrying sacks, one in the loft, the traction engine operator and his mate, together with Owd Ned and the two of us you would have thought that many hands make light work, well, none of it was light work of that as I am sure as it is one of the hardest jobs I have ever done.

There were however moments of light relief when, above the deafening noise of the traction engine and threshing machine and the constant dust cloud there was the occasional shout of triumph which signified that the hailer had seen and caught a rat. This was proven by holding his arm aloft with pitchfork in hand and on the end would be a rat firmly skewered to one on the pointed tines, wriggling and writhing in the final throws of life.

We worked for three long days and it was barely a day or so after that the two of us fell ill. As I recall it was like a bad bout of hay fever with probably a hint of over exhaustion mixed in too. It took the best part of a week for us to recover. Whenever I think back to the whole experience the first thought that springs to mind is, ah yes, that was the time when we caught threshing disease.

I was so pleased to find this photo which is the actual traction engine and threshing machine busy working at Waleswood Hall Farm

There had been small scale opencast mining in and around the Rother Valley sometime prior to the mass destruction of farms and farming that had survived and thrived for centuries. This small scale coal harvesting had not encroached on the tranquillity of the valley and its inhabitants to any great extent and few could see or comprehend what was to come.

Clarence Smith went to his grave leaving his farm and his valley much the same as when he had arrived. He died at Brookhouse farm and though my research has been unable to confirm, I suspect also the he was probably born there too.

He died around 1970 although it could have been a year or two either way. The farm and its contents were a monument to a bygone era and the subsequent farm sale by his executors revealed a collection of treasures that brought people from far and wide, not only to see what had been hiding away for years and years but to also to hopefully make a successful bid to takeaway with them a piece of history.

I remember the spring of our first acquaintance with Owd Ned when, one day when his master was away from Brookhouse Farm he took us on a tour of the many outbuildings around the farm. Like most farms built before mechanisation evolved, when the powerhouse of agriculture was man, horse, donkey and oxen, the buildings were grouped to create a quadrangle with the farmhouse dominant on one elevation while the other three elevations formed a square open court yard commonly called a crew yard. The crew yard was where the animals lived during the winter months and was often covered by some sort of roof structure fashioned from any material that would fit the purpose and such was the structure at Brookhouse Farm.

To the rear of one elevation was a lean too building that stretched its entire length and it was this long low building that held the most fascination for me.

It was deep, with the interior barely in half light where it abutted the back wall of the large barn that supported the roof. The roof at the front of the lean too was supported by stout wooden pillars sat on square foundation stones which had kept the wooden supports from contact with the muddy wet earth and therefore guaranteed their longevity.

The equipment stationed between each of the pillars was old. The tractors that we would later see in the fields at harvest time were there, together with the binder, the drays and much more. It was the equipment that was in the second and third rows in the rear darkness that we looked at in wonder. They were beyond use as no longer were there carthorses or oxen to pull them, harnessed between the shafts that still adorned the many hand crafted carts. Some of these relics were painted to add further charm and character to this wonderful glimpse of farming history before our eyes.

Owd Ned beckoned us to the far corner of the lean too and was keen to show us firstly a two wheeled pony trap and to the side of that a four wheeled carriage. The carriage was covered in straw and dust accumulated from years of storage and the elegant canopy that sat above the now decaying leather upholstered seats was full of holes but little imagination was needed to see how splendid a sight this would have been in its heyday. Ned was keen to tell us that when he was a nipper he had once rode in the carriage all the way from Brookhouse Farm to Waleswood and back!

I didn't go to the auction sale but I do remember seeing a photo of the carriage on the front cover of the order of sale taking its rightful place as the star attraction.

Thinking back to the story my father told of the stage coach charging past him in the darkness along the lane by the mission hall, could this have just possibly been the spirit of Clarence and his carriage taking his final journey into the history books??

Another farmer that I had the opportunity to work for was Reg Smith.

Reg Smith's farm was Wales Grange on Church Street in Wales. Wales Grange sat immediately opposite the village church and like the array of buildings I described at Brookhouse Farm they were set around a quadrangle courtyard although much smaller in scale. The gable end of the farmhouse faced onto Church Street with a narrow raised path running alongside which was shielded from view by a stonewall that denoted the boundary of the farm and the street. This path led to the rear of the farmhouse where a large but overgrown orchard stretched downwards parallel to Church Street and only stopped when reaching the boundary of a large red brick detached house on the corner of Church Street and Orchard Lane. Orchard Lane provided the short cut from Church Street to the school on School Road without the need of walking through Wales Square. There is no doubt that before the construction of this house the orchard would have thrived there and naturally gave its name to the lane. The mere fact that this orchard was overgrown and uncared for was an open invitation to "scrump" its produce, which we often did, safe in the knowledge that escape routes were plentiful.

I don't recall if there was a family relationship between Clarence and Reg Smith but I suspect there was. With such a common surname as Smith they could have been related to so many but, living only two miles apart as the crow flies and both being men of the land then there is little doubt in my mind that their gene pool was pretty close.

A further endorsement of this theory was their chosen method of farming. Their respective ages suggested that that Reg Smith was a generation younger but that was not the case with their farming methods which were both firmly in Clarence's era.

In my early teens, just like many of my peers, I wanted to earn some pocket money and a Saturday job was just one way forward. Typically in the 1960's the salary for a day's toil on a Saturday was £1 and regardless of what the work involved this seemed to be the standard wage.

It was not an insignificant amount as according to the office of National Statistics £1 in 1965 is equivalent to £18.24 in 2017

Unlike Reg Smith, who was a grumpy old sod, his wife Mrs Smith was the opposite, not so much in age but certainly in character.

She was approachable and friendly and I often met her at the gate of Wales Grange when delivering the Sunday papers (which was another money making scheme that I will return to later) and it was at one of these chance meetings that I broached the subject of a Saturday job.

Mrs Smith said she would ask the question and let me know.

The following week she was waiting at the gate for her copy of the Sunday Times and with her usual friendly greeting told me that she had arranged for me to start work the following Saturday however I was not to report Wales Grange but to their chicken farm opposite the school and behind the Methodist Chapel on School Road. I was aware of the chicken farm but had never associated it with Reg Smith.

As my understanding of Smiths chicken farm unfolded I could see that they had already built a new bungalow which they were soon to move into alongside two large chicken houses after which they would forsake Wales Grange which, for a number of years following their move was still used as a base for machinery and general storage. Even the farm house had new tenants as Chickens and geese wandered freely through the permanently open front door.

On my arrival for work the following Saturday Reg Smith was there to greet me. Come on lad al show thee rarnd and get thee on wi some work. He showed me the chicken houses and more buildings beyond. A keep me pigs over thea in them there sty's, he said, but thall ave nowt to do with them, chickens ul be thar job und sows al be mine.

What a lovely place to build a new house I thought. Not only was there the pungent aroma of the chickens and pigs to be endured but also, just beyond and alongside the rear boundary fence that ran the entire length of the property was an embankment at the bottom of which was the M1 motorway with the constant hum of traffic as it passed, going North or South. Not exactly Location, Location, Location.

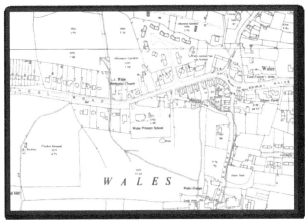

Pre M1 Motorway

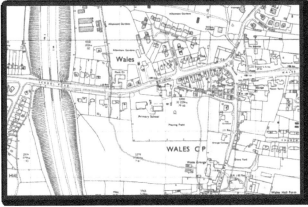

Post M1 Motorway

 A study of the maps above show Wales Grange and its orchard (circled in red) both before and after the arrival of the MI Motorway. The arrowed red line goes across the fields to the left and along a lane between the second and third houses by the school and then, emerging onto School Road crosses the road and on down a lane by the side of the chapel and into a field (pre M1) and the chicken farm (post M1). On the pre M1 map only one large red brick house stood between Wales Grange, the orchard and Orchard lane, soon after the Smiths were settled in their new bungalow the orchard was given up to new houses that gradually multiplied in number which no doubt swelled the coffers of Mr & Mrs Smith. The arrival of the M1 also swallowed up and deprived the school use of the cricket field which resulted in an extension of the existing school grounds into land that had previously belonged to the Smiths which boosted the Smiths coffers yet again.

The land on which the chicken farm now stood had previously been part of a much larger field, again swallowed up by the M1. The arrival of the M1 brought great changes to many lives and not least to the life and livelihood of the Smiths. However, what with compulsory purchase of some of their land to roads and playgrounds and the orchard gradually sold for residential development it assured them a bright future with their chickens and pigs.

Reg Smith opened the door of the first chicken shed and ushered me inside, quickly closing the door behind us. He explained that currently it was night time and the chickens were all roosting.

He went on to explain that the chickens had three days to our one and the commercial term for these chickens was 8 week broilers. Chickens and their care was not alien to me as at school I had opted to take GCE Agriculture and with a school farm containing chickens, pigs and other livestock (albeit in smaller numbers) I was in familiar territory, or so I thought. I was aware of a chicken being referred to as an old boiler, meaning that due to their advanced age they had to be boiled in water for a considerable length of time before they were tender enough to eat rather than simple roasting but a broiler was a new one on me.

Reg explained that from day old chicks they were subjected to 3 days to our one and consequently they would eat 3 times as much and by the time they reached 8 weeks of age they were actually 24 weeks old! This rapid aging process produced extremely tender, plentiful, and desirable meat at a much reduced cost to the farmer, a win win for both producer and consumer. There were literally hundreds of birds in each of the two sheds and during their short day the noise was deafening. My job was to walk through the crowd of birds and collect any that had died from perhaps over eating, fighting, or other terminal ailments and remove them from the shed. It seemed that if this was not done each day then the corpses would eventually be set upon by the remaining brood. Once collected I would clutch them by their feet and as their bodies hung limply in my grip I would take them outside and deposit them in a large covered bin. Every Saturday was the same and gradually my appetite for chicken waned somewhat.

One particular Saturday evening following my usual knock on the bungalow front door to ask for my wages, I was greeted by Mrs Smith who cheerfully invited me in to the kitchen while she fumbled in her handbag for a £1 note.

 She thanked me for the day's work and after handing me the crumpled green £1 note she continued to hand me a brown paper bag that had been laid on the kitchen table. I thought you would like this she said. It's plucked and dressed and ready for the oven, I hope you enjoy it.

The chicken was roasted the following day and it was the best chicken I had ever tasted!

My least favourite task that I was often required to do was stone picking. I felt sure that this was the fall back job to give the Saturday lad if there were no other jobs to do. I could almost guarantee that if it was cold and raining then stone picking would be my task of the day with just the occasional appearance from Reg. I was instructed to gather any stone bigger that a golf ball that lay on the surface of the freshly harrowed field and put them into piles to be collected later with Reg's help. The first time I stone picked I waited expectantly for the help that had been promised but it was not until the afternoon that Reg finally put in an appearance. However, it was not to pick up stones but to ride around the field on his aging grey Massey Ferguson tractor pulling an equally old trailer onto which I had to load all the stones that I had lovingly collected and all by hand. As each pile was loaded he would move on to the next as I followed on behind.

Occasionally Reg would take me to Wales Grange where he kept most of his farm implements. He didn't have a lot of land and following the compulsory purchases for the M1 and school playing fields his estate had reduced even more. What few fields he did have were close to Wales Grange while the chicken farm stood in relative isolation on the other side of the village.

On one particular Saturday morning Reg announced that he had a field of grass that was ready for cutting and my help was needed. Well at least this was a change to the usual Saturday toil I thought but my recollection of cutting grass on other farms didn't involve more than one man with tractor and machine? Reg beckoned me towards his pig sty's where his old Grey Fergie was parked. On the back of the tractor was a small open backed platform suspended from the ground by the tractors hydraulic system. The suspended platform allowed various items to be placed upon for ease of transportation. A number of food stained empty metal dustbins currently occupied the platform which we removed to reveal 5 perfect circles where they had stood. Inside each circle the metal platform was visible and clean but beyond the Olympic symbol that the bins had inadvertently created the platform was thick with deposits of all manner of dry and crusty foodstuffs that were firmly adhered to the platform.

I sat on the now empty platform in a vain attempt to place my backside on a clean circle while Reg fired up the old tractor and off we went to Wales Grange, crossing School Road, along the narrow lane between the two houses and up the fields to Wales Grange at the top of the hill. This approach to Wales Grange was so different to that on Church Street where, unless you were aware of what lay beyond the stone walls that abutted the Street then you would pass the farm without a thought whereas arriving as we were from the fields below the Grange stood majestically on the crown of the hill with the Church tower visible beyond on the skyline.

The ride on the platform afforded no comfort from the lumps and bumps of the field and together with the thought of the crusty seat that I was sat upon then arrival at our destination could not come soon enough.

The platform was removed from the tractor and Reg then proceeded to open up a pair of large barn doors to reveal an array of aging farming implements. That's what we need today he said pointing to what certainly looked like a grass cutting machine but not of the modern era!

The two wheels that supported the machine were metal and devoid of rubber tyres. Instead the outer rim of the wheel was also metal with large studs evenly protruding around its circumference which were intended to give some grip to the ground on which it was pulled along.

While in storage The scythe or cutting blade on the machine sat vertically and was lowered by the hydraulics of the tractor to a horizontal position for cutting, or at least that was my understanding of mowing machines that Mr Coulson and other farmers in the locality now used but Reg's machine was different. At the rear of the machine and in a commanding, elevated position was a seat supported by a sturdy curved metal bar which I later learned afforded the occupant of the seat a modicum of comfort as it flexed up and down from the undulating ground that the mower travelled on. To the side of this seat was a large lever which was not unlike an oversized handbrake.

I had certainly seen a similar machine in Clarence's collection however Reg's machine had one subtle difference. This machine had been converted from a horse drawn mower to a tractor drawn mower.

Once the mower was safely coupled to the old Grey Fergie we set off out of the farmyard, this time with me on foot while Reg led the way on the tractor retracing the journey that we has made earlier to a point where we reached a field gate. Reg dismounted, opened the gate and then, once I had caught up with him, proceeded to explain to me my role in the proceedings.

Na then lad, a whant thee to sit on that theea seat and mak sure tha owds on tight (to what I thought) an when I gi thee ma signal a whant thee grab that lever, squeeze it tight an push it forward. When tha does that thea cutter ul drop darn and start cutting grass. Na then, when we get to top o field a whant thee to grab lever again and pull it ard and mek cutter gu back in air, then a can turn raand and we can start again. As tha gorit lad?

There were no further instructions as I was deemed to have gorit. I climbed aboard the mower and found the seat surprisingly comfortable but inwardly I was terrified as there was absolutely nothing to stop me falling forward into the machine that trundled along beneath either falling sideways into the wheels or chattering cutter or backwards into fresh air. How would Reg explain to my parents what he had had me do for my £1 Saturday job if I didn't return home? The old grey Fergie's engine built up speed and we were off, and I followed Reg's instructions to the letter. After two circuits of the field I was feeling much more confident in my duties and at the end of the day's work I was rather disappointed that it was all over.I have one more farming story to tell of Reg Smith but first let me take you back to where my farming adventures started on New Lane by the pit head baths on Mansfield Road. I described earlier how the land lay on the roadside from New Lane at Waleswood to the start of East Terrace at Wales Bar at the time of my arrival at Wallingfield. The cricket field, Coulsons field, allotments and general scrubland bridged the two landmarks but back then change was just around the corner. The Cricket field survived in place the longest until its eventual relocation in the 1980's as did Coulsons field but the allotments and scrubland changed beyond all recognition in just a few short years.

The scrubland was bought up in part by a Mr Gratton who, being a mechanic, built a garage complete with petrol pumps and servicing facilities. It was not an all singing all dancing service station that we associate with a filling station of today but a much more muted affair where the occasional car was serviced and a few second hand cars bought and sold along with a gallon or two of petrol.

Not long after this business venture had started there were rumours that a large warehouse was to be built between Mr Grattons garage and East Terrace and exactly opposite Wallingfield.

The warehouse was to be the distribution centre for McVities, Crawford's and Macfarlane Lang biscuits, a national company which had become collectively known as United Biscuits some years earlier. When complete, large vans emblazoned with pictures of Jaffa Cakes, Rich Tea and Crawford's Wafers busily ferried back and forth distributing their wares. Mansfield Road Traffic was on the increase and there was so much more to come.

The front of United Biscuits warehouse soon after it was built

Closer to Sheffield in its northern suburbs was a local chain of supermarkets by the name of Dels and their expansion dictated that they too needed a storage and distribution warehouse and soon this became a reality as their new facility was built, squeezed in between United Biscuits and Grattons garage. Handsworth near Sheffield, some 7 miles from Wales Bar was the home of E T Sutherland & Sons who were famous for their potted meat. In the early 1960's they decided to open a new factory and this was to be located at Wales Bar. The allotments and extensive land that remained between Coulsons field and Grattons garage was the chosen location for this expansion and the new factory was quickly established. Local employment received a major boost with scores of men and women joining the ever expanding workforce. Vehicular and pedestrian traffic on Mansfield road increased yet again and there were even signs of a "rush hour" emerging as Sutherland's workers started and ended their working day.

So, now that Sutherlands have arrived on the Waleswood landscape let me take you back to Reg Smith, the pig farmer.

I was not allowed to be involved with Reg Smiths pigs other than to see them from a distance and to listen to Reg's continuous commentary of just how wonderful they were. Everything to do with these pigs was firmly under his control. Like all animals his pigs needed food, lots of food as lots of food meant fat pigs and fat pigs produce lots of pork and bacon.

Reg Smiths venture into pigs very much coincided with the arrival of E T Sutherlands and their food business at Wales Bar and looking back it seems clear that Reg was quick to take up on this fact.

Any business involving food processing would invariably also produce food waste and while Sutherlands food waste was beyond human consumption it was ambrosia for his pigs.

Every day in the early afternoon, Monday to Friday, Reg could be seen on his old Grey Fergie wending his way along School Road and on to Mansfield Road towards his destination. The platform behind his tractor loaded with five empty metal dustbins.

By 4pm he was on his return journey, the dustbins now full to the brim with whatever was Sutherlands surplus food of the day. As his tractor rode the humps and hollows of the road the dustbins would sway gently back and forth allowing the brimming contents of food to wash over the sides and gently run down the dustbins to the platform that supported them.

No wonder I had reluctantly sat on the Olympic symbol for my ride to Wales Grange.

However, not all the food that his pigs were fed was the best. Reg also collected leftover food from the kitchens of Wales Junior School and as a former pupil I can vouch for the fact that some of these left over School dinners were certainly not and had never been fit for human consumption but no doubt his pigs thought differently.

Sunday papers and other jobs.

By the age of 15 I was holding down 4 jobs in addition to attending my last year of School. Our parents were very strict on school attendance and we all had a 100% attendance record however my attendance record most certainly didn't match my attention record!

School work was boring, as were the subjects, or at least most of them. I have already told you that I took GCE O Level Agriculture and I firmly believe that the only reason I failed that subject was due to a change in teachers mid way through the course. Old Aker Parkinson was an excellent teacher and could hold the attention of the whole class with ease however his successor was the opposite. Half the class simply messed around during lessons which quickly brought the other half to the same level of behaviour and from then on all was lost.

For those who already know me then guessing my other favourite subject is easy, woodwork of course! I left School in the summer of 1970 with just one O Level pass in this very subject.

Of course I should have paid more attention in class but who needed to speak French in 1970's Yorkshire? What a waste of time. Now, 47 years later and having lived the last 9 years in France I know now that I should have paid more attention but no one has a crystal ball, c'est la vie!

It is perhaps worth noting here that in the summer of 2008 I doubled my GCSE (GCE O level) tally by sitting and passing my French exam, Mrs Bennett who was my frustrated French school teacher would have been proud.

I had three paper round jobs and my Saturday job with Reg Smith brought the tally to four.

The first paper round that I took on was in the evenings, delivering the Sheffield Star in and around Wales Bar. Our local (and only) newsagent was Harold Prestige and his shop was in Wales Square.

The shop was run by Harold and his sister Mary who had taken over the business following the death of Mr Prestige senior. Old Mrs Prestige still busied herself around the shop but was fast becoming a liability due to her declining health and advancing years. Harold and Mary were unmarried as was their younger sister and although they all lived "over the shop" this youngest sibling chose to work elsewhere.

The shop was double fronted and actually consisted of two shops in one. The newsagents was on the left which and in addition to its core merchandise it also sold sweets and other childhood treats, this side of the shop was the domain of Harold Prestige while on the right was a haberdashery run by Mary. In my formative years I had often visited Mary's side with my mum where she bought various items needed to darn, sew and generally repair our clothing but now it was Harold's side that I visited six times a week to collect around forty Sheffield Stars to take on my paper round.

On School days I would arrive home at around 4.45pm after the school bus had dropped us off at Wales Bar and then walk from the Bar Corner to Wallingfield which already felt like a route march following a day at School. After a quick change of clothes I would grab my grubby white canvas paper bag on which were emblazoned Sheffield Telegraph and set off back along Mansfield Road to the Bar Corner, then up and over Wales Bar hill and along School Road to Wales and Prestige's newsagents. The Sheffield Star was the evening paper of The Sheffield Telegraph group and I would have much preferred the name of the Star on my paper bag to advertise the paper that I was actually delivering but Mr Prestige was not the type of person who would understand such a thought, a bag was a bag as far as he was concerned.

My round was of average size and each Monday Mr Prestige would give me an updated list of all the delivery addresses although it rarely changed from week to week.

Forty newspapers were very heavy and it even though the canvas bag was the perfect size in which to carry them it was necessary to continually swap the bags shoulder strap from one shoulder to the other a number of times on the long walk back to Wales Bar where my first delivery was at Radford's the Butchers'.

Pashleys was next with the front door and its letterbox hidden behind the trees that in turn hid the bungalow from view and then on to the few terraces that still existed behind the houses with Waleswood Hotel that fronted Wales Bar Corner being my next port of call.

Then South Terrace which for some reason few of the residents here had the Star delivered, perhaps they shared the paper with their neighbours? Which was all very well but what would they have had to hang on the nail behind the outside toilet door?

East Terrace was very long with thirty eight houses in total although not all were Star readers. I was at least grateful that my paper round consisted mainly of terraced houses as a similar number of deliveries on a housing estate would have taken considerably longer.

I had just three stars to deliver on Waleswood villas before returning home to Wallingfield with my final Star newspaper and my tea. I would barely get through the door where I was met by my father expectantly waiting for his evening read.

I had my Star round for about three years and it paid the princely sum of 7/6d per week and the pay didn't change throughout that time, inflation wasn't a consideration then as it seems to be now and the welcome income was never questioned.

One evening while I was collecting my Stars Mr Prestige asked me if I would like a morning round.

I had previously expressed an interest for doing the mornings as I knew that it was much better pay and for that reason paper boys and girls rarely gave up this more lucrative round.

Mr Prestige explained that the round almost covered the same houses as my Stars so would be perfect for me. I agreed and with pay of 12/6d per week I was set for a big rise in income. Mr Prestige presented me with a brand new white canvas bag for my new job which looked extremely smart especially with the bold black writing on it advertising The Star and Green Un. Now that I had two canvas bags I was able to correctly advertise the contents of my morning and evening rounds!

At least my Star round had an open ended finishing time although if for some reason I was particularly late on the round some customers would be already standing at their gate waiting for me, no doubt my untimely arrival upsetting their routine.

By comparison the morning round had neither a casual start or finishing time. It was hard enough to get up for school in the morning let alone to get up at hour or two earlier to face whatever the days weather had to offer while trudging all the way to Wales to collect the papers and then all the way back to deliver them. It was always a close call to finish the round, change into my school uniform, have breakfast and then change my paper bag for my school bag and get to the school bus stop at the Bar corner before 8.10am. Thankfully mum was always there to make sure that deadlines were met by first getting up before me and then waking me from my slumber in order to get me up to do my round and then have a full English ready for breakfast when the round was done!

The Green Un was/and still is a Saturday only paper which was not on the list for deliveries as it was a late edition containing all the sport of the day. At the time I recall that all professional football matches across the land kicked off at 3pm, unlike today when kick off is dictated by the TV sponsors who plough millions into the game. The Green Un contained the half time scores of the day but was already printed and out with the street sellers by the time the final match whistle was blown. Needless to say that the seller's cry of Green Un Green Un would also be mixed with tantalising suggestions of what the final score might be. The newspaper used for this paper was green so it was aptly named using the local dialect as those not of Sheffield would have called it the Green One.

Having a Saturday job and 2 paper rounds earned me £2 per week (£36.50 in 2017) which was more than enough for a young teenager to take on but, temptation came my way when my friend told me that he had heard that there was Sunday paper round coming up for grabs in the near future with a wage of 35 shillings !
The distribution contract for the Sundays was not owned by Mr Prestige but by a family in Kiveton called Tye. Their operation was totally different as they had no shop and operated from the back kitchen of their terraced house. Very early on a Sunday morning the papers were delivered directly to where ever the delivery boy or girl lived so the Tye's had no need for a newsagents shop and simply collected the sale proceeds. Even this part of their business was easy for them as on completion of their respective rounds each paper lad or lass had to make the journey to Kiveton to the Tye's house where in their back kitchen Mrs Tye would sit and collect the day's takings. They

commanded sales of the Sundays from Hard Lane at one end of Kiveton and all the way through to Wales and Waleswood at the other extreme with all places and housing estates in between. The round that My Friend and me took on was enormous. It Started in Wales Square, covered the entire length of Church Street and Orchard lane before continuing from Wales Square along School Road to Wales Bar and all the houses that my morning and evening rounds covered and some. Initially all the papers were delivered to my friends house from where we started the round. We had been forewarned of the amount of papers on the round and that we should acquire some form of transport to carry them so we had spent the previous days searching for something suitable.

Like all lads back in the day we were experts in trolley construction, nothing like a supermarket trolley of today but a go cart trolley. Made from the wheels and running gear of an old pram, and sometimes even the old pram frame too.

Prams of the 60's were evolving into the Smart Silver Cross models that are now enjoying a comeback as Retro prams, confirming the old adage of what goes around comes around. These new style prams were lighter in both weight and colour with a much smaller set of wheels and constructed on a frame suitable only for its intended purpose however this style of prams predecessor was a totally different animal. The pram of the 40's and 50's which were now out of fashion were being discarded in their masses and were an instant attraction to us lads. Firstly by pushing each other around having pram races and such, and then later with the realisation that with some cutting and carving of these aging baby carriers we could fashion the pram into something much more streamlined and most importantly, much faster. They were solidly made with good sized spoke wheels. These wheels resembled a bike wheel in most aspects but were usually half the size and had a solid rubber tyre. The wheels were fixed to separate axles on the front and rear of the pram and when cut away from the surrounding bodywork they made the perfect starting point for constructing a go cart or trolley.

Often the rear wheels of the pram were larger that the front wheels but with the axles set at different levels within the pram frame then the body of the pram would sit level. The sometimes elaborate and always black body of the pram with its integral fold down hood and perhaps best described as a scaled down version of Clarence's old carriage was of no use to us and was discarded after its removal from the frame and running gear below. The framework, axles and wheels were of robust construction and following some work with a hacksaw we would soon have all the components required to fasten to a new wooden frame made from anything that we could find and finish up with a mode of transport altogether faster and much more fun than the pram we had been pushed around in as little nippers.

A typical example of a superfast trolley

I already had a trolley and it was my trolley that we used to carry the newspapers on from house to house. The trolley worked well and so did our new paper round but a few weeks in we began to realise that the round was simply too big as it often took us 4 hours or more too complete so we came up with a cunning plan. We asked the Tye's if we could split the round into two with my friend doing Wales and me doing Wales Bar which they agreed to. This was a great move for both of us as we knew that we could easily work single handed on our new rounds and complete it in no more than two and a half hours. The pay was the same as each new round paid 17/6d so the future looked good, and it got better which I will come too later but first a few memories of people and places I remember on our paper round.

***

Remembering People & Places

Yes Boy

Our round started in Wales Square and then along Church Street
which gradually climbed up hill, past the church and onwards
until it reached the cemetery that had been established after the
Churchyard had become full. From this point a lane continued
downwards along Stockwell Lane towards Norwood tunnel top
where I described some of our earlier adventures.
Ironically the first delivery was to Harold Prestige's newsagent!
And then the Lord Conyers Arms.
In addition to the newsagents and haberdashery run by Harold
and Mary there were 3 other shops in the Square. The post
office, a butcher, and a ladies hairdresser. All 3 shops and a good
part of all the buildings around them were owned by one family
the matriarch of which was one Mrs Walker.
Thinking back she was not unlike Annie Walker of the Rovers
Return in many ways in her looks and manner and most
definitely in her perception that everyone was subservient to her
social standing.
Mrs Walker was the Village Post Mistress and consequently was
in a position to know all that went on in a typical 1960's village.
She handled the post, paid out old age pensions and was the
contact point for every type of communication that anyone and
everyone needed to make; she therefore knew something of
everyone's life that chose to use her services. She was also
selective in who she chose to serve and when. The post office
counter occupied one side of her shop while the rest of the shop
was given over to general provisions where she was occasionally
assisted by her long suffering husband Harold Walker. Harold,
being a butcher was often out on his rounds in his van or in his

own shop next door, so it was Mrs Walker who was usually on her own in the shop. She took her role as Village Post Mistress very seriously and deemed it to be a position of high importance. So much so that if she were busy serving a customer with general provisions and another customer arrived for post office services then regardless of how far advanced she was with her non post office customer she would leave them to attend to the much more important matters that were HER Post Office customer. Furthermore, if there were two or more customers in need of Post office services Mrs Walker had no respect of the time honoured British system of queuing, instead she would decide in her opinion who in the queue in front of her had the better social standing within the village and it would be they who was served first.

The customer she had left in general provisions had just one hope that Mrs Walker would return at some point to complete their purchase. If, after she had worked through the post office queue there happened to be a minor i.e. a child, the definition of which in her eyes at least, was anyone less than 21 who had perhaps been sent on an errand for a stamp or postal order, then that lowly being would be totally ignored and passed by in favour of her 'ordinary' general provisions shop customer. Only when there were no more customers in the shop would Mrs Walker stoop to a level that forced her to serve the waiting juvenile. I don't know how she addressed a girl but her acknowledgement of the presence of a male was always the same, 'Yes Boy' followed by silence as her greeting was delivered in the tone of a question to which you had to respond to quickly to avoid further belittlement.

A view along School Road towards Wales Bar before the MI dissected School Road

In the foreground of this view of School Road is Harold Walkers Butchers van parked outside his son's house. The four detached houses and two bungalows immediately behind the van were demolished to make way for the M1 motorway. Most distant is the brow of Wales Bar hill which then descended in almost equal distance to Wales Bar. This distance was roughly half of the total walk I made each day and each way to collect and deliver the daily papers.

Harold Walkers butchery business must have been a profitable enterprise as working alongside their father were sons Peter and Harold Junior.

Next door to the butchers shop was a ladies hairdressers where Dorothy Walker (Harold juniors wife) practised her profession.

Attached and to the left of the Post Office was the home of Harold and Dorothy while Old Mrs Walker and Harold senior lived over and behind the post office.

A mass of stone barns surrounding a large yard sat prominently and opposite Harold and Mary's newsagent and completed the ensemble that was also part of the empire that was the Walker dynasty.

Some further research has revealed to me that Wales Square really was the nuclease of their empire that spanned many generations as in the 1800's George walker (who I presume to have been Harold Walker seniors father) was the tenant farmer of Manor House Farm which dominated Wales Square at that time and he also ran a shop there after previously being the landlord of the Leeds Arms on Church Street. This obviously explains why so much of the property that formed Wales Square was in their hands. It also provides the answer to the sign writing on the butchers van which read: - G Walker & Son Family Butchers. Perhaps a more apt advert would have been G Walker & Son, Grandsons and one or two more to come?

A view of Wales Square taken from the cenotaph with Walkers shops on the left, the Lord Conyers on the right and the old farm buildings in the middle which some years later were developed to create a home for Harold junior and his family.

Wales Square, the shop on the right is the Post Office where some feared to tread with the attached house also being part of the Walkers portfolio. Behind the cenotaph are the cottages which contained the meeting room for Sunday school which is the doorway on the far left of the picture.

Sunday School

Dominating the Square was the Cenotaph erected in commemoration of the dead of two world wars and behind the memorial was a group of dilapidated cottages, one of which had been used as a meeting room and held childhood memories for me inflicted by my parents. Sunday school!

Not only were we thrust into school life at the age of five having previously never set foot in a school playground, let alone a school building and worse, school days lasted the whole day and 5 days a week. We were force fed school dinners too that were a far cry from the real, lovingly, homemade, home cooked food that mums made but our parents also thought it was sensible to get rid of us for a while on Sunday morning and sent us off to school again but this time it was to experience the glory of Sunday school for god's sake! It was certainly not for our sake that's for sure!!

Sunday school was conducted from the front room of one of these dilapidated cottages. The room consisted of a lino floor with an eclectic mix of rickety wooden chairs neatly placed around the room's perimeter. The room was cold and damp regardless of the time of year and that smell was the same that I later came to despise, the sweaty smell of the school gym. From memory there was a hardcore of attendees of around a dozen. Occasionally as a "treat" we were ushers out of the meeting room and led up Church Street in single file to the church where our Sunday schooling would continue. Only one memory really stays with me from the teachings delivered to us, or, more specifically the teachers that delivered them. There were 2 young ladies, sisters, and I can only presume that their parents were "big" in all things Churchy and had brought their daughters up with the same beliefs. Admirable for those who choose the church as a focus but perhaps in the case of these 2 young ladies their focus had been chosen for them?

Me being still in my formative years it was not the female form of our teachers that attracted or intrigued me but their names. The bigger of the two and presumably the older was called June while her sibling was called May!

What were their parents thinking?

Perhaps one was born in May and the other in June?

Or possibly conceived in these late spring and early summer months?

It was their parents choosing for whatever reason and for them was the right thing to do.

Given the era and the ever popular daytime airing by the BBC of "Watch with Mother" then perhaps had their parents they been blessed with 2 boys our Sunday school teachers would have been called Bill and Ben!

Bill and Ben with Little Weed

Thinking of names brings to mind a family who lived in the next village of Kiveton. They had 3 boys, all of which I knew by sight as they all attended the same comprehensive school as me but in different years as it was the case back then at school that we tended to stick with our own year group and interaction with other year groups was minimal. The oldest of the 3 brothers was called Harry Bull and was not one to mess with. He stood out from the masses of comprehensive education initially because of his uniform attire. From the age of 11 and entry into secondary education boys went through the transition from short to long trousers and of course to wear a school uniform for the first time. To arrive on that first September day of the autumn term as a newbie in short trousers would have been the height of embarrassment and certainly attract unwanted attention when all that was desired as a newcomer was mingle and dissolve into the masses. Of course as new arrivals it was impossible not to be noticed, wearing a brand new uniform with a blazer two sizes too big which your parents had assured you that you would grow into very soon! This of course was totally contradicted in the final year of school when your blazer sleeves finishes just below the elbow and it was impossible to engage the blazer buttons with their button holes and despite all the pleading for a new blazer you were told by your parents that there was no point in buying a new blazer that you would only be wearing for two or three terms!!

Now Harry Bull was the opposite to his fellow classmates as he wore short trousers for the whole four years that he was at our School.

Being in the year above me he left school at age 15 whereas my year was the first to be subjected to a compulsory leaving age of 16

Harry could also look after himself and was not to be messed with, and few did. Perhaps it was his choice to wear short trousers to ensure that he was noticed but either way his reputation went before him. Not only could he look after himself but he also made sure that his two younger brothers enjoyed the protection that came with being Harry's brother. If anyone messed with Gerry or Ivor then they had to answer to Harry. So, why were these brothers names so memorable?

Harry Bull (Horrible) Terry Bull (terrible) Ivor Bull (I've a Bull) Didn't their parents realise what they had done?

Like all villages Church Street had its varied mix of characters and I feel sure that my recollections that follow will bring back memories of them or of similar types from your past.
As we walked up Church Street, on the left with its imposing stone gable to the street and its enormous form stretching away the size of four or more terraced houses was Wales Hall. Wales Hall was what I believe to be the original Vicarage for the parish. The front elevation looked up Church Street and at the time of its construction would have had full view of the church beyond where only two stone dwellings existed between it and the church. This was the home of Miss Talput. She was the Girl Guide Troop leader of the village. We met her each Sunday to hand over her paper and she always tipped us. She was extremely well spoken and thinking back on what her profession may have been then I think the Civil Service would be a strong contender.

Wales Hall

*The current vicarage at that time was a large Victorian red brick pile on Manor road that lay in the opposite direction to Church Street and a small distance behind the mass of stone barns of the Walker Empire. In the 1980,s this vicarage also became the old vicarage as in an attempt to reduce costs the Sheffield Dioceses embarked on a programme to built new residences for their Vicars. Often a vicarage would have enormous grounds around it or the Church would own swathes of land within the parish that afforded readymade building plots. Wales parish was in such a position and I won the contract to build what is now the current vicarage on Manor road and built partly in the garden of the old Victorian vicarage and some further church land that lay alongside.

In all I built 3 vicarages within the Sheffield dioceses but they are for another book*

The Victorian red brick Vicarage on Manor road.
The land in the foreground on the left is where I built the
current Vicarage and the building on the left was, in the
early 1900's the village doctors surgery but as I was growing
up it was an even more inhospitable place, it was the
headquarters of the 54th Rotherham Scout Troup of which I
was reluctantly a cub and then briefly a scout.

Wales Square and Manor Road

How places change !

The roofs in the foreground are the former shops of both
Walkers and Prestige's.

The collection of buildings in the centre left are the converted
barns of the Walker Family
Bottom right are new houses where the Lord Conyers once
stood.

Very top right and behind the trees is the old Victorian
Vicarage with the current Vicarage in front of the trees.

The long low building to the right of the new Vicarage is
the old Scout hut

Cubs and Scouts

My parents were obviously keen on extracurricular activities for myself and my siblings. Perhaps it was because having four children it meant that we were not under their feet out of school hours although by the time my younger brother arrived I don't recall the same torture befalling him.

I suspect the idea of me becoming a Cub came from our butcher Mr Desmond Radford as his son, also Desmond, was the same age as me and already enrolled in the pack.

As I mentioned earlier the Radford's shop and home was at Wales Bar and each Tuesday evening at 6 o'clock I would meet up with Des at his house and then the both of us would walk on to the scout hut at Wales Square for a 6.30pm Start (mum or dads taxi services was for future generations).

For the first few weeks of Cubbing I was in civvies which was presumably to see if I could hack it before my parents splashed out on a uniform? On the other hand I doubt I had an option as until I reached my teens I simply went along with what came along as to question anything was met with a frown at best and "no, we know best" at worst. I am not suggesting that I became a rebel without a cause in my teens, far from it, although I doubt my parents would have agreed!

The Scout shop was on Trippet Lane in Sheffield and one Saturday morning my parents announced that today was the day that I was to be fitted out with my new cub uniform. It was not the first time I had been to the shop as a year or two earlier I had been there with my sister for the kitting out of her Brownies uniform as she had joined Miss Talput's Brownie & Girl Guide troop.

More than 50 years on the Scout and Guide shop is still trading from the same place and I hope now that youngsters of today are much keener than I was when visiting there

The cub uniform consisted of a green woollen jersey, grey short trousers, and green knee length socks with two yellow hoops at the neck that were exposed when the sock was turned down over a sock garter that had a red tassel to hang below the turned down sock.

The headwear was in the style of a traditional school cap with yellow piping on a green background and above the peak of the cap an embroidered badge sporting the face of a wolf because that's what we were, wolf cubs!

Each troop had a different coloured neckerchief; ours was green with a red border and was held in place by a woggle. Folding the neckerchief in the correct style was an art form and once complete it was kept in place by the leather woggle which sported the emblem of a wolf's head. The neckerchief was actually a simple square piece of cotton material bordered in red but as it was rolled and folded it took on a whole new life form with a triangular corner placed around the back of the neck and the twisted square then wrapped around the neck and passing through the woggle to hang down the chest like a tie. The twisting of the neckerchief created a spiral effect with the red edging and looked rather spectacular. The best way to keep the neckerchief in shape was to iron it once the correct twists and folds had been achieved. Mum did that of course!

A typical Brownie and Cub Scout uniform of the 1960's and my very own leather Woggles and scout belt complete with whistles

Today there is so much political correctness about bullying in all walks of life and while it may be possible to cap it to a degree it is hard to suppress in growing children as it comes to them as naturally as breathing. Bullying was often experienced and as a consequence always expected from the scouts as they targeted us young cubs. They simply didn't like us cubs, even though they had been one once.

 Tuesday night was cub night and I enjoyed most of the activities that we did but occasionally we would have a joint meeting with the scouts and as soon as Skip's (The skipper, our pack leader) back was turned the scouts would stick the boot in, sometimes literally.

 I survived the cubs and earned a number of proficiency badges along the way. These beautifully embroidered badges which depicted the task that you had successfully undertaken were lovingly sewn by mothers onto the green woollen sleeve of your cub jumper.

One particular thing that sticks in my mind with the cub uniform was the green jumper. It was made of the coarsest wool possible and was so stiff it was like wearing chainmail and boy oh boy was it itchy; it also had a very distinctive smell like wet wool even when it wasn't!

The 54th Rotherham cub pack was made up of a number of teams. Each team consisted of 6 cubs, led by a Sixer and a Seconder who were the leader and vice leader of the team. I was in the same team as Des but as the most recent incumbent to the pack, when lining up for inspection I was at the back of the team's line.

My first promotion up the line was when I received my uniform; I was no longer at the back of the queue. As time moved on Des moved up the ranks and made it to the head of the team and became our team Sixer. The rank of Sixer meant that you were rewarded with two yellow stripes that were sewn onto the arm of your green itchy jumper, much like a police sergeants strips. The lesser rank of Seconder was afforded one strip! Des was my nemesis, I made it to Seconder but it was not until Des moved on to be a scout that I finally made it to a Sixer. There was just one activity however that I always excelled in and much more than Des's efforts which was Bob-A-Job-Week!

Bob-A-Job-Week was an annual event that was held in spring and coincided with our school Easter holidays, no doubt cleverly planned so that we had no excuse for not participating.

An explanation of Bob-a-Job-Week

The scheme, officially known as Scout Job Week, was launched after the Second World War in a bid to encourage young people to assist friends and neighbours in their community.

Bob-a-job week was first introduced as a good turn day in 1914 by scout movement founder Lord Baden-Powell and officially started during Easter week in 1949.

In exchange for a small payment, boy scouts turned their hand to gardening, shopping and household chores from dog walking to window cleaning.

The scheme got its nickname from the five pence - roughly a shilling, colloquially known as a 'bob' - that the youngsters were paid for completing their good turn.

The eager scouts would knock on doors in their local areas, offering to mow lawns, clear out garages and carry out all kinds of domestic chores for neighbours and friends or even their parents.

I soon worked out where the best payers were and some customers would even contribute their Bob (or more) and not want a job doing, although they were always keen to acquire a "Job Done" sticker from me to place in their front window to signify that they had done their bit and didn't want any other callers. This was my first experience of entrepreneurial skills together with the rewards it brought and although for this particular enterprise it was our scout troop that benefitted it certainly stood me in good stead for the future. Des was not an enthusiastic Bob a Jobber and my efforts made me top earner for our troop on more than one occasion.

As Cubs and Scouts we were made to participate in Church Services. Easter, May Day, Harvest Festival and Remembrance Sunday and on Remembrance Sunday we marched.

We would gather at Hard Lane in Kiveton and along with numerous groups of people representing their particular organisation we marched in a long procession to the Cenotaph in Wales Square.

The older scouts carried marching snare drums strapped to their waist so that the drum hung on their hip. Skip would carry the big base drum hung from a double shoulder harness that suspended the large drum on his chest, the position that this drum was carried meant that he was barely able to see his way forward, but he managed.

Skips pounding of the drum signified our marching speed as first the left and then the right drum stick hit the taught animal hide, Left Right Left Right.

The drum sticks that the scouts used were just that, a shaped stick with a rounded end to beat the drum but Skip's sticks were different, they were like mallets with a leather bound head. The sticks also had a leather strap that secured the stick to Skips hand so that he could beat the big drum with all his might without fear that the stick might take flight and hit an innocent bystander.

Both Skip and the scouts must have done plenty of practice prior to marching as they were very proficient. In addition to the scouts keeping in time with the beating of the drums they would also play their sticks by tapping them together in total unison, the overall presentation was certainly impressive.

Like all grand occasions it brought the great and the good out from the woodwork to take pride of place like they were the all important leaders while those who were the real stars of the show had to be satisfied to play second fiddle.

Two such dignitaries of the 54th Rotherham Troop were Harold Headley and Harold Waite. It was on my first march that I saw them. They were dressed in very smart scout uniforms and wearing hats the same as Baden-Powell, the Scout movement founder, had always worn. They certainly looked the part as they took the lead and we marched along bringing up the rear.

I later learned that Harold H was our troop leader and not Skip as I had previously thought, and Harold W was the elder statesman of the troop who had handed over command to Harold H some years earlier. It was not until I became a scout that I had any interaction with Harold H as it was he who was in charge of the scouts.

Moving from a cub to a scout followed the same path as the move from junior to comprehensive school other than it was your 11th birthday that was the benchmark rather than your 11th year.

It was for this reason alone that I attained the rank of Sixer in the cubs as Des was 3 months older than me so my promotion was rather short lived!

Having earned a number of proficiency badges while in the cubs, as soon as I became a scout I was disappointed to learn that I had to start the process all over again! Perhaps if I had been allowed to carry my qualifications forward it would have helped maintain a focus but that was scouting rules. I did gain some scout badges which involved similar tasks to the cub badges but with a more advanced content and the one that I particularly remember was my fire lighting badge.

As mentioned earlier Friday night was Scout Night when we met at the scout hut to do basically the same things that we had done at Cub Night, but with a more grown up twist.

This particular Friday Night Harry H picked out three of us as suitable candidates for our fire lighting badge and instructed us to report to the scout hut the following morning and be sure to wear warm clothes and wellingtons as our task ahead could only be completed in the great outdoors.

The three of us stood as instructed outside the hut the following morning on what was a cold wet and thoroughly miserable Saturday morning. We all thought and hoped that when Harry H turned up he would cancel the morning schedule but, no such luck.

Harry arrived in his car and once we were all safely aboard he exclaimed that the day was perfect for our task ahead. We drove to Kiveton Park Steel works, which, being beyond Kiveton Park proper it backed onto open countryside so as Harry explained it was the perfect place for our trial. Harry told us that Kiveton Park Steel was his place of work, so he wasn't just a scout leader then, I thought.

With the wind and rain in our faces we climbed up the steep lane that led from the old quarry floor in which the Steelworks had been built after stone quarrying had long been exhausted until eventually we were above the quarry face and in scrubland that had no particular use.

Right, said Harry H as he gave us each 3 matches and a sheet of newspaper, you now have to make a fire fit to boil water and cook on and you have 30 minutes to complete the task.

Of course, we all failed, it was hopeless. The wind and rain didn't give us a chance although to be honest I doubt we would have fared better if it had been the height of summer and tinder dry.

I suspect that Harry H already knew what the outcome would be and to show his prowess he proceeded to do what we had failed to do. Despite the rain he found some dry grass from under a decaying tree trunk and sheltered the dry grass and his single sheet of rolled up newspaper from the rain under the same decaying tree trunk and then struck a single match on a dry stone that had also been revealed from under the tree trunk and with a single match we had flame which quickly turned into a small fire, need I go on?

Obviously we were suitably impressed but equally embarrassed at our failure, so much so that we kept the morning's outcome of events to ourselves.

The following Friday we went to the scout meeting as usual and when it came to the time when everyone's recent achievements were announced. Harry H asked the 3 of us to step forward.

He handed a fire lighting proficiency badge to each of us, with a simultaneous handshake.

Looking back I wonder how many of my scouting friends had worked as hard for their reward?

Scouting ended for me by the time I was 13 as other more exciting extracurricular activities began to appear on the horizon. Some things you never forget yet and until I started doing my research for this book I didn't have a clue what was meant when Skip shouted DIB DIB DIB and we shouted back DOB DOB DOB followed by a group recital of our cub scout promise. I now find out that Skip was actually saying DYB DYB DYB which was an abbreviation of DO YOUR BEST and our reply was an abbreviation of DO OUR BEST!!

The scout promise was simple and straight forward and was, and in my opinion still is, the best motto any individual should follow, more or less, to lead a good life :-

We'll do our best
To do our duty to god and the Queen
To help other people
And do a good turn every day

Amazingly, Queen Elizabeth who we vowed our duty to all those years ago had already been on the throne for some 12 years and as I write she is now the longest-reigning British monarch at 65 years and still counting.

***

Wizards, Winners & Losers

Getting back to Church Street one of the original stone dwellings that stood between the old vicarage and the church was no. 7 The Garth. Interestingly the ancient meaning of "Garth" is an open yard or garden which fits perfectly to the name of this dwelling being built in what was most certainly the garden of the old vicarage. I don't recall the old ladies name at No. 7 but she was a sweet old dear. We would knock on her door to alert her of our arrival and from the depths of the rooms beyond she would shout us to enter. The first room following the front door was anything but what we expected. It was unused, other than for a store room. It was fitted out with a counter and shelving was on every wall with stone flagstones underfoot, polished from years of wear. We were intrigued as to why this room resembled a shop rather than a home and on asking the question our customer was only too pleased to explain that before the relocation of the Post Office to its current position in the village Square the room that we were now standing in had been the village post office and she had been its Post Mistress.

Many times when delivering her newspaper she would insist that we stayed for a cup of tea and she loved to tell us stories of her time in the village. She never addressed us as paper "boy" but by our names, unlike her successor.
Behind the Church was another farm, Brabb's farm. Three brothers lived here. Two brothers worked the farm while the youngest brother was supported by his older siblings. The youngest was called Merlin and as his name suggests he was somewhat of an eccentric.

Looking up Church Street The Garth is on the left with the old Post Office shop front. The trees on the right are the orchard of Wales Grange with the farmhouse immediately beyond where Mrs Smith would wait for her Sunday newspaper to arrive.

He was certainly skilled with his hands as he spent his days building all forms of contraptions, some useful and some not. The first of 2 memorable projects was probably one of the very first camper vans. It was a sight to see. He had purchased an old flat bed lorry and an equally old caravan which he fashioned together to create his leisure vehicle. As the saying goes "Beauty is in the eye of the beholder" and to Merlin this was surely true but, to the eyes of others his handwork was just what it looked like, a caravan minus its wheels, bolted onto the back of a lorry. The farm had obviously been prosperous in previous years as in the garden was a swimming pool.

Of course this swimming pool could have been another madcap project of an equally madcap Merlin but that I can't confirm.

His second project that I recall was still all about leisure but this time of the nautical type. Merlin set too to build a boat the size of which was dictated by the size of the swimming pool as that is where is was made, not in a dry dock but as soon as the hull was complete it entered the water of the pool and remained there until its completion. It never made it to open water as it lay moored in the swimming pool until it eventually sank and was broke up. Merlin was certainly the most eccentric madcap resident in the village but was no less loved for that.

This Ariel view of Brabb's farm. The garden in front of the farmhouse was where the boat was "launched"

Through the years of coal mining deep beneath Wales and the surrounding area many properties suffered from subsidence and none more so than those on Church Street. My next recollection is from the 70's and 80's but worthy of note here. Opposite the Church was the Leeds Arms, a public drinking house that would have been at the very heart of the village in the 19th century. Behind the Leeds arms was a bungalow that was entered by driving through the pubs car park and at the driveway entrance to the bungalow was a garage. The bungalow had been constructed in the early 60's and with mining subsidence already prevalent the problem had dictated that the bungalow had to be built on a raft foundation rather than the more traditional strip foundation. The purpose of the raft was in the name. The property was built on a large single reinforced slab of concrete that in effect floated on the ground beneath so that any movement of the strata below meant that the raft would move as one and not cause any damage to the structure that was built upon it.

In Bricks and Mortar I described how we bought our first house in Killamarsh in 1974 and then sold it a few years later. At the time we were selling we had an interested couple come to view by the name of Mr & Mrs Moore's. They made an offer but nothing came of it and the reason why became apparent a short while later, they had won the pools. There was no such thing as the National Lottery back then, it was either Littlewoods or Vernons Pools. The pools was a form of gambling on the results of football matches by suggesting which teams might draw their match, with a score draw awarding the player the most points and the winners receiving large sums accumulated from the entry money.

The arrival of the National Lottery some years later was the death knell of the pools and the term "He's come up on the pools" was then replaced with "He must have won the lottery ". The Moore's won about £750,000 pounds (over 8 million in today's money) which quickly set their sights way beyond a mid terraced house in Killamarsh!!

Over the next few years they worked their way through their fortune buying a fancy house, race horses, stables, a country manor house, a minibus to treat their new found friends on trips and holidays, and of course a Rolls Royce. By the 90's it was all gone, easy come easy go.
The following is a clip from a Magazine all about winners and losers of pools and Lottery wins:-

One way of keeping old friends is to stay in the same job. It doesn't always work. Some decide they want to leave in order to start their own business. 'People say they've always wanted to own a pub or a sweet- shop,' explains Mr Crawford. 'I have to explain it's the worst thing they can do. It's bloody hard work, and a sure way to lose money.' Take Peter Moore's for example, he won over £750,000 in 1983. He bought a 16th- century mansion which he decided to convert into a pub. He also bought race-horses and stables. A decade later, he had lost most of his money. The bank had repossessed the mansion, and the stables and horses had all been sold. Today he says he feels 'sick, definitely', at what happened. Still, he didn't regret winning.

In the late 70's, Gerry, a dear friend of mine asked me to have a look at a bungalow on Church Street that was up for sale and he was interested in buying it. It was the bungalow behind the Leeds Arms. He explained that it had been affected by subsidence but had no cracks or structural damage as a result. On viewing, the raft was testament to its design and purpose as indeed it had protected the bungalow built above it from any damage but from one end to the other the whole bungalow was 6 inches out of level!!
Gerry didn't buy but a friend of his did and following some work lived there quite happily. Some years later while chatting to

Gerry he told me that the bungalow was up for sale again and would I like to see all the work that his friend had done, as he was holding the key while his friend was away.

The Bungalow was still 6 inches out of level but the work that had been done was a credit to the owner and he had certainly bagged a bargain in those heady days of rising property prices. As we walked back up the driveway towards the Leeds Arms car park and passed the garage by the entrance, Gerry said "come and have a look in the garage I want to show you something ". Gerry opened the doors and beckoned me in and behind a pile of boxes that were stacked in the doorway.

It was a large garage, big enough to take a good sized family car and still leave room for all the other accumulations that we all have in our garage but, whatever vehicle lay in this garage beneath the sheet that totally covering it was certainly no ordinary sized car.

Gerry had mentioned to me on a number of occasions that his friend was an acquaintance of the pools winning Moore's but I had never really taken much notice to the fact.

So, Gerry said, what do you think is under that sheet? And as he said it he slowly pulled the sheet away to reveal an ice blue Rolls Royce with cream leather interior. It was looking rather shabby and being about 15 years old was in need of an awful lot of TLC if it were to have half a chance of seeing the open road again. What on earth is that doing here? I exclaimed.

Well said Gerry, you remember I told you that my friend was a friend of the Moore's who won the pools, well, But, I interrupted, what is his Rolls doing here, I thought he'd gone bust ?

Gerry explained that Peter Moore's had managed to squirrel his car away to here in the hope that one day he can sell it, but Gerry continued, I somehow doubt that will ever happen looking at the state of the car now.

The bungalow was eventually sold and no doubt the Rolls Royce was moved on to another hiding place where perhaps it remains to this day?

***

The Cresta Run & Cottage Hospital

Beyond the Leeds Arms, Church Street reached its peak and continued almost level to the cemetery where Church Street ended. On the right of Church Street all the houses commanded an uninterrupted view from their high vantage point as the land dropped away steeply to the valley below where the M1 motorway would soon be built and then further to the hill beyond over which was Wales Bar. Above the line of this hill ridge Norton and Gleadless could be seen on the high hills beyond which then gave way to the Sheaf Valley and the city of Sheffield in the next valley below.

Between the houses on the right was a small field entered via a permanently open gate.

The field continued over the brow and dropped steeply into the valley. Halfway down the steep slope was a ditch running the full width of the field and in the centre of the ditch was a bridge supporting a cart track that led to the next field that descended even further to a high hawthorn hedge that marked the end of the field.

This was Mallenders Hill and was the focal point for everyone and anyone when the snow came.

This was our Innsbruck, our Cresta run. It was fast, very fast and possibly dangerous too but we never thought of danger, only of speed, thrills and the spills.

The perfect run was to navigate the sledge over the bridge and cart track to the field beyond or risk finishing up in the depths of the ditch that the bridge spanned which was more often than not the case. Steering a sledge single handed was relatively easy to master but if two or more had piled on the sledge sat one behind the other, or worse, laid on top of each other then it was almost a certainly that disaster loomed somewhere along the downward slope.

The snow thankfully provided a good cushion against injury and we all seemed to get through the day unscathed, but totally knackered.

Looking down Church Street the lorry is parked outside the Leeds Arms.
The white post just visible in the hedge in the centre of the picture marks the gateway to Mallenders field.

Kiveton through to Wales Bar was served by a practice of three doctors in the 60's.

On arriving at Wales Bar in 1954 the doctor's practice was located just beyond Wales Square in the front room of a large house that was both the doctor's house and the surgery. This later moved to new purpose built premises further down the road on Walesmoore Avne in Kiveton to cater for the growing population of the area.

One of the practice doctors lived on Church Street, above the church in a house that had previously been a farm but was now made over to a family home.

This doctor was a mixer, not only of drinks but also with people. He was very popular and everyone liked him, as did the women as at the time I remember that he lived with the lady that would become his 3rd wife!

Over the years I have worked for many doctors, building both surgeries and working on their private homes. While working on the latter often we would see the human side of their stressful lives when their guard was down. Most like a drink and doctors are no exception. Vodka seemed to be their favoured tipple as it leaves little or no trace on the breath but our Church Street doctor was a pints man. He was a local of both the Leeds Arms and The Lord Conyers and was a good egg.

He was known to hold informal consultations at the bar which meant that buying his own drink was a rare occurrence.

The surgery operated standard hours but in the case of an emergency it was not a visit to A&E that was the first port of call but to the doctor's house. In the less serious cases he would do or prescribe what was required to give comfort to the patient so that they would last through to the next scheduled surgery opening or in the more acute cases he would speak to the hospital so that on arrival his patient would be fast tracked through the system.

I had the misfortune of trapping my fingers in a sliding sash window one Saturday afternoon while at home. It was extremely painful and all the more so as I was unable to free my fingers from the window on my own. It took more than 15 minutes to attract my parent's attention to my predicament. There was no thought given to the possibility that further injury might be inflicted to my fingers as my father grasped the sliding sash window and thrust it upwards to release my trapped digits and the sight of my hand when freed certainly suggested that was a possibility.

A towel was wrapped around my throbbing hand and within minutes we were speeding along Mansfield Road and on to our destination of Church Street which had followed a phone call to confirm that there would be a Doctor in the House when we arrived!

The operation to remove the remains of my fingernail from my twisted and mangled finger was performed on the doctors kitchen table and a dressing and antiseptic duly applied.

I attended the surgery the following week as instructed and all was well, time would be the healer I was told. 50 years on I still have a twisted finger and a strange looking nail but I can still pick my nose so all is well.

***

Eye Eye

At the end of Church Street was a new self built house. This was the home of Mr and Mrs Norman Horsley. Mr Horsley was a jack of all trades and probably master of them all. He owned a large black Humber Hawk car which he used as a taxi and if he was not ferrying his fares back and forth he also had a lorry in which he could carry almost any load that would pay its way.

A fine example of a Humber Hawk

My first recollections of Mr Horsley were not so much of him but his car. As a young lad it was decided for me that I could not see very well. Admittedly I had a lazy eye which was quickly seized upon by fellow school friends to use to their advantage in name calling, and my older sister had had more serious eye problems which I can only presume led to the assumption of my diagnosis.

The upshot was that I was condemned to wearing national health glasses which were far from trendy, although that trend was totally reversed years later when John Lennon adopted similar styled glasses as his trademark look. My glasses were blue wire framed monstrosities (the same style was available in pink for the girls) and were issued to me as a result of regular trips to Sheffield Royal Infirmary hospital. The hospital, with its impressive roundhouse was some distance from the city centre and Ponds Street bus station so my parents decided that hiring Mr Horsley's taxi would be the best option. The car was enormous from the outside and just as cavernous on the inside. The seats were dark red leather and the carpets a contrasting dark red. The interior smell of an old leather upholstered car is unique and unforgettable in much the same way as a Sunday roast beef dinner!

Mr Horsley would glide up to our front door at Wallingfield and after alerting us of his presence would stand by the opened rear door of the car while my mum and I climbed in, closing the door behind us. The ride was an absolute treat for me although the business between our outward and homeward journey was less so as each hospital appointment seemed to take forever.

 No matter what time we emerged from the Royal Infirmary Roundhouse building that was the eye hospital, Mr Horsley would be waiting for us. I hope he didn't leave the meter running!

My mum and me would sit patiently beneath the domed roof of the roundhouse until we were called to one of the many doors that continually opened and closed around the buildings perimeter as people and patients went back and forth. It was the same door for us every time. It led into a large room with tables along each side. On each table was a large piece of apparatus at which one of them I was told to sit in front of. With the eye doctor sat behind the apparatus I would then place my chin on a rest protruding from this contraption and have to look into what was to all intent and purposes a very large pair of spectacles mounted on the apparatus in front of me.

What followed was a sequence of numerous slides inserted before my eyes of lions, elephants, giraffes, monkeys and more. I was asked to identify each one and say if they were in a cage or not, if they were in black and white, or in colour (I never saw a zebra for some reason?), if they were upside down or not, were they blurred or clear. Next I would have a patch placed over my left eye and then my right and go through the whole sequence again.

The result of all this testing was blue wire framed NHS spectacles. The temples, being the long arms on the sides of the frame that extend over the ears to keep the glasses on the wearer's face and more commonly known as earpieces, were made of uncontrollable springy wire that expanded in length to ensure that one size fits all !

Sometimes between one appointment and the next one of the lenses would be blanked out with Elastoplasts so that vision was through one eye only. I was told that this was necessary to strengthen my lazy eye. All well and good perhaps but what about the covered eye? Would that not get lazy from lack of use?

I am sure that the eye doctor meant well but each school day I would keep those stupid glasses in their blue glasses case in my pocket and when asked at home if they were helping my eyesight I would answer in the affirmative. Perhaps that is why I had so many hospital appointments?

On the positive side the spectacle wearing era didn't (unofficially) last long and officially not much longer than a year or two.

Perhaps training the menagerie of animals to go in and out of their cages was not in vein as I was almost 50 years old before I next wore glasses and then only for close work and to this day nothing has changed (except for the strength of the lens).

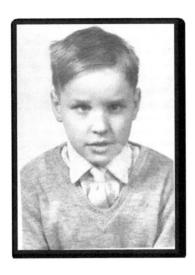

Look into my eyes!

Research tells me that the Roundhouse is still there as both it and the buildings around it are grade 2 listed. It now serves as an office park. The establishment opened in 1792 under the name Sheffield General Infirmary, renamed Royal Infirmary in 1897 and closed in 1980. Many of the establishment's features made it unique. An innovative octagonal outpatients department was built in 1884, and was lit by a cupola (the Roundhouse). It had a roof of wrought iron lattice girders and a tiled waiting room with the consulting rooms leading off it.

**Photos from around 1906 show the newly named Royal
Infirmary with the Roundhouse on the left
The waiting area within the Roundhouse on ironically shows
many patients with eye patches so it seems that many years
before the NHS became a reality this building was where eye
problems were treated.**

Living some 10 miles out from Sheffield to a large extent we
were spared from the smoke and grime that hung over Sheffield
caused by the heavy industry that the city was famous for the
world over.

Sheffield, the City of Steel. The source of energy to power this industry was coal and the beautiful stone buildings that had appeared as the City grew wealthy eventually paid a heavy price as they turned black from soot deposits from the polluted air of the two centuries that followed the start of the industrial revolution .

I remember the Roundhouse and the surrounding buildings being black and as a child I simply assumed that this was their natural colour. Unlike so many Sheffielders whose good health and lives were all too often cut short by the affects of the soot and grime, theses buildings were much more resilient. The 1960's brought the realisation that the air we breathe should be cleaner and in the following years the industry that had made Sheffield great cleaned up its act and in doing so brought the steel industries demise.

Gradually all the black buildings were cleaned to reveal both the true colour of the natural local stone and red brick used to construct them, together with the wonderful architectural features of their design. Thankfully, like the grade 2 listing status that protects the Roundhouse and Royal Infirmary buildings, so much of Sheffield's architectural heritage has the same protection and the once blackened forms now stand proud in their original colour and splendour for future generations to enjoy.

Mr Horsley's taxi service was used by many in the village as it was the only alternative form of transport to the bus however, as the 1950's turned to the swinging sixties more and more families became car owners and the need for Mr Horsley's taxi service diminished.

His love of cars continued and the Humber Hawk gave way to his new pride and joy, a Rolls Royce.

It was black and in the classic style. It was no longer used as a taxi but did make the occasional appearance around the village. His one man and his lorry haulage business became his only source of income and by all accounts a profitable one.

Some years later my sister Jane was to be married with the wedding taking place at Wales Parish Church. It was a grand affair and my parents arranged all the usual things, flowers, reception, invitations, and more. Everyone was ready to leave home for the church as expectations rose as to how the bride would get there when once again Mr Horsley glided up to our front door at Wallingfield but this time in his gleaming Rolls Royce. He climbed out and stood by the open rear door waiting for his fare to arrive just like he had done all those years ago. Not this time was it a blue bespectacled lad in short trousers and his mum, bound for Sheffield and the Roundhouse but the father of the bride and the bride to be. Thanks Mr Horsley.

Get me to the Church on time! Our proud Dad helping the bride from Mr Horsley's gleaming Rolls Royce and the blushing bride with husband Steve leaving Wales Church after the wedding.

All dressed up for the wedding day.
Pamela looks a picture but what on earth were me and my
brother wearing?

I'll recall here one further memory of Mr Horsley.
He was an animal lover and always kept a dog as his companion.
Man's best friend at the time of this memory was an Alsatian.
A beautiful specimen of the breed and like all his dogs was
highly trained and extremely faithful.
His dogs were never kept on a lead as they always obediently
stayed by his side.
Mr Horsley achieved the high level of obedience between man
and dog as most trainers do by rewarding with food morsels of
one kind or another.
His preferred fuel for heating the house was wood and as he had
his lorry he was able to collect and deliver vast quantities of the
stuff to his house. The front of the house faced down the valley
and had views of the hills beyond and the outskirts of Sheffield.
The back of the house faced onto Stockwell Lane which started
where Church Street finished. This was the business side of the
house where he parked his lorry and cut and stored his firewood.
For this purpose he had an enormous bench saw with a circular

blade the size of a dustbin lid which cut his firewood to the required size with ease. Often when close by or passing his house the noise of the saw could be heard as he replenished his firewood stocks.

It seems that one day he took his eye off the ball and while pushing a log towards the spinning saw blade his hand got too close. In a split second his finger was gone. Before the pain of what he had done registered with his brain, he heard the severed digit rattle through the sawdust extraction pipe and fall onto the large pile of sawdust beyond the saw where his faithful friend would always lay.

Being a practical and knowledgeable man he knew that if he could retrieve the digit quickly and store it on ice then there was every chance that it could be reattached. Clutching his damaged hand he quickly ran to the bloodstained pile of sawdust but found nothing. He searched through the sawdust in vein, as did his faithful hound.

Mr Horsley never found his missing finger that he so desperately searched for, nor did his dog find the second morsel of food that he was looking for!!

***

The kitchen sink

Our last Sunday paper delivery on Church Street was to Mr
Horsley after which we would race back downhill riding our still
well loaded newspaper trolley, turning into Orchard Lane and
then on to School Road and Wales Bar.

Orchard Lane provided a shortcut between Church Street and
School Road without the need to re-enter Wales Square and the
best bit was that we were still able to deliver our papers to the
houses whose front doors we had missed by our short cut as the
rear of these missed houses faced on to Orchard Lane. These
houses were semi detached but not in the modern style. They
were best described as Terraced houses in design in that each
kitchen at the rear of the house had a window facing the kitchen
window of the house next door but, unlike terraced houses where
the rear yard to which these windows faced was usually shared
these houses had their own yard and a pathway between them.
The pathway provided access from the front to the rear of the
house via a 3 feet passageway flanked by the towering gable
brick walls of each house. This passageway gave the impression
that a row of terraced houses had been prised apart just so that
the householder could feel one step up the housing ladder.

My good friends Gerry and Betty lived in one of these houses.
Their next door neighbour was a parish councillor and was very
much a stereo type for the roll. He smoked a pipe and sported a
very hangdog expression with his chubby jowls drawing his lips
to an inverted new moon giving him the look of a cross between
Clement Freud and Harold Wilson but I doubt he would have
welcomed the likeness to the latter as our parish councillor was a
staunch conservative. He was extremely well turned out; he was
the man about town. He was a sociable sort, as his position in the

village dictated. He also oozed with over confidence and wittingly or otherwise always looked down on his subjects in a rather condescending way.

Villagers knew not to engage in in-depth conversations with him of what they may be planning or who had done what as it would always go further but, despite all that he was liked as the busying busy body that he was, exuding with the confidence of his own importance but in reality he was no more than a bag of wind full of hot air. He would have been horrified if there was any possibility that his clean cut, whiter than white image became tarnished and he made sure that it never did.

He did however have one unfortunate habit that would have made him the laughing stock of the village had it every become public though I doubt that anyone would have believed it had they known and simply think that it was an attempt to smear his good name!

Gerry's pre work ritual each morning of taking breakfast and preparing his packing up for the day ahead kept him in the kitchen for most of that time and as his kitchen and window faced East it was often lit by the early morning sun so he had no need to use the kitchen light. The opposite was the case for our councillor, he too was up and about at the same time as Gerry but with a West facing kitchen it was always artificially lit. These opposites meant that Gerry was almost invisible in his unlit kitchen whereas his neighbour could be seen in full light, although this fact must never have dawned on him as we shall soon discover.

Almost every morning Gerry would watch his neighbour appear at the kitchen sink after he had taken his drink of morning tea where he would proceed to rinse his cup under the tap. At this point he would glance furtively to the left and right to make sure that his wife or children were not about to enter the kitchen and when he considered it safe he would quickly zip open his fly and relieve himself in the kitchen sink !

Gerry being a public spirited type of guy kept what he saw each morning to himself, well almost!!

***

A Pinta Milka Day

The last house on Orchard Lane and next door to the Primary School was the home of Mr and Mrs Bradley. It was not only their home but also their business. Their garage had been converted to a giant fridge in which there were many hundreds of milk bottles. The Bradleys were the village milkmen. Milk was delivered daily, direct to the doorstep with a double delivery on Saturday as Sunday was a day off! To be absolutely precise the deliveries were made by 3 young lads in the Bradleys employ. These lads were school age and just like me doing the morning paper round they instead had chosen to do the milk round. Their job never really interested me as they had to get up much earlier than me and their milk round took much longer. They had to load the van with crates of milk before starting the deliveries and then perch themselves on the van floor between the open rear doors of the van with legs dangling and the soles of their feet brushing the tarmac as the van sped from door to door. Mr Bradley sat firmly in his driving seat shouting out instructions of how many pints at which house.

Mrs Bradley didn't help on the round during the week but Saturday was different, Saturday was their pay day. She was a glamorous lady and always wore makeup and jewellery. In order to show off her precious stones to thier best advantage she wore her hair up. It was kept in place with a silk scarf, meticulously woven through her hair like a film star. Her earrings hung gracefully from her lobs and her necklace lay around her neck on skin that looked 20 years younger than her age. She obviously had looked after herself in addition to being blessed with youthful looks. The opposite was the case of Mr Bradley, he was a stocky dark haired chap and always unshaven which was presumably because of the time constraints he battled with on his early morning start. I particularly remember with some surprise his clean shaven and well dressed appearance when delivering the Sunday papers around 9.30am, his body clock which dictated his early weekday starts had obviously not stopped ticking and had allowed him plenty of time to himself and his appearance prior to our arrival.

The milk round took much longer on a Saturday as Mrs Bradley called at each door to collect payment as her lads struggled with a double delivery.

All their customers knew how much to pay and would leave their payment beneath an empty milk bottle on the doorstep and if their requirements were different for the following week then a message was left on a scrap of paper neatly rolled and placed in the neck of a milk bottle.

I loved milk and still do. There is nothing better than a cool glass of milk, unless of course it was fresh unpasteurised milk from Coulsons farm, drunk from a cup dipped into the frothy head of a full milk churn, lovely.

The range of products that the Bradleys delivered was limited almost exclusively to milk but they also carried orange juice and eggs on request. The orange juice was not the 100% pure juice that we take for granted today but instead had no more than 10% orange content! That said, it did taste of orange and it was orange in colour but without the additive control that exists today I suspect that it was not just the minimal orange content that gave it its colour.

It was a still, refreshing drink, not fizzy, and came in a milk bottle with a sealed metal foil top. There was no fancy bottle or labelling neither..

On the occasions that we were treated by our parents to a bottle of orange with the milk delivery I recall that I often got into trouble if I had been thefirst the first to see and then open the bottle, The thing was that once the bottle of orange was open then it was so easy to drink, I could down a pint of orange as quickly as I could down a pint of milk and often did, much to the annoyance of my siblings!

There were 4 types of milk, gold top, silver top, red top and sterilised. Gold, silver and red were fresh pasteurised milk and the equivalent of full cream, half cream and skimmed milk that we have today.

Sterilised, better known today as long life milk was not very popular but I adored it. This milk came in a narrow necked glass bottle and sealed with a beer type bottle top. The milk had a taste like tinned evaporated milk (Carnation Milk) and was quite rich and unlike pasteurised milk the sterilised milk was not graded. On the rare occasion that for whatever reason the Bradleys had run out of pasteurised milk we would wake up to these strange looking bottles on the doorstep. This was a real treat for me as no one else really liked it so, more for me!

We had 6 pints of milk delivered every day with 12 on Saturday allowing Mr & Mrs Bradley and their milk lads their day of rest the following day. Next to our back door step we had a metal milk crate in which the days deliver and the used bottles were kept. Keeping milk at the right temperature today is easy but not back then. In the heat of the summer we would stand the full milk bottles in a bucket of cold water on a cool stone shelf in the pantry which went a small way towards preventing the milk turning soar and in the winter we would leave the milk outside in the crate and let the cooler weather work in our favour. However, this was not always the case as when the snow and frost came the milk was at risk as some mornings when it had been particularly cold the milk would freeze and in doing so expanded, pushing the foil milk bottle top upwards as it formed a column of frozen milk high above the neck.

In mid winter when bird food was scarce the sparrows, tits and robins knew where they could find nourishment as we often found holes in the bottle tops!

The bird that got the cream, unless it was frozen

Sterilised milk was safe from the birds

We had silver top milk which in reality was much richer than its semi skimmed equivalent of today.

The cream in the milk would settle in the neck of the bottle and was clearly visible by its rich colour.

We were always told to shake the bottle before opening to distribute the cream evenly which was a shame for a creamy milk lover like me. The trick was to open the bottle out of sight, gently tip the bottle to drink off the cream and then, placing the palm of your hand over the top of the opened bottle, give it a good shake and no one would know. But, they did as often the cry would be, Johns had the cream again, this milk is watery! The red top milk was like coloured water but the gold top, oh the gold top.

This milk was the crème de la crème, literally.

The milk was from Jersey and Guernsey cows that grazed on the best pastures and were renowned for their rich milk yield. The milk was as rich as the cream of the silver top and the cream on top like double cream on Wimbledon strawberries.

When the bottle was opened a spoon handle was often needed to break through the thick neck of cream to release the milk below. We were not allowed gold top but just occasionally on a dark morning when the milk lads could not spot the difference between gold top and a silver top in the stacked crates of the milk van there would be a gold top on our doorstep, heaven! Thinking of the metal milk crate that stood by our back door for our daily pints brings to mind an incident, or perhaps more precisely an accident that happened in my early teens.

All youngsters love bikes and me and my siblings were no exception but, as we lived on the A614 Mansfield Road our parents strictly forbid us to ride our bikes on the road, in fact we were not even allowed to venture beyond the front gate with them ! This would have been a severe restriction to most cyclists but fortunately we had a very long driveway which ran some 80 yards from the front gate to the house and then continued to circumnavigate a large oval ornamental pond surrounded by a shrubbery and tall hedge before linking back to the long straight driveway again. This was our road and we even made tracks around the garden to extent our circuit.

One Monday morning school day I was dressed and ready for school and on this particular morning I was wearing brand new school shoes for which I was under fear of death, or worse, if I were to scuff, scratch or damage them in any way. I can hear the words now that were so familiar to us "Those shoes cost good hard earned money and they are not for you to ruin, they have to last a long time, you had better look after them".

I had spent the weekend tinkering with my bike and was really pleased with the result although the brakes still needed tweaking to be at their best. This was not really an issue however as the inefficient braking system was easily compensated by using the soles of my shoes to add friction between them and the ground.

I had time in hand before going to catch the school bus and was desperate to ride my bike. A few times around the driveway circle and then top to bottom from the front gate to the house, the bike was performing well. At the bottom of the descending drive there was a gate then passageway that led to the yard by the back door. The yard was large enough to enter, turn, and exit with my bike without the need for dismounting although braking played a big part in the success of this skilful manoeuvre. I approached the gateway at some speed and then into the passageway and the yard beyond. At that same split second I remembered that braking had to be achieved via the bikes braking system and my feet while also remembered my new school shoes! No matter I thought, I will simply turn and come back out of the yard, I've done it loads of times before.

I remember flying over the handle bars and then feeling very drowsy as I came around in a heap on the floor. My bike was some feet away and the milk crate and bottles in which my head had landed lay upturned by the side of me.

It must have taken a moment or two for me to come round as by the time I realised what had happened my mum was stood over me pulling me to my feet with a very concerned expression on her face. The metal crate had done its worst and had inflicted a large gash on my forehead and blood dripped from my mouth where my front teeth had penetrated my upper lip.

Being a weekday I was taken to the doctor's surgery where our Church Street Doctor was waiting to patch me up. He was good at his job and stitched my wounds as I lay on the surgery table, had my accident been the day before then I have no doubt that he would have stitched me up at his kitchen table!

As the day progressed, which I spent at home recovering, my upper lip expanded massively just as I had been forewarned as it had been impossible to stitch the internal damage to the aresa. The following day I looked and felt like I had been on the losing side of a boxing match but, having parents that were very strict on school attendance I was packed off to school. That week at school was much worse than normal and normal was bad!

My school shoes survived and so did I and 50 years later I still bear the scars of that eventful day.

***

White lines, Skid and lollipops

Leaving Orchard lane we would make our way along School Road where on the left the school lay before us, first the junior school class rooms, then the headmasters house and garden behind which was the juniors playground, and finally the school gates where the entrance opened into the large infants playground in front of the building that housed the three infant classrooms. The infants and junior playgrounds were separated by a long low stone building that was the school toilets.

A painted white line on the tarmac playground that stretched from the toilet building to the perimeter hedge of the headmaster's garden was the line that no infant or junior dare cross into the others space. There was another white line marked on the infant's playground about 20 feet in from the entrance gates and parallel to them. This line created a no go zone between it and the gates.

Virtually the first thing that we were told when ripped from our mother's apron strings and thrust into the schools care at the tender age of five was the importance of these two lines . By crossing one then the big children would get you and crossing the other took you into a world fraught with danger from passing vehicles and any other danger that may lurk beyond the school gates.

O f course curiosity would always play its part and it was not long before we realised that it was possible to actually stand almost on the line without some accident occurring. The problem was that if we were to stand too close to these two lines there would always be some bright spark that thought it hilarious to push us over it and in so doing would shout "Arrrrrh, I'm going to tell on you for crossing the line".

These two lines and both playgrounds were policed by Mrs Platt.

Mrs Platt was a very enterprising lady as she held down 3 jobs. She lived at the house that was directly opposite the School gates and this was probably why she had been the perfect candidate for her jobs.

She was the lollypop lady both before and after school insuring that there was a safe passage of children from her side of School road to the school gates and to the white line beyond .

At morning and afternoon play she was on playground duty, guarding the white lines and all the screaming and shouting children in her care.

At dinner time she was a dinner lady along with three other women who served out our school dinners.

She had a uniform for each job. In the morning she wore a full length waterproof white coat with black peaked shiny cap and in her hand she carried her lollypop stick. When not in use the stick would be placed neatly between her front garden wall and privet hedge, hidden from view and easily accessible for the next shift. At lunchtime she wore a pale green cotton smock with matching hat and a pinner tied around her waist of no particular colour. For her playground duties she cast aside her two uniforms in favour of her everyday clothes.

Mrs Platt was small, round and big bosomed which served as comforting protection when the need arose for her to hug away a child's troubles. She was like a second mother to all her school children and loved us all as much as we loved her. If you felt upset, ill or generally out of sorts she had the knack of knowing and would always offer comfort or, if you tumbled in the playground she was the first on the scene to wipe away the tears and sometimes the blood from scraped knees or elbows.

The outside toilets were the only convenience for us. There were no toilets inside the school buildings, at least not for children, and come rain, sun, frost or snow we had to use them. We were always discouraged from asking for a toilet break during lesson time so each playtime the toilets were a very popular place. They were smelly, and wet underfoot in the boys toilets although I cannot say if the same applied to the girl's side. Toilet paper was by request and Mrs Platt would always oblige by tearing off a sheet or two from a role of shiny medicated IZAL toilet paper that she kept in her coat pocket. For those of a certain age you will recall that the adopted name for this type of toilet paper was "skid" and the name quickly became apparent when using it. The boys and girls toilets were obviously different in that the girls consisted of a row of five in line doors behind which was the toilet which has no seat but a shaped wooden strip fixed to each side of the porcelain base did offer some protective warmth from the white pottery and exposed flesh . Each door offered little privacy as there was no lock. There was a gap both above and below the door big enough to climb over or crawl under and as often as not a face would appear in the gap asking "have you done yet?

The boy's toilets had a row of just three toilets and to make up for this loss of convenience there was a urinal. The urinal was at the end of the row of toilet doors and was at right angles to them. It occupied the wall that divided the boy's toilets from the girls and where the girls would stand on their side waiting for a free cubicle.

 The urinal was made of earthenware and as all earthenware products was predominantly brown in colour with a shiny glazed finish; it was wide enough to stand three abreast.

Now, boys being boys and having excellent peeing pressure at a young age the architecture of the outside toilet block was either good, or bad depending on your gender.

The very design of these urinals encouraged us to pee on the wall rather than to the floor and as young lads it soon became a competition as to who could pee the highest. Needless to say the target got higher and higher until the top of the wall above the urinal was our aim when screams would quickly follow from the girls standing on the other side!

Of course as new arrivals at school each boy thought that this game had never been played before and we were all eager participants. It was invariably a shock for the girls when water droplets cascaded over them like a waterfall as we stood there in fits of laughter listening to their screams. Hearing the screams Mrs Platts knew not to go to rescue the girls but to go directly to the boy's toilets where she would stand at the entrance with hands on hips and wait for the offending boys to turn around to be confronted by her rounded silhouette in the toilet entrance.

School Road circa 1960 looking from Wales Square. The houses on the left are the large semi detached terrace style houses whose gardens back on to Orchard lane, our short cut from Church Street to School Road. Orchard Lane enters School Road beyond these houses where the school begins.

Thinking of Mrs Platts and her school "lollipop" patrol duties
brings to mind a formidable lady that I got to know some years
later. I don't know her name and perhaps she is best kept
anonymous to avoid any repercussions!! This Mrs Lollipop
patrolled the school crossing outside school in the nearby village
of Harthill. Whether or not she had other jobs with the school as
Mrs Platt did I don't know, but I'm sure that she was well loved
by the children in just the same way that we loved Mrs Platts.
The era of this Mrs Lollipop was some 20 years on when the
roads were busier and everyone seemed to be in a hurry,
particularly at rush hour which coincided exactly with her hours
of patrol.
She was thoughtful to passing motorists and always gave good
advance warning of her intension to stop the traffic to allow the
safe passage of her children across the road. She would stand at
the pavement edge holding her lollipop stick aloft to attract the
attention of oncoming traffic to make clear that they should stop
and then she would move to the middle of the road with arms out
stretched and lollipop stick firmly rooted to the road allowing
her little children to cross in safety. Responsible motorists would
wait patiently at a safe distance until Mrs Lollipop signalled that
it was safe to continue but, as often as not, just as the last little
person had arrived safely at the school gates another would
appear from between two stone walls that flanked a footpath
leading from the many houses on the hillside overlooking the
school. Mrs Lollipop would always stand in front of the hidden
footpath when not holding up the traffic. She knew only too well
that emerging children might not think to stop at the railings at
the pavements edge that was their only protection between them
and the busy road. For this reason, if a child was spotted coming
down the descending footpath while she was at her post in the
middle of the road she would wait until they emerged from

between the two stone walls and then, with a sharp left and right
turn to negotiate the gap in the railings that was a few yards
away from the hillside path her children could safely cross the
road via the safe passage that Mrs Lollipop had created. The
problem with all this were the impatient motorists. From the
drivers position in their waiting vehicle it was not possible to see
up the secluded hillside footpath, or for that matter read the mind
of Mrs Lollipop.

To the waiting motorist, who had probably already left home
later than intended and was now getting later and later for work
while this stupid Lollipop woman was holding up traffic for no
apparent reason as no children were visible was quite simply,
like a red rag to a bull. Motorists would start to rev their engines,
or edge forward, or even toot their horns in annoyance of this
apparent needless reason for holding up the traffic and as these
impatient bulls raged then so did Mrs Lollipops lollipop!

With one swift arm movement her lollipop would become her
weapon of choice as she swung at the nearest waiting vehicle,
clattering her stick across the vehicles grill and bumper, like a
child running along railings with a stick. With her point made
she would then return to her position to wait for her children to
appear and cross the road in safety.

Her frown at the offending driver when they were finally sent on
their way was enough to tell them the error of their ways and to
keep their distance, and be more patience in the future.

Passing by Mrs Platt's house the next building of note was Wales
Chapel and while for obvious reasons this building was not a
recipient of a Sunday Paper on our round it holds many happy
memories of which I shall recall here.

***

M.A.Y.C.

Youth clubs were widespread with almost every village having one and it was natural to gravitate to the club closest to you and your peers. During my 6 years of primary and junior education Wales Bar and Wales formed the nucleus of my friends as that was the schools catchment area however, as extracurricular activities seemed to always be already pre-planned by my parents as I alluded to earlier, a youth club was never one of them.

On moving into comprehensive education at Dinnington High School everything changed.

My year group at Wales was around 25 whereas my year group at Dinnington was upwards of 350 as the catchment area of the school was enormous. We were split into 12 forms of similar size so the chance of one of my peers from Wales being in the same form as me was pretty slim so it was only the playground where we might meet.

Wales Bar and Wales were small villages on the periphery of the Dinnington school catchment area so making new school friends was a necessity although breaking into groups who had previously been in much larger primary schools was not easy and being introduced to their local youth clubs never really worked.

I had known my fellow Sunday paper lad almost from the first day of primary school and while the odds of us both being in the same form at Comprehensive School were stacked against us that is exactly what happened. I made new friends but they were not the same as old friends and we both continued to pal around together and indeed in the greater number of the adventures that I have already described my friend was there too, thanks for your friendship VW.

Kiveton was our nearest Youth Club and like all similar clubs everyone was welcome but even though it was only in the next village it still seemed too far to travel and its members were relative strangers to us.

We had heard that there was a youth club that met in the rooms adjoining the chapel and some of our primary school friends already attended, perfect we thought our own youth club on the doorstep and so it was that we turned up and met the youth club leader Mr Roy Staniforth. Roy was the son of Mr Staniforth from Waleswood Hall Farm and the scene of our threshing exploits. We were made very welcome and before long we felt part of the family, it was a great place to be.

Initially we were oblivious as to why the Youth Club should be enjoying the hospitality of the Chapel buildings and never really took much notice as to the emblem of the youth club, Wales MAYC or to give it the full title, Methodist Association of Youth Clubs.

It was only when Roy suggested that if we wanted to continue enjoying the Youth clubs hospitality that we should think about attending Chapel that we realised the link. This was not what I had envisaged, having already been through the trials and tribulations of Sunday School and then moving on to Cubs and Scouts, only to find that they too were linked to the Church, surely religion had not infiltrated this youth club?

Our immediate reaction was to ask why all our friends who attended the youth club didn't go to chapel but, as Roy explained, they had earned their right by association as their parents were Chapel goers and our friends as children had attended numerous chapel meetings, a Methodist chapel Sunday School !!!!

Roy was loved by everyone within the youth club, the chapel and beyond and in a few short weeks we knew that MAYC was the place to be, but attend chapel too?

Roy knew that teenagers didn't want to attend chapel but to sweeten this bitter pill he held a Sunday evening Youth Club that was open to anyone who attended the weekly Sunday evening Chapel service and so it was that just when I thought that religion was behind me I found myself on the chapel pews on Sunday evenings.

It's worth pointing out that during the 1960's Sundays were to be endured, they were boring as hell.

No worthwhile TV, which could also be said for the other 6 days of the week and doing homework ready for school on Monday morning, No shops open, in fact nothing open anywhere, so the thought of a youth club on Sunday evening was just great even if a Chapel service had to be endured first.

I should add that there was a Sunday highpoint that broke up a long boring Sunday which was of course Roast Beef and Yorkshire pudding with all the trimmings.

Our dinner was at midday as we were northern folk! Breakfast, dinner, tea and supper were our four meals of the day. We took dinner money to school to pay for school dinners and after school we came home for our tea.

Continental breakfast, Lunch, and evening dinner was an alien concept.

Against my better judgement, I found that a chapel service was quite interesting, at least some of the time. The hymns were much more upbeat than the ones that I was familiar with and the preacher (not a vicar) wore normal clothes. To my surprise at the second service that I attended it was conducted by a different preacher and only when I questioned what had become of the

previous weeks preacher was it explained to me how the
Methodist preaching system works.

*A Methodist local preacher is a lay person or deacon who has
been accredited by a Methodist church to lead worship
and preach on a regular basis. ... Local preachers continue to
serve an indispensable role in the Methodist Church of Great
Britain, in which the majority of church services are led
by lay people*

During the many services I attended in order to keep my
"membership" of the youth club active there were a number of
memorable preachers, some quite young, some female and some
would even bring a guitar along for a musical interlude. Many of
the sermons were actually quite interesting to listen to being
relevant and up to date with no mention of the bible and its many
stories. But, not all were good orators, there was also a fair
sprinkling of boring old fuddy duddy's that would drone on and
on about something and nothing although I'm sure they kept the
older members of the congregation entertained.
There was so much going on at the youth club which was held on
Tuesday, Friday and Sunday evenings. It was a club for the
youth of the village and so much more. Roy was born for the job;
he was tireless in arranging numerous activities both at youth
club meetings and beyond.
Roy's forte was writing, producing, directing and acting in the
lead role of pantomimes. He had been writing them since the
1940's and his bands of actors were the members of the youth
club.
Every year he would take sometimes 40 or more of us on a
week's camping holiday in August which would coincide with
the bank holiday weekend, we camped on land in the woods

above Oughtibridge on land that belonged to one of Roy's farming family relatives.

A 20 mile sponsored walk was another highlight of the year. Another year a few of us spent a week cruising on the Norfolk Broads.

I was an active member of the youth club for 6 or 7 years and after that still continued to keep in touch and participate in fund raising where possible, they were great times.

Pantomimes are a traditional Christmas time extravaganza and to keep the Christmas spirits flowing at our youth club Roy's annual Panto was presented around March!

Aladdin, Puss in Boots, Cinderella, Sleeping Beauty, Jack and the Beanstalk, Ali Baba and the Forty Thieves, Snow White & the Seven Dwarfs, Roy wrote his own version of them all and each had many references to local people and places which would bring fits of laughter and rapturous applause from the audience.

Auditions would start around November time following the long awaited announcement of which Panto it might be that year. We all wanted a good part but we knew that parts like the principal boy, played by a girl, and the principal girl, also played by a girl, together with the villain of the peace, the fool, and the fairy had already been selected and Roy wrote his Panto scripts around them to bring out the best in each individual. He also made sure that everyone else got a part that would encompass their talent, or otherwise, that they were capable of. The outstanding actors came and went as they grew into the part and then grew up and moved on although even as adults they would return years later either to act again or assist with the various chorus boys and girls of which their offspring would by then be one.

The Pantomime Dame was always Roy's part to play. It was Roy's show after all and his writing, acting and total dedication guaranteed its success year after year.

Health and safety of today is there for a reason and often when confronted with that reason why such a regulation is in place you have to research the reason for the reasoning behind the regulation, if you get my drift!!! Of course back in the 60's we had rules and regulations to follow but more importantly we applied common sense and self preservation, and it worked, with most of us still being here to tell the tale.

Back stage at Wales Methodist Youth Club Panto presentations it was absolute chaos, and in the hall audiences were packed in like sardines which together made for a great atmosphere. The youth club room that was attached to the rear of the stage became the girls changing room while the kitchens to the side of the hall became the boys changing room. There was a further large meeting room behind the hall where the junior chorus would get ready too so we each had our own space to prepare for our big moment, so far so good you might think. Then there was the logistical problem of getting from the changing room to the stage both quickly, and above all quietly. The girls were best placed for this whereas the boys had to dash from the kitchen, across the chapel yard and into a side door behind the stage that led into the girls changing room! The same stage access applied for the multiple chorus girls and boys after they had been shepherded by their bustling parents from the meeting room, across the chapel yard and into the girls changing room. I leave it to your imagination as to the pandemonium that ensued when virtually every panto player was packed into the girls changing area waiting for the que to go on stage for the finale.

The final curtain is about to close on a performance Of Aladdin at Wales Chapel.

There was one further challenge which came at the interval when tea, coffee, orange juice and sandwiches with cake were served. A few minutes before the interval the chapel women elders would appear exuding an authoritarian air and take over both the kitchen and the meeting room to prepare the interval feast that was to be laid out on tables that had until that moment been stacked in a pile in the corner of the meeting room. Their mission was, to them, all important and the thought that the panto players had to retake the two rooms for the second half of the show never entered their heads. This was their time and nothing else mattered.

**A scene from Aladdin, left to right Andrew Crowther, Me
and Neville Fairbrother.**
**Andrew went on to join the RAF as a trainee fighter pilot
and while training in his aircraft somewhere in the Scottish
highlands he crashed and sadly lost his life.**
Neville is the streaker you will see in a picture a little later!

The hall seated probably 100 and due to the panto's year on year
success the audience swelled annually as a result and it was not
uncommon to put on 7 or 8 performances to satisfy demand. I am
not sure if it was the sheer numbers of eager panto goers that
brought to an end the Wales Chapel venue or Health and Safety
requirements or perhaps both as by the late 60's we moved to a
new venue, and it was a bold move. The bright lights of the big
city beckoned when Roy announced that the forthcoming Panto
would be performed in Sheffield at The Montgomery Hall. We
were all both disappointed yet excited at the same time, it was
the end of an era a Wales Chapel but to perform in a real theatre

would be amazing. I had been to this theatre a few years earlier to watch a performance of Gilbert & Sullivan's HMS Pinafore with my father, impressed? It was boring and I was desperate for it to end but I had remembered how grand the theatre was with seats at stage level and a whole lot more above them on a balcony, or circle to give its correct name. I think perhaps the only reason I was taken to the D'Oyly Carte Opera Company's performance was to get me from under mum's feet for a while. Montgomery Hall was a real theatre with dressing rooms, an enormous stage that sloped from front to back, and stage curtains that swished back and forth at the push of a button; there was even a white safety curtain that came down from above the stage to cut off the audience from any contact with the happenings and preparations' on stage pre performance. During performances at Wales Chapel scenery changes happened in a crazy panic stricken few minutes while the front curtains were drawn. One or two players would entertain the audience with a song or a gag as the canvas scene from the previous stage set was lowered and rolled onto a pole to reveal the next canvas painted scene already hung in sequence behind it, but not at Montgomery Hall. This was a proper theatre and with seamless efficiency as each scene moved on to the next so would the painted canvas scenery rise upwards into the enormous roof space above the stage. This was such a slick operation and it was done as players continued to act with the scenery change all part of the act.

Back stage, below stage, stage left and stage right was a rabbit warren of corridors that allowed the players to get to where they needed to be in order to make a grand stage entrance. There were also four screens on both stage left and stage right so that an entrance could be made at the front, middle or even up stage. It was a world away from the Wales Chapel Stage and we all felt like real stage actors.

Of course with our new venue being so much bigger the performances were fewer and our first year at Montgomery Hall we played to just two full houses but moving the show to the big city had also attracted bigger audiences and within a year there was a Friday night performance with an afternoon and evening performance on the Saturday following. Roy's fame as a pantomime writer, producer, director and performer was assured.

Roy created so many wonderful memories for all those who knew him. Roy Staniforth MBE passed away earlier last year in 2017 aged 89 but for me and the many thousands of others who were touched by his tireless generosity to life he will be forever young. RIP Sir Roy.

The following is one of many obituaries that appeared in both the local and national press earlier last year:-

Roy Staniforth, who has died at 89, enjoyed a remarkable stage career that spanned seven decades on the boards in South Yorkshire. A noted pantomime dame, he made his acting debut at 15, during the war, and remained active into his eighties.

He set up the Methodist Panto Players in his home village of Wales, on the edge of the Rother Valley Country Park, from where he treated audiences to a coterie of outrageous characterisations, in performances that became a village tradition. But by the end of the 1960s the show had become such a favourite that it had outgrown its roots and moved to the Montgomery Theatre in Sheffield city centre. His show was the last one on stage before fire swept through the Montgomery in 1970, but the company was back as soon as the auditorium had been rebuilt. Never one for scaling back a production, his shows regularly featured more than 50 speaking parts and a full chorus.

For the company's 50th anniversary he managed to squeeze a cast of 120 people onto the Montgomery's stage. Mr Staniforth wrote, directed and acted, and his productions helped keep the sense of community alive in Wales and nearby Kiveton. He was awarded an MBE for his work in 1997. After his retirement from the stage in 2012, he said: "I will miss the fun of it all and seeing people's faces as they are laughing. I will miss being on stage but I have no regrets. I have enjoyed every minute; it's been a big part of my life. "I will remember the happiness we have brought to people and the laughter we have had in rehearsals. It's been such a joy.

A week of camping in the wilderness above Oughtibridge was the best fun ever. It was looked forward too by everyone at the youth club. The camp site was a field that was grazed by cows for 51 weeks of the year and lay some 200 yards beyond the entrance to a farm where a family relative of Roy's eked out a living from the unforgiving terrain on the moorland above the woodland that surrounded the farm. The field lay in an area of flatland with woodland both above and below it.

There was a fresh water spring that tumbled down the hillside above the campsite and formed a pond by a rock face close to where we pitched our tents and from where the water then continued its flow on through the woods below.

Milk was provided by the absent bovine tenants of our campsite and provisions for the week came from catering sized cans of food together with heaps of potatoes and other fresh produce. Over the years Roy had amassed tents of various sizes together with tables, benches, pots, pans and every conceivable utensil, vessel and general paraphernalia item required for a battalion of campers to survive the wilderness that was our billet for the week.

We would arrive at chapel on Friday morning with our nap sacks on our backs all stuffed full with sleeping bags, clothes and a few toiletries of which usually remained untouched, or at least that was the case for us boys!

The camping equipment that I have just described created a major logistical operation in getting it all from the store room at the chapel to our campsite in the woods but as ever Roy had not overlooked anything. One of our group was the son of a local farmer and his dad provided the transport we needed to get both the equipment and us where we wanted to be. We would load all the tents and supplies required into the open cattle lorry and when all was safely aboard we all climbed on top and had an open air ride to our camp.

Our camp "village" was extremely well organised. We had a marquee as a dining room complete with folding trestle tables and benches and a kitchen tent that was completely open on one side with an overhead canopy under which all the kitchen equipment was set out.

For our sleeping arrangements Roy had his own tent while we had 4 large ex army bell tents, two for the girls and two for the boys, which when erected were not unlike a large Indian tepee. Tents of today almost erect themselves but have you ever tried to erect a bell tent?

It is not a job that can be done single handed in fact for this task many hands certainly made light work!

The key was first to decide where to pitch our tent and once that location was decided then for us the first job was to remove the cow pats from the area that had been left by the previous week's tenants. Next we would spread out the canvas tent on the floor and then assemble the central wooden pole to its full length of some 12 feet, on the top of which was a large metal spike. One of us would then crawl into the canvas to locate a bound hole that denoted the very top of the tent and where the spike of the pole had to be located, so far so good. Fastened around the outside of the bound hole were 4 long guy ropes that were to be the key to the stability of the tent when finally erected. So, the next stage was ideally when 10 people gathered around to get the tent into a secure upright position although I doubt the previous military owners of our bell tents had needed as much manpower! Two of us would place the base of the pole in the preselected centre point of where we hoped the tent would finally be pitched while four more sets of willing hands would each take hold of one of the four guy ropes and position themselves in an imaginary corner of a large square plotted around the limp canvas currently laying on the ground. Now, for the next stage everyone needed to know their role and no matter how well the briefing had been prior to our starting this stage it was always accompanied by frantic shouts of pull, hold it there, no, that's too much, to your left, to your right, I can't hold it much longer, he/she is making it worse, and so much more.

The plan was for the two pole holders to grip the pole to keep it firmly anchored to the ground in its allotted spot while two guy rope holders, standing on the same side of the imaginary square, pulled hard on the guy ropes while walking backwards and away from the tent. This action saw the pole and the tent around it rise to its full height as the two pole holders disappeared into the folds of tent canvas that enveloped them. The next crucial moment was, as the pole got closer to its vertical position, for the other two guy rope holders also to quickly walk backwards to take the strain of their guy ropes so that the pole was prevented from passing a vertical position and hopefully, if everyone had worked to the plan, the central tent pole would be upright with the two pole holders within a mass of hanging canvas still clung to its base and four guy rope holders each stood at the corner of the imaginary square.

So, that was it, we would have the makings of a well erected bell tent, but, I did say that ideally ten body's were required for a successful outcome. Now it was the turn of the four individuals who had until now stood at a distance shouting and yelling numerous instructions between fits of laughter as the pole had swayed first left and then right as each of the four guy holders had under or over pulled and the pole holders, hidden from view in the folds of the thus far limp canvas, had hung on for dear life to the swaying pole.

The remaining four bodies each had a wooden mallet and a tent peg. Their job was to drive a peg into the ground at the point where the guy holder was standing so that the guy rope could then be looped around the peg and final adjustments made to the guy rope tension by sliding the wooden tensioning toggle of the guy rope up or down and finally achieving a secure framework around which the erection of the bell tent could be completed. Every year we went through the same performance and every year we had forgotten what we had learnt from the previous year's fiasco which perhaps was just as well as it would have been only half the fun had we known what we were doing!

An example of properly erected bell tents

We had a spring for water, a farm for milk and eggs and a kitchen fully stocked with provisions for the week, we had it all, well not quite. The last job (although it should have been the first) was to erect two toilet tents and all the necessary equipment to go inside them. Basic sanitation would be the best description for the two conveniences as they certainly wouldn't have passed muster in today's practically perfect environment.

Like the bell tents, we had one tent for the girls and one for the boys and they were pitched at a discrete distance from each other and a good distance from our canvas village. Each tent was a basic 4 feet x 4 feet canvas cubicle supported at each corner by a tent pole and guy rope. The toilet was a galvanised dustbin on top of which neatly fitted a plastic toilet seat and lid. Each dustbin was filled with 2 inch covering of water in the bottom mixed with and a dose of Elsan Blue toilet fluid. There was no toilet roll or holder as that was the user's responsibility to take on their visit.

The guy ropes to the toilet tent were a constant form of amusement, particularly for the boys, as we would lie in wait for the girls to "spend a penny" and then creep up and slacken the ropes to allow the tent to gently settle onto the occupant. Of course we were always told "now that's not funny" but I suppose it depended on your point of view!

We all had duties for the day around our camp and some were better than others. There was firewood duty when you were charged with not just keeping the camp fire burning as this was the only source for cooking food and boiling water, but also foraging in the wood for the fuel. Cooking duty was ok and certainly better than washing up duty. Water had to be collected from the fresh water spring some distance below the camp and while the outward journey carrying the empty containers to the spring was a breeze, bringing them back full to the camp was a chore and made the duty undesirable. We were 200 yards and more from the farmhouse and it needed two campers on milk and egg duty. The milk churn had a handle on each side for transporting, leaving a left and a right hand free to carry the eggs. Again the outward journey was ok but bringing back a full milk churn and the eggs was hard work. The best or worst duty, depending on your point of view, was toilet duty.

All the duties, bar this one, meant that you could be called on at any time throughout the day to fulfil your obligation but toilet duty was different. The toilets had to be emptied once a day and it required a team of two. The toilet tents were pitched below the campsite on the edge of the woods and the drill was to first dig a hole between the trees, always remembering where the previous hole had been dug, then retrieve the by now very full dustbin from the toilet tent and each carefully clasp a dustbin handle and carry the dustbin to the hole in which the contents were poured and then quickly to return the excavated material to cover the dustbins contents. A quick rinse of the dustbin and dose of Elsan and it was job done. Fortunately we were both of similar height and were able to keep the dustbin level during transit, most of the time!

For the daily chores we had to draw straws but a bit of bartering meant that me and my mate always did toilet duty. Lots of practice meant that we could get the job done in 20 minutes so the day was then our own.

The marquee dining room to the left of the tennis players with the kitchen tent beyond and the camp fire burning well. A game of tug of war by the marquee with a view up the long valley to the farmhouse that the milk monitors had to trudge every day.

As these campsite photos show we had plenty of fun between our daily duties and as it was August and some 45 years ago then my memory, or perhaps my imagination, tells me that every youth club camp was under blue skies and whether or not the sun was actually shining it most certainly was from the from within. Games by the pond of water that gathered by two small cliff faces where the fresh ice cold water passed from the spring above and on to the woods below were a frequent occurrence with water fights between rival teams or simply enjoying an impromptu dip to wash away the grime of campsite living although as teenagers that was not a high priority. The streaker pictured on the next page was honouring a lost bet!

"Jack Jack shine yer light blow yer whistle" was the best game of all and was talked about throughout the 51 weeks that we were not camping. For those going to camp for the first or even umpteenth time, we could not wait for darkness to fall as Jack Jack could only be played in the hours of darkness. To add excitement to this commando style game it so happened that on our journey out of Sheffield and on into the hills above Oughtibridge and riding in the back of our laden cattle truck, we had need to pass an austere looking large stone edifice that was a Convent. No doubt occupied by the Mother Abbess and her nuns seeking their solace from the world but to our group of intrepid campers this was where the Blue Nuns lived and as "Roy's Story" often told of the ghosts of the Blue Nuns that walked the moors in the dead of night above the woods of our campsite. Of course this legendary tale had the desired effect to all who entered the woods at night. It seemed that the best chance of catching a glimpse of these ghostly figures floating on the horizon of the bleak moorlands was on a moonlit night, and Roy knew the best vantage point from within the woods to see and experience this phenomenon.

I remember my first year at camp and the nervous anticipation that built up inside me as I went into the woods on a bright moonlit August night along with my fellow campers as Roy led the way towards the moors above us, all the while he talked in a whisper telling us of the strong feeling he had that we might just get a sighting that night.

Seeing the three Blue Nuns was just as I had imagined as they moved across the horizon dressed in a flowing veil from head to foot and walking slowly one behind the other with the bright moon enhancing their silhouettes until they seemed to disappear slowly over the horizon.

When we later returned to camp full of wonder of the phenomenon that we had just experienced the three older campmates that had chosen to stay back in camp that night tending the campfire listened in awe to the cacophony of voices trying to explain what they had just seen.

In later years I remember only too well racing down from the moors to get back to camp and the campfire to wait for Roy's young group of ghost spotters to return to camp and tell us the tale of the Blue Nuns that they had seen earlier walking over the moors!!

So, back to Jack Jack. We had the entire woods as our playground, there was a ravine and stream that ran almost the entire length, intermittent glades covered in waist high ferns, boggy areas, grass areas, large trees, small trees, fallen trees and even the occasional rocky outcrop.

Jack Jack was basically a variation on hide and seek but much more besides.

We had two teams of up to maybe a dozen or so and when it was sufficiently dark the first team would set off into the woods as far as a ten minute start would take them before the second team set off in pursuit. The intense darkness beneath the wooded overhead canopy was the first teams shield against being found as the second team set off to seek and find. Of course in such a large area it would have been almost an impossible task to find anyone and this is where our game got its name from.

After a fruitless search the seeking team would shout "Jack Jack shine yer light blow yer whistle" to which the first team had to respond by either a blast on the team leader's whistle or a flash from their torch beam to indicate their whereabouts. Team two would then set off towards the location from which they thought the sound or sighting had come from. Easy you might think? Well not so as once team one had revealed their location they would be up and away to find another hideout while all the time listening for the possible approach of team two. And so it went on, this game of cat and mouse with team two gradually closing in on their prey. The ravine in the woods was deep with a small track running along one side before the wooded slope continued on to the valley below, this was a total contrast to the other side which rose steeply from the ravines stream at some 60 degrees angle with trees of varying maturity clinging precariously to the rocky slope reaching upwards towards glimpses of sunlight from above the woods canopy that was there lifeline.

One particular night we were the seeking team and after a while we had tracked team one to a point where we could hear them moving along the track in the ravine. We were so near yet so far to finally catching them due to our team being high above them looking down the steep slope on the opposite bank of the ravine. Thinking that this obstacle gave Team one the protection they needed to make their escape they shone their torch upwards and towards us through the clinging trees while all the time laughing at the impossible task that lay before us to catch them.

We were not going to be beaten and without thought of fear or safety two of us took a leap of faith from the top of the steep ridge that separated us from them. We could have died!! But luck was on our side as within seconds of launching ourselves over the edge we were in, then out of the stream and quickly pouncing on the rearmost team one member at which point the whole team was obliged to admit defeat. Shell shocked by their capture, Roy, who was heading team one, said that in all the years of playing Jack Jack he had never seen anyone brave enough, or stupid enough to do what we had just done. I still remember like it was just yesterday, flying through the darkness with hands, feet and backside briefly touching the ravines unforgiving terrain while somehow miraculously missing the numerous clinging trees. Lady luck was with us that night and from then on whenever the exploits of Jack Jack were talked of it was our commando style antics that became legendary.

One fund raising activity that was always great fun and allowed all ages to take part was the 20 mile walk. It was intended as a leisurely Saturday walk in the summer sunshine and indeed that is what most participants did. Whole families of sometimes 4 generations would walk the route along with scores of other eager fundraisers. (Well at least 3 generations would walk as the 4th would be in their pram or pushchair!)

For us we saw the walk as a challenge and walking around the course was not an option. We saw it as a race and had every intention of winning it.

The crowd of walkers would gather in the chapel yard laden with picnics, rucksacks, spare shoes, socks and anything else that they thought would be indispensible for the intrepid trek that lay before them. We travelled light with jeans tee-shirt and plimsolls and of course our sponsor sheet. The sponsor sheet was most important as it was to verify that everyone had completed the walk. Along the route we had to find the Methodist chapel of each village that we passed through and waiting for us would be refreshments and a member of the congregation to stamp our sponsor sheet as proof of our visit.

Thinking back now at the route of the walk, while I imagine that all the chapel staging posts are still there, the beautiful open countryside and rural roads that we passed by, and on, have mostly disappeared with development of land and remodelling of infrastructure that has seen much of our rural idle change to urban sprawl. Some call it progress, but others don't agree and that includes me.

The majority of sponsored walkers completed the course in a leisurely 6 or 7 hours but for us we had to be the winners and for 3 years running I was the first one back home, arriving back at the Chapel gates from where we had set of less than 4 hours before. Perhaps not quite a good marathon equivalent time but it certainly felt like it.

One more highlight of the youth club year was the Annual M.A.Y.C. London weekend. This was a gathering of all Methodist youth clubs from around Britain with the centre of all the activities being non other than the Royal Albert Hall. We would travel down to London by coach on Friday afternoon on a journey that would take 6 or more hours and on arrival we would make our way to one of the many local chapels around London where the local youth club were are hosts for the weekend. We slept in the chapel school rooms or halls in neatly set out rows in our sleeping bags. Using the minimal sanitary and washing facilities was quite novel the following morning as upwards of a hundred or more queued to use the 2 or 3 toilets available but as Oughtibridge camping experts we could easily cope with these basic conditions! On Saturday morning we would be back on the coach and making our way to Central London and the Royal Albert Hall. On my first weekend in 1969 I could hardly believe just how many Methodist youth club members there were, it seemed like they had all converged on London for the weekend. It was the first time I had been inside the Royal Albert Hall and only my second visit to London, having been on a day trip to the capital 2 years earlier with the Scouts.

The Hall was an amazing building from the outside and even more so from within. We were sat on seats that seemed almost vertically tiered around about 75% of the auditoriums circumference and to lean forward felt like you were going to tumble downwards into the seats below.

There was plenty of singing, dancing and presentations with the highlight of the morning's events being an appearance by Cliff Richard who was well into his religious period at that time. After the morning's events within the Hall we all spilled out onto the concourse surrounding the Hall where various youth club groups participated in friendly rivalry of chants and shouts in support of their club. We had bunked down the previous night in Rickmansworth and we were back there for another night that evening. We needn't have worried about finding their chapel again as they kept up their chant all day long while walking around London on an afternoon free of activities which allowed us to explore the capital city.

The screaming chant of "Ricky Ricky Ricky Ricky Rickmondsworth" was everywhere and simply had to be followed.

While waiting outside the Albert Hall after the morning's presentations we happened to be standing by an entrance where vehicles would come and go to gain direct access to the inner sanctum of the Hall. As we stood there a brightly polished purple Jenson Interceptor luxury sports car appeared from behind a pair of large doors that had been swung open to let it and its occupants out of the Hall. The car slowly made its way past just where we were standing. Cliff Richard was at the wheel and he gave us all a broad smile. Fame and fortune was well and truly his.

My ticket to the MAYC Weekend 1969 costing the princely sum of one shilling (or bob)

MAYC Weekend 1970 with Roy Staniforth taking centre stage

Wales Methodist Youth Club and all my friends associated with MAYC played a massive part in my life throughout my teenage years. I could continue to recount so many more adventures but will save them for another time and now move on past the Chapel and make my way along School Road and beyond to Wales Bar.

Wales Chapel when it was first built

Wales Chapel today, who thought red bricks would look better?

***

I Told 'Em – Oldham

Passing the chapel and immediately on the left was the lane that led to Reg Smiths chicken farm followed by a selection of detached and semi detached houses and bungalows. First was the home of Peter Walker the butcher, then Mr and Mrs Brian Mills. Brian's claim to fame was having his name over the door of the Lord Conyers pub in Wales Square telling everyone who passed through the door that he was the pub landlord. Then there was the Plant family who lived in a fine red brick detached house which surely was their pride and joy. Their house escaped demolition when the motorway came through but became the last house before the new motorway embankment and having Reg Smiths new chicken farm rise up at the bottom of their garden I think the bubble that was their dream had surely burst. In the photo that follows taken midway through the motorway construction the Plant's house is the first from left to right with the scaffolding in place to temporarily prop it up!

I have no doubt that like today, government compensation was paid out to those who suffered disruption to their properties and lives but I doubt that then, as now, it was ever enough. Mr and Mrs Meese were the Plants near neighbours and lived in a beautiful bungalow with manicured gardens on all sides of which I have no doubt was a reflection Mr Meese's profession as a hairdresser. It remains a matter of opinion as to who was the least fortunate, the Plants, or perhaps the Meese's. The Meese's gave up their home to three lanes of the northbound carriageway while the Plants stayed put. The Meese's didn't move far investing their compensation in a new bungalow built just around the corner on Mansfield Road in Wales Bar on land between Waleswood Villas and the Waleswood Hotel.

Just along from the chapel was the home of Mr & Mrs Waite. Remember I told you earlier about Harold Waite who was the retired scout troop leader? Well this is where he lived along with Mrs Waite who was a teacher at Wales Primary School; she practically lived on the job! Mrs Waite taught the top class of three in the primary school. She was tall and slim with short permed hair and large spectacles, the type with large lenses and butterfly wings and fancy temple arms. She spoke with a soft deep voice and I assume she was of similar years to her husband although life had been much kinder to her.

She was the perfect teacher to take on a babbling class of 7 year olds. She was kind, patient and considerate, every child loved her.

I would suggest that perhaps Harold Waite's occupation was better known around the village than he as personally as the tool of his profession was always parked on the grass verge by the garden wall of their house. He worked for Oldham Batteries who, in the 1960's were the market leaders in the manufacture of car batteries together with all types of batteries used in the mining industry which I suspect were his main customers in the area. His van was an Austin A60 in the company colours of red and cream and emblazoned on each rear side panel of the van was his companies slogan "'I told 'em – Oldham" which was an iconic catchphrase for the company.

**This Austin A60 van is in the same colours as that driven by
Harold Waite
but the logo of "'I told 'em – Oldham" is missing.**

Before the late 60's the walk along School road from Wales to
Wales Bar was tranquil, quiet, and devoid of a mass of road
traffic but, as surrounding villages developed in tandem with the
construction of the now completed housing estate flanking both
the West and East facing slopes of Wales Bar Hill the villages of
Wales and Wales Bar had been linked together forever. The
times and landscapes were changing rapidly. The New Tree
Estate, thoughtfully named by the locals as each road on the
estate was named after a tree! Cherry, Almond, Fir and Green
Oak. By today's standards they were large houses but typical of
construction methods and materials of the early 60's, they were
built on a budget. I am extremely grateful for this fact as the
continuous improvements that the proud owners of these new
homes undertook over the following years provided a steady
stream of work for my Construction Company. Had the new
householders and their families who now lived on the Eastern
slopes of the estate realised that Wales Sports field which spread
out along the bottom of their quaint estate gardens providing a
very pleasant outlook but without the responsibility of upkeep
was soon to disappear then I suspect that they would have chose
to live elsewhere. As it was, the Sports ground disappeared

forever to make way for the M1 Motorway. I have already recalled my adventures during the time that this colossal feat of civil engineering took place but one more event is worthy of note.

The building of a bridge to carry an existing road under or over a new development is bound to cause disruption to everything and everyone that wishes and needs to continue to use it and so it was that the bridge builders of the the School Road motorway bridge came up with a cunning plan.

Their idea was to build a temporary horseshoe shaped road some 100 yards distant and parallel to the current road on the site of the cricket field with links back to the existing School Road at each side of the proposed new bridge allow both road and pedestrian traffic to make their journey without undue interruption.

The idea was a success, or at least it was until the mass excavations on either side of this new temporary link got deeper and deeper towards the levels required for the new motorways foundations. The temporary road became more and more prominent, sat on top of steep embankments to either side as two way traffic continued back and forth. One day some movement was observed in the tarmac surface of the temporary road suggesting that the cracks that appeared were due to more than the effects of the passing traffic so it was decided that a one way traffic light controlled system should be put in place. Today's health and safety regulations linked with a climate of damage limitation and litigation would have closed this road link instantly but the one way system continued until eventually the road had become so distorted that the passage of traffic was halted.

Of course this action had massive implications to commuters and locals alike and for a while Wales and Wales Bar returned to their roots of two quiet country backwaters that no one other than its inhabitants visited.

During all the major disruption that the motorway building brought, those lucky enough to have cars to get to and from work had quickly varied their routes in order to avoid bottlenecks such that the cricket field diversion created. It was all well and good for the lucky folk with cars but for those who relied on public transport courtesy of Sheffield Corporation Transport or The Booth and Fisher bus company the disruption that the road failure caused was unavoidable and every delay had to be endured.

As this picture shows, taken soon after the temporary road was opened and before its sides were excavated into steep embankments, the traffic flowed freely with a Sheffield Corporation Double Decker making its way around the diversion towards Wales Bar while pedestrians walk towards Wales.

The closing of this link road meant that the bus companies had to devise a plan. If you were a Double Decker commuter the bus service ended at the Wales Bar side and started again at the Wales side. After alighting at one side or the other there was a 10 minute slot allocated to allow the passengers to walk around the diversion and re board the service at the other side. Looking back now it seems strange that the powers that be decided that although the diversion was unsafe for vehicle use it was perfectly fine for pedestrians to use! However it did give us a bird's eye view of the construction works as they progressed, deep down in the cutting below us.

The Booth and Fisher bus service adopted a different plan. Booth and Fisher was a privately owned bus company based in nearby Halfway. I should enlighten my readers here to say that they were not based halfway from here or there but actually based at Halfway, a village equidistant between Killamarsh and Mosborough and consequently very aptly named!

"Boothies" as we preferred to call them, owned the bus route that eventually terminated at Worksop some 10 miles distant from Wales Bar with the route winding through many outlaying villages along the way so for those rural inhabitants without a car and not in reach of a the Sheffield Corporation bus route then Worksop was their metropolis. The bus drivers and conductors of this service were often on first name terms with their passengers, such was the intimacy of the service. in fact I remember well that one of the bus crews were husband and wife with husband at the wheel and his wife as conductress.

Boothies bus fleet was nothing like the size of Sheffield Corporation so they were compelled to thinking of a way to keep their service running with the limited resources that they had available to them.

The bus and passengers would arrive at the Wales Bar side of the diversion having left the bus depot at Halfway a while before and amassing its passengers en route. Following their arrival at the Wales Bar side the driver would park the bus, lock it up and both he, his conductor and their passengers would walk around the diversion to where a locked and empty Boothies Bus was waiting for them at the Wales side of the diversion and the service would then continue to its destination in Worksop where, after a short rest at the bus station, the same crew would retrace the route back to Wales, disembark from the bus and walk around the diversion once again to the waiting empty bus to get the crew and passengers back to the terminus at Halfway. The total closure of the link road continued throughout the summer months and although many never signed up for a motorway in their back yard it was certainly a relief to see the bridge completed and to get School Road back.

***

My Profitable Pram

The motorway bridge is the perfect place to put a temporary halt to my recollections of the people, the places, and the adventures that they inspired as it was at this point that my friend and me decided to split our enormous Sunday paper round. I was to take on what few customers we had on the New Tree estate together with everyone else who lived along School Road to Wales Bar and all those in and around my home village.

The Tye's were in agreement and they arranged for my batch of newspapers to be delivered directly to Wallingfield where they would arrive at some unearthly Sunday morning hour and left on the front door step for me to gather up and sort out ready for my morning deliveries, News of the World, Sunday Mirror, Sunday Times, Sunday Telegraph, The Observer all together with their relevant glossy magazines and 2 copies of The Peoples Friend, one for Mrs Saxby and one for her neighbour Mrs Askew. What I could never understand about these next door but one neighbour's was why, out of the entire round were they the only two to read this magazine and even more strangely why they didn't buy just the one Magazine between them?

This was now my paper round and I was in charge and it was not long before I realised that there was more to be had out of it than just getting a wage for my labours.

Each week I had to compile a list of newspapers and magazines that my customers wanted the following week and I would present this list to my employer when delivering the current week's takings to their house in Kiveton every Sunday after the completion of my round. My order would arrive on our doorstep the following Sunday and my first job was to check that the delivery tallied with my list.

The papers would first arrive at Sheffield Midland station by train from London or Manchester in the small hours of Sunday morning where wholesalers then packed them for distribution to their clients or in my case to their client's paper lad. The neatly packed bundle of newspapers was extremely heavy and within seconds of handling them the black ink that filled the pages of the broadsheets was also all over my hands. I don't know what process the wholesalers used to count the papers, perhaps by weight, thickness, or an experienced eye cast over the folded edges of a pile of papers? Whichever method they adopted then it was not accurate. Fortunately this inaccuracy aired on the side of excess as each week I would have some 10 to 20 spare newspapers. So what was I to do with them? Should I take them back to my employer when I had completed my round? Or, profit from the wholesalers cavalier attitude to mathematical counting. Now that I had my own round I also needed to upgrade my means of transport. The home made trolley had worked well for us but on rainy day it was very hard to keep the newspapers dry so we used an old overcoat to throw over the papers as we trundled along from house to house. The process of splitting up the round had taken a few weeks and it was during this time that I started my search for new reliable transport and I had put the word out that I was looking for a good, sturdy and above all complete pram. As I mentioned earlier, as lads of a certain age we all looked out for old prams to remodel into a trolley to race up and down the street and I knew where to find the perfect pram but dare not ask although I was perfectly aware that this pram was no longer used. All my previous requests to convert it into a trolley had been turned down point blank by its custodian. Imagine my surprise when this untouchable pram was offered to me. It had already had 3 previous careful owners and I was told quite firmly that if I promised to look after it and not do any unnecessary modifications then I could have it for my paper round. It was perfect, 2 previous careful female owners and one equally careful male owner from new and each of them had been accompanied on trips out by a responsible adult at all times to ensure that the pram was driven carefully. The prams last male owner had used it most days but the pram had been garaged for the last 10 years or so but always kept covered by a sheet and was in excellent condition.

Here it is, my Sunday paper transport, pictured with all its previous owners.
From the left, me, Sister Jane, Mum and Sister Diane.

I should say at this point that the old pram did indeed stay in one piece for almost 2 more years in which time it covered many miles on my paper round. After it was finally retired from the round the wheels and chassis became the running gear for a replica vintage car that I made for one of Wales Chapels pantomime performances!

No longer did I need an old overcoat to protect the newspapers from the rain as the pram had a hood and cover. Even better were the two clips that when released allowed the rear section of the pram to extend and it was here where I kept my "spare" newspapers.

During my round I was often stopped and asked if I had a spare copy of one or other newspaper and always willing to oblige I was able to offer a choice from my "spare" collection!

Of course, I was aware that surely all my fellow Sunday lads and lasses would get a similar glut of broadsheets placed on their doorstep and indeed I had noticed that as I queued at the Tye's kitchen door to wait my turn to deliver the proceeds from my round that each of us would also have a small number of papers to return and of course this practice soon became obvious to me, it was a token gesture to our employers.

When I finally gave notice that I was retiring from my round in the summer of 1970 due to my imminent start of work in the real world then no wonder that there was a long waiting list for my round of eager would be employees for the Tye's to choose from. By the time I finally finished the job my wage was exactly 20 Shillings (£1) but I suspect the real attraction that had created such a long waiting list was the unofficial bonus scheme that went with the job. Depending on how lax the counters and packers had been in those early hours of Sunday morning at the Midland Station I would regularly get a weekly bonus of around 10 shillings.

My employers when placing their weekly order with the wholesaler would have surely only settled their account in line with the quantities ordered and indeed the wholesalers would have followed suit to the news printers, so, if the London and

Manchester printers chose to overprint their broadsheets we were surely doing them a service by selling their newspapers and spreading their printed word to new readers.

Certain members of the 60's population got up to no good just as they do now. I have a copy of the Sheffield evening Star in front of me with headlines reading :- Riddle of City Shop Raid, Youth crashed Brothers car, Boys fired catapults (not me guv), Ice cream man fined (what's that all about?) but there was one significant difference. We all had possessions of value but the value was to each individual and had no worth to others. Drugs were not on the streets and streets were a safe place to be in town or village.

Cash ruled the day, there were no credit cards, chip and pin or contactless payment, day to day spending was in pounds, shillings and pence, real money.

By the end of my Sunday paper round I would have collected a significant amount of money which I kept in my pram in a toffee tin. Harold Prestige, my morning and evening paper round employer would walk the streets of Kiveton to Wales bar on a Thursday and Friday evening with his leather money bag hung over his shoulder, collecting the proceeds from the papers that I and my fellow paper lads and lasses had delivered throughout the week. Mrs Bradley the milkman's wife would do the same on Saturday mornings. The butchers Messer's Radford and Walker would always have cash with them as they sold their meat, sausages, tripe, and liver from their butchers van. The conductress and driver on Boothies bus would walk around the M1 diversion with their passengers alongside and the proceeds from ticket sales casually hung in a bag over her shoulder.

We all carried our takings generated by our jobs and never gave a thought of being robbed; such was our idyllic, carefree and above all safe life in the 60's.

The summer of 1970 marked a big turning point in my finances. My new career as an apprentice joiner for Sheffield Public Works Department began (of which you can read all about in my book "Bricks and Mortar") and my Saturday job with Reg Smith came to an end along with my 3 paper rounds. My starting wage for the PWD was just short of £6 per week and after deductions for tax, union subscriptions, bus travel and weekly board to my parents I was actually better off at School doing 3 paper rounds plus bonuses and a Saturday job which earned me £3 and no outgoings !!

***

Life at 100 mph

Wales bar did see changes during the 1960's as I explained in my last story about Reg Smith. The development of this area with the arrival of Mr Gratton with his garage business, the biscuit warehouse, Dels supermarket distribution centre and E T Sutherlands from where Reg Smith obtained the swill to feed his pigs certainly changed the landscape and what follows are some memories and experiences that these places bring to mind.

Mr Gratton made the first change to the landscape by building his garage and petrol station. It was a far cry from today's petrol forecourt s of neon lights, mini markets, cash points and snack bars but still provided what the customer of the day wanted, petrol, car repairs and even car sales.

Mr Gratton was in the garage business but he didn't get grease on his hands, he was always well dressed and chose to be the front man of the operation, serving petrol or buying and selling cars while his long suffering mechanic worked tirelessly in the garage workshop that was just big enough to house 2 cars and the enormous pile of car parts that lay in one corner of the garage. There were probably enough pieces of engine, body panels, wheels and axles to make at least another 2 cars but the pile merely served as reminder to his customers of just how many cars had passed through the garage and resulting in greater or lesser success of repair. His mechanic was good, or at least that was what I heard my dad say after entrusting his car to the mechanic to repair the front wing of our family car which had happened to come in contact with another car while on our family holiday.

We were a family of 6 plus our pet Labrador Mandy and we needed a big car. My dad loved his big cars although none of his cars loved him as he was a terrible driver! I will say at this point that the damaged wing incident was definitely not his fault as we were stationary in a queue of traffic at the time when a car pulled out and hit us. It was a black car but the air was blue!!

Our car at the time was a 1964 Ford Zephyr 6 and my dad loved it. I remember going to Cross Scythes Motors in Sheffield to buy it. The car was just 6 months old when my dad became the proud owner of what he was reliably informed had just had 1 previous careful owner. I guess that the car dealership was no less scrupulous than similar outfits of the day and was just one of many garages selling "dodgy motors". Some things never change.

Prior to the arrival of the M1 motorway any great speed attained on the single carriageway road in Yorkshire was fraught with danger, however there was a stretch of dual carriageway not too far from us which provided the opportunity to put your foot down.

The A1 was a road that followed the ancient coaching route that stretched from London to Edinburgh and in the 1950,s a slow but steady programme had begun to build by-passes around bottlenecks towns along its route. These bypasses relieved congestion but were still single carriageway roads. In 1961 work was completed on the very first section of dual carriageway of this bypass programme and it diverted traffic away from the town of Doncaster, hence it was named the Doncaster by-pass. Soon after my dad had taken possession of his flying machine he announced that he was going to "test her out" and the following weekend saw our entire family en route to the Doncaster by-pass. The Zephyr's interior was different to cars of today although quite normal for back then. The gear change was on the steering column and the front seat was the same as the rear being a bench style seat meaning we sat three in the front and three in the back.

Seat belts? Not in 1964, just sit still and don't wriggle was the rule.

It wasn't until December 1965 that a temporary speed limit of 70 mph was introduced on Britain's motorways and trunk roads which was then made permanent 4 months later. Before that time there was no limit, which I am guessing was not such a problem as it would be today as few cars of the day were capable of such great speeds.

We arrived at the southern end of the by-pass with the road stretching out before us like an airport runway. Two lanes going North and two coming South, separated only by a small central grass strip which was devoid of any crash barriers which only began to appear in later years.

Are you ready? And off we go.

The 6 on the car maker's badge of our Zephyr was there to confirm that under the bonnet was an engine with 6 cylinders and not the usual 4 cylinders meaning that our car had more power and could go faster.

We gathered speed with a running commentary from my dad, 50, 60, 70, 75, 80. Then there was a long pause while the rush of wind and the roar of the engine got louder and finally commentary resumed, 98, 99, 100, we all shouted with delight, we were travelling at 100 miles per hour!! Our joy was short lived as suddenly the suspended vinyl interior roof lining of the car began inflating like a balloon and expand down and around our heads. It was quite terrifying but at the same time rather amusing as 11 arms struggled to push the roof lining back into place while our family's 12th arm held on tight to the steering wheel. The reduction in speed and desperately flailing arms had the desired affect as by the time we were below 90 mph the roof lining had receded to its rightful place. On reaching the Northern end of the by-pass we turned around and headed back South but this time maxing out at a mere 95 mph with the roof lining staying in place.

The chances of doing the speed that we attained that day were rare and knowing that 100mph was the trigger point for inflating the roof my dad watched his future speed and didn't give the problem another thought, unless of course when we often brought the incident back to mind.

Following the holiday incident and the damaged wing, the car was booked in to Mr Grattons garage for repair which when complete looked as good as new. I walked from Wallingfield to the garage with my dad to collect the car which was parked on the garage forecourt waiting for us. Mr Gratton arrived and as we admiring his mechanics good work he asked if my dad had experienced any problems with the car? Only at 100 mph when the roof expands was dads reply to which our garage man smiled knowingly, that explains it then, explains what? My dad asked. It explains why we have found broken glass under the carpets and body filler under the paintwork! replied Mr Gratton. But the car is only a few months old! Maybe, said Mr Gratton but it has definitely been in a big accident and then put back together again. "Will the car be ok" asked my dad, looking rather worried? "I don't see why not" said Mr Gratton, just keep it below 100mph he said with another smile.

The Zephyr continued to give our family excellent service for another 5 years before it was traded in for a newer model.

The family Zephyr

My grandparents spent time with us at Wallingfield in the summer months for 2 or 3 weeks at a time. They lived in Somerset and would drive the 230 miles to see us in their beautiful Lanchester car, which my grandma drove with the journey taking them upwards of 10 hours to complete as the entire route was devoid of motorways or by-passes.
today with modern transport and more direct routes the same journey takes just less than 4 hours with a distance of 203 miles
One year they arrived with the car making very strange noises from under the bonnet. The following day the car was taken to Mr Gratton for him to hopefully discover and then repair the problem. After a few hums and arh's the car was taken into his workshop and didn't emerge for almost a week. My dad took matters into his hands and paid a visit to the garage to find out what progress was being made to be told that all was repaired and the car was ready to go.
The car managed about a week before the same problem returned so it was back to the garage for a further diagnosis. This time Mr Gratton announced that the car was beyond economical repair and should be scrapped! But, not to worry as he had just bought

a nice little car that he had planned to place on his sales forecourt and it would be the perfect replacement for my grandma's old pile of junk. And so it was that the poor old Lanchester was exchanged for the "nice little car" that Mr Gratton had quite conveniently just bought. My grandparents left for Somerset a week or so later in their newly acquired Morris 1000 and made the journey safely, and in better time, but without the comfort and majesty that their dear old Lanchester had in bucket loads. The Lanchester that Mr Gratton described as an "old pile of junk" remained at Grattons garage for a few weeks, then one day it was gone. I was about 11 years old at the time and like most boys had already developed a passion for cars. I was as convinced then as I am now that the deal that Mr Gratton did with my grandparent's car was not in their best interest but in his own.

The Lanchester that was my grandparents pride and joy would now be around 70 years old. Some would say that it had long since gone to that great highway in the sky but I have my doubts. Research shows that there are still many Lanchester's in the hands of enthusiasts today and I firmly believe that one of them once belonged to my grandparents.

What do you prefer a Lanchester or a Morris ?

Soon after Grattons garage and the biscuit warehouse were
established another warehouse building sprang up between the
two. The big supermarket chains were growing as they made
acquisitions of smaller regional supermarket companies, but
others either resisted this trend of takeovers or were too small for
the big boys to bother about as the large nationals knew that
sooner or later there marketing model would put these small fries
out of business.

One such business was Dels supermarkets that had a small chain
of shops in the local area and this new warehouse building was
to be their shops supply hub from which they could stock their
shops. All went well for a while, however, by the early seventies
the pinch from the big supermarkets was taking its toll and Dels
warehouse space was downsized by renting off half the
warehouse to Richard McClure for his pallet business, who I
have written at length in "Bricks and Mortar".

By the mid 70's It was all over for Dels and their former
warehouse was shared by Richards timber and pallet company on

one side and The Doncaster Meat Company on the other. This meat company was essentially a wholesale meat supplier employing a number of butchers who worked tirelessly behind closed warehouse doors, cutting and carving at animal carcasses that arrived daily from the abattoir from which they produced desirable joints, cutlets and chops that were then transported away to any shops that chose to buy and then retail the companies produce.

Being naturally inquisitive the village locals often gossiped as to what actually went on at the meat processing warehouse, or some would say that they were just downright nosey! Rumours spread of various goings on but I suspect that the rumours were a creation of their own imagination through frustration of not knowing but it was not long before all was revealed. The warehouse opened its doors as a freezer centre. The meat was cheap and tasty and they had a great range of sausages and burgers too and the aroma that was emitted during their preparation was wonderful, or was it?

Development of the swath of land along Mansfield Road had not been restricted to just biscuits, a garage and a supermarket warehouse. Below the garage E T Sutherlands had established their business on a site twice the size of all the above put together and as I recalled earlier, thanks to the company's arrival Reg Smith had very contented pigs when dining on his daily collection of leftovers.

The smell of food cooking is always a joy and brings with it both expectation and anticipation of what delights are soon to be tasted and we all associate certain smells to different eating times. The smell of roast beef is surely the most reminiscent and memorable of all? Sunday was a boring day in the 60,s. Sunday School, forgotten homework to finish, no television unless Songs of Praise floated your boat, bath night, or worse, hair washing too, they all had to be endured. But, one thing that Sunday was the best for was Sunday Roast Dinner complete with Yorkshire puddings and the deep brown colour of rich gravy made from the juices of the roast beef joint. Just to be clear for those South of Watford gap, or perhaps those reared with a silver spoon "in thee gob", our Sunday roast was eaten at dinner time which was anytime between 12 noon and 1pm. It was worth having Sundays and all the bad things that came with it because for an all too short hour or so we were firstly savouring that unforgettable smell drifting from the kitchen and then stuffing ourselves until we almost popped, wonderful.

Both Sutherlands and Donny meat, as The Doncaster Meat Company was affectionately called locally, were in the food preparation business but they were not preparing food to be eaten at a certain time, their produce was prepared at anytime. The smell of cooking food at the right time is the best, but at 8oclock in the morning or, at some midnight hour when the night shift at Sutherlands fired up the ovens and Donny meats burger and sausage preparation plant was working 24 hours a day, then the smell that drifted over the residential area of Wales Bar when the wind was blowing from the north was not the nicest of smells to fill your nostrils at the start of the day.

I loved Donny meats sausages and burgers and would often pop in and buy some after a Saturday working for Richard McClure. One day while talking with one of Donny meats butchers he asked if I would like to see how these delicious creations were made and he proceeded to lead me to an outside enclosure surrounded by high fencing to the rear of the warehouse. This compound contained 2 large shiny steel vats each of which stood over a lit gas ring of some 3 feet in diameter and gently heating the contents of the vats above which, not having a lid on were giving off a column of rising steam into the darkening evening air, not unlike a witches cauldron cooking up some evil spell. As we stood there the rear door to the warehouse opened and one of his workmates backed out of the door carrying a plastic bread tray full of bones of all shapes and sizes with morsels of blood red meat still attached that the butchers knife had failed to remove when jointing up the animal carcasses.

My guide quickly sprung to his assistance by setting up a step ladder that had been leaning up against the warehouse wall and positioning it by one of the vats. Between them they manhandled the full tray up the steps and slowly tipped its contents into the vat.

"That'll be ready int morning" they both said in unison as my guides mate disappeared back into the warehouse with his empty plastic bread tray.

I have to admit that the smell coming from the bubbling vats was appetising, at least at certain times of the day but I was intrigued as to their use.

My butcher friend explained that every 3 or 4 days the vats were emptied and the "broth" from the meat was removed together with a good percentage of the remaining bones which were then ground to dust and all remixed with the broth to go on to make their prize sausages and burgers !!!

I didn't buy anymore of their prize sausages or burgers and it wasn't that many months later that Donny Meat closed down. The official reason was that the company had gone bust which was perhaps just as well for their sausage and burger eating customers.

***

Pies Hav' Come

Unlike Donny Meat, E T Sutherlands was a slick professional outfit. The company had been established in the 1920's in Sheffield and relocated their factory to Wales Bar in the 1960's. The business had been built on the success of the company founder's wife, Mary Sutherland, who regularly made potted meat using home minced beef mixed with her own secret blend of spices to produce a tasty filling for her husband's sandwiches as he travelled around local shops in his job as a salesman for Lyons Tea. One day Eddie Sutherland shared his sandwiches with a shopkeeper who suggested that the potted meat filling was so good that he was sure he could sell it for Eddie in his shop. The potted meat was a success but eventually Eddie got caught selling the potted beef to his shopkeeper customers and was sacked from his job with Lyons Tea so Eddie decided to go it alone and in 1927 E T Sutherlands was born.

By the time the new factory was established at Wales Bar E T Sutherlands had expanded their product range. The potted meat was still a family favourite and as locals we always knew when a new batch was being made!!

I was not the only one of my siblings that had a job before leaving school. My sister Diane got herself a job during school holidays working on the production line at Sutherland's food factory. It wasn't long before she learnt that workers were allowed to purchase any of the companies produce that for whatever reason was deemed not to the standard that the company wanted. Reg Smith's pigs were already feasting on Sutherlands excess ingredients from the manufacturing process but the produce available to the staff and workers were the finished products that were perhaps under or overcooked, misshapen or badly packaged. We always looked forward to whatever treat my sister might bring home following a day's work and there was one product that was my absolute favourite. Occasionally my sister was put on the production line for Cornish pasties. The method for making the pasties was somewhat back to front in that the pastry of the pastie was baked first and then passed along a production line conveyor where staff would take the baked pasty case and inject it with the meat filling by way of an oversized syringe, then the completed pastie moved on to be packed. A simple and effective way of making pasties which you would imagine to have a very high success rate of perfect production.

The pasties that my sister brought home were delicious and crammed full of meat and were 100% better than the same Sutherland pastie that could readily bought in the local shops, but why?

The workers on the pasty production line knew that, if they held the syringe inside the baked pasty casing for twice the allotted time then naturally twice the amount of filling would flow into the pasty and voila! The pasty would be rejected. Of course, human error was always blamed for the mistake and I have no doubt that mechanisation ultimately solved the problem but thankfully during the time that my sister was employed the plump pasties were never wasted as the same workers that had made the mistake were always more than happy to buy them at half the price with twice the filling!!

The pasty story brings to mind another treat that my sister would bring home from school every Thursday afternoon. The school curriculum of the 60's displayed excessive prejudices towards boys or girls in so much that certain subjects were taboo for one or the other. In sport boys played Rugby, football or cricket while the girls played netball, hockey or rounder's and in the classroom the boys did metalwork and woodwork and for the girls it was domestic science. All these subjects were specific to boy or girl participation and the thought that each might be interested in the others subject was decades away. For me the boys craft subjects were the best and I have made them my life's work but thinking back I would have also liked to learn the art of cooking at an earlier stage rather than the trial and error attempts I had to make after leaving home. In the 60's to even consider a culinary skill as a school boy would brand you a sissy, or worse. The subject title of domestic science suggested that girls were being taught to look after the home while the boys were taught manly craft subjects that would allow them to enter the workplace and bring home the weekly wage for their wife and family. That was the norm in the 60's being a throwback from earlier decades, but thankfully the world was changing yet 50 years later there is many cases of inequality of the sexes in the workplace and beyond to address.

Anyway, back to domestic science. Thursday was the day that my sister was taught domestic science but of course different school years were taught on different days. It was easy to tell which year group's turn it was as the girls would arrive at school with their school bag over their shoulder and a large biscuit tin clutched in their hands and taking every care that the tin was held horizontally to protect the ingredients inside which had been lovingly prepared from the teachers list by mums the previous evening.

Domestic science was always an afternoon lesson if cooking or baking was involved, with the end of the lesson coinciding with the end of the school day when the girls would emerge from the classroom, again clutching the biscuit tin tightly but this time full of sweet smelling butterfly buns, a cake or perhaps a savoury pie.

Butterfly buns, now more commonly called by the American name of cupcakes, look and taste just the same, it's all about marketing !
The girls would stand waiting for the school bus to arrive with their biscuit tin held tightly, looking forward to getting home to show off to a proud mum their culinary skills but, there were always lurking predators intent on 'just a look' at what was in the tin. Suddenly the girls were even more attractive to us boys than was usual as we circled them and muttered all manner of niceties in the hope of just a glimpse inside their biscuit tin. For the girls who succumbed to our advances the possibility that their mum would see anything other than an empty tin suddenly became very real. We knew which girls to target and we all had our fill.
My sisters baking always arrived home in one piece but it didn't last long although we always had to leave one specimen for dad to enjoy when he came home from work.

Warning, the next few paragraphs should not be read by the squeamish amongst you

I do remember a sort of coming together of the sexes in my last 2 years at school however. Dinnington comprehensive school also had a farm which offered a GCE 2 year course in agriculture. As I had a love of all things farming then it was a no brainer that I took the course. While me and one or two others had a genuine interest in the subject, sadly it also attracted the less studious types which had the effect of bringing the whole class down to their level which resulted in only one of the class of 1970 making the grade, who just happened to be a farmer's son.
The farm livestock consisted of some chickens, a pig and its piglets. It was these breeds that brought together both the

agriculture class and the girl's domestic science class. In our first year it was the turn of the chickens to participate when we were taught to ring their necks, pluck, and dress them, before handing them over to the domestic science class to do the roasting. It was total carnage on the farm during the lesson that our chickens met their maker. The term "running around like a headless chicken" springs to mind as I can assure you that once they have been necked, if the chicken is released from your tight grip before its life is totally extinguished then it does indeed run around like a headless chicken.

In British and near continental countries dressed poultry are presented on the sales counter already plucked however in continental Europe the head, neck and feet remain attached while the British way is to detach these extremities. We were taught how to remove these unwanted body parts and then dress the bird ready for the oven which I have never forgotten and the skill has proved to be most useful over the years. The head would come off first with a sharp knife detaching it at the top of the neck and then by cutting the skin from the chest to the point of the now severed head the skin of the neck was pulled back to expose the long neck which, with a twist and a pull was easily removed. Then it was the turn of the legs. The same sharp knife was used to cut through the skin at the knee joint but no deeper than the skin as to do so would also sever the guiders that control the chickens feet and toes and if the guiders were left in the remaining drumstick it then made them impossible to eat. After a swift crack of the knee joint and a pull of the foot then all being well the leg would break free from the drumstick with it the guiders now hanging from the detached leg like pieces of string.

Why have I gone into so much gory detail I hear you ask?

As I mentioned earlier the agriculture class attracted a number of the less studious type and our chicken dressing skills was the catalyst for them to have fun.

Following our macabre lesson of slaughter it was not unknown for some innocent sole in school to open their schoolbag during lessons and find a chickens head staring up at them but our favourite trick was with a chicken's foot. It was scary enough for the girls (and some boys) to be tapped on the shoulder and suddenly, on turning round t be confronted by a chicken's foot yet worse, if the holder of the chickens foot held on to the guiders hanging from the severed end and pulled on them it would make the feet move as though the leg was still alive which resulted in an awful lot of screaming and shouting.

The pig's demise was far less exciting but just as tasty. The porker was also so much more versatile as every part of the animal was edible, nothing was left to waste, except of course the squeal!!

Welcome back

These changes in the landscape during the 1960's were just the start of expansion and development that has continued to the present day, changing every corner of the vistas from Wales Bar to Waleswood with yet more major changes planned for the future but that is for someone else to tell the tale. I will always be grateful for the memories of my time at Wales Bar have given me and of the joy these memories still hold as I mentally recall each one of them. Some of which I have now shared with you and others I dare not! If at some point in the future I might happen to forget the thrills and spills of my youth then I can always flick through these pages or better still to sit quietly in what I hope will be many twilight years still to come and listen to my grandchildren reading these words to me and asking "did you really do all those things granddad?".

***

Wallingfield - Where it began

It's now time to show you around Wallingfield, my family home for 60 years. I want to tell you of its past before my family arrived in the summer of 1954 and the many memorable adventures and experiences I was lucky enough to enjoy while living there. Also of its ongoing history after I had flown the nest to set up our first marital home in nearby Killamarsh and finally, the end of an era as Wallingfield became Wallingfield Court. So sit back, read on and enjoy Wallingfield, my home.

During the latter part of the nineteenth century the vast majority of land in and around Waleswood, Wales Bar, Wales and Kiveton was owned by The Earl and Countess of Yarborough which consisted of tenanted farms and farmland or in the case of Wales, being the oldest of these villages, a settlement of a number of houses and hostelries grouped around the church, all of which were tenanted.

The historic ownership of the area came down the line of the Countess, Marcia Amelia Mary Pelham; The Countess of Yarborough was the eldest daughter of the 12th Baron Conyers and on 5th of August 1886 she married Charles Alfred Worsley Pelham the 4th Earl of Yarborough and in doing so she became the Countess of Yarborough. The grand title that she took on by marriage was only one of the perhaps even grander titles that she held previously as she was already the 13th Baroness Conyers and 7th Baroness Fauconberg and even more, she held the position of the Order of the British Empire or OBE as is it more commonly known. Through her titles she was a British peer and therefore had a seat in the House of Lords. The landed gentry always moved within their own circle of friends and acquaintances and there is little doubt in my mind that that was how she met her husband. The Baroness was from landed gentry in Yorkshire while her future husband hailed from a family of equal standing in the neighbouring county of Lincolnshire, and with them both being of a similar age and background it was probably not just a marriage of love but also a positively planned match by their parents.

Charles Alfred Worsley Pelham the 4th Earl of Yarborough, who's title was Lord Worsley until 1875 when he inherited his title of Earl on the death of his father and then took up his seat in the House of Lords, had a successful career in politics and around the turn of the 19th century was appointed Lieutenant Colonel of the Lincolnshire Imperial Yeomanry which was later called the Lincolnshire Regiment. Then in 1921 he was appointed Lord Lieutenant of Lincolnshire which he remained until his death in 1936.

A quick look down the ancestral line of the Countess reveals some familiar local names, The Duke of Leeds and the Lord Conyers being the names of the former public houses on Church street and in Wales Square. George Osborne. which was the birth name of the Duke of Leeds gives his surname to Osborne house being one of the school houses at nearby Dinnington Comprehensive school. Hatfield, Athorpe and Segrave were the other 3 school houses at Dinnington Comp. also deriving their names from local gentry. The Earls ancestral line turns up just one name of Pelham. Pelham is the name given to a schoolhouse at the Public School of Worksop College.

The Countess in fancy dress attending the Devonshire House Ball, London in 1897.
The Earl is seen here as a caricature drawn in 1896.
Devonshire House was the London residence of the Dukes of Devonshire of Chatsworth House in Derbyshire.

The other principal land owner in Wales Bar and Waleswood and the surrounding farmland at that time was the mining company of Skinner and Holford. My research shows that before the mining of coal became the dominant source of energy and the source of power behind the industrial revolution in Britain the Skinners were a local farming family of some wealth with the Holfords arriving from Lancashire around the time that coal was about to be exploited in the area.

The land on which Wallingfield was soon to be built by the Skinner and Holford Company was purchased from the Yarborough Estate in 1913 and the construction of Wallingfield took place during the First World War years. While young men were fighting and slaughtered in foreign fields England remained visually much the same, unlike 20 years later in the second world war when the fight was brought to English soil from the skies by the German Luftwaffe. Those who were not miners or farmers in the Great War went to the trenches and coal production was increased to help the war effort. Somewhat perversely the increased coal production also increased the mining company's profits which may well have contributed to the costs of building Wallingfield.

The first 40 years of Wallingfields before our arrival in 1954 was particularly eventful what with two world Wars, King Edward VIII's abdication in 1936 and then on the 1ST of January 1947 "Vesting Day" when the newly created National Coal Board took over the mining industry together with all the mining companies' assets which included Wallingfield. The labour government of the immediate post WWII years that had come to power with a mandate of mass nationalisation had a notice posted outside each colliery on Vesting Day which read: - "This colliery is now managed by the National Coal Board on behalf of the people".

Clement Attlee's post war labour government certainly had communist tendencies!

During these first 34 years the house was certainly enjoyed by its owners and the architecture of both the house and gardens mirrored that of a stately home in miniature with much of the facilities of its larger cousin, which I will come back to later. Collieries were taken under temporary government control during the first and second world war years and coal reserves that lay beneath the land that had previously been owned by its land owners was eventually nationalised in 1942 during the Second World War. These coal reserves were placed under the control of the Coal Commission, however the mining industry still remained in private hands. At the time, many coal companies were small of which Skinner and Holford was one.

The Coal Industry Nationalisation Act received its Royal Assent on 12 July 1946 and the NCB was formally constituted on 15 July 1946. On the 1st of January 1947 the National Coal Board not only acquired Wallingfield but also 958 collieries together the property of about 800 private mining companies of which Skinner and Holford was one. Compensation of £164,660,000 was paid to the owners of the collieries and £78,457,000 to former owners of other assets including 55 coke ovens, 85 brickworks and 20 smokeless fuel plants with Skinner and Holfords coke oven works at Waleswood being one of them. The National Coal Board also took over power stations situated at some collieries along with the dedicated railway sidings and networks that brought the coal to the power stations. It also managed an estate of more than 140,000 houses and over 200,000 acres of farmland. At its inception the NCB employed nearly 800,000 workers which was around four percent of Britain's total workforce.

Now that was some company to manage!

***

A Strange Course of Events

Ok, So that is a brief resume of the Wallingfield ownership history in the first half of the 20th century from 1913 to1947 of which I will return later. Little else changed hands in terms of land and property in Wales Bar and Waleswood during this same period with both Skinner and Holford and the Yarborough Estate happily coexisting.

I have read extensively conveyances that I have in my possession that relate to Wallingfield and in such documents it is standard practice to record any land and property transactions linked to the conveyance by way of previous ownership and it is here that I have discovered a rather extraordinary chain of events. The reason for some of the events seem to me to be very clear although some are less so and leave me only with supposition, so please read on and see what you think.

For century's large swathes of land across the length and breadth of Britain was in the hands of nobility or as it was more commonly referred to "the landed gentry" and this was certainly the case in and around Waleswood with the Yarborough estate being the principal landowners.

The industrial revolution started in Britain towards the end of the 1700's and from that time forward it not only provided employment opportunities for an expanding population but it also created wealth and fortunes for those who chose to be captains of industry in those great times.

In Sheffield like many other towns and cities, markets thrived, selling their wares to the expanding industrial workforce. Also there were wholesalers who would sell their wares to the market trader and some of these wholesalers along with other entrepreneurs became very wealthy.

They were the nouveau riche of the 19th and 20th centuries who could even match, in some cases at least, the wealth of the landed gentry who's domain they were infiltrating but the big difference was that these "new kids on the block" were not of noble birth but commoners, grafters, leaders of men.

Herman Jennings is described as a "Gentleman" wherever there is reference to him in the conveyance. He lived at a property called "Newstead" in Dore with his wife Gertrude. Dore was, and still is, an affluent district of Sheffield. The house still stands today, it is a fine substantial stone residence set in large landscaped gardens however the size of the gardens are now much reduced as a number of more modern properties have been built within the grounds, such is the modern way of maximising building land and profiting from what is certainly a prime location to live. It is a residence of which I have no doubt would have employed a sizable team of gardeners and domestic staff in order to run the house and gardens seamlessly and efficiently.

Taking a look at the word Gentleman in order to give me a clue of Herman Jennings standing and character it tells me that such a person of that time might be a man of high social position and wealth, a chivalrous courteous and honourable man, a man of noble birth attached to a royal household, a man of good social position, especially one of wealth and leisure or even a courteous title for a male fellow member of the House of Commons or Lords.

He could perhaps have been any of these but first and foremost he was a Yorkshire man, a man of Sheffield, a market wholesale trader and his vocation in life had made him a very rich man and a very clever businessman, right up to his dying day.

The various descriptions of a gentleman suggest that Herman Jennings would also be totally comfortable in the presence of titled aristocracy such as the Yarboroughs and indeed he may well have moved in the same circles and more likely as not even knew them with perhaps more than by mere acquaintance?

In 1936 Herman Jennings made his will naming his wife Gertrude as an executor and benefactor to his estate along with 2 more executors who were probably family friends. One was a local Fruit merchant by the name of John Thomas Dobson and the other one Walter Edward Moore who was an incorporated Accountant. Both lived close to Herman Jennings, the former in Abbey Lane and the latter on Millhouses Lane, Sheffield. Both their homes also still exist today as fine detached stone houses but of slightly less grandeur than that of Herman Jennings yet they still indicate these two local businessmen were successful in their own right and trusted by Herman Jennings to be able to deal with his affairs in the event of his death.

I have searched long and hard to find how a Sheffield market wholesaler could have attained his wealth and I came across this newspaper cutting :-

263

Egg Trade Possiblities.

Mr. Herman Jennings, managing director of Herman Jennings and Co., Ltd., egg and butter importers of Sheffield (Eng.), is now in Sydney with the object of developing the egg trade with England. In an interview with the "Sydney Morning Herald" Mr. Jennings said that, by exercising proper supervision, Australia could capture the greater part of Britain's trade in egg pulp, which amounts to more than £750,000 a year. Mr. Jennings said he had already purchased eggs for delivery in Melbourne to the value of £100,000. Discussing the methods of packing, he said that all the States should employ uniform packs, preferably those adopted by New South Wales—14 and 16 lb. per long hundred. The quality is highly regarded in England, and the methods of packing are also excellent. Last year one shipment was tainted as a result of being shipped on a vessel which had previously carried oranges, and care should be exercised in this regard. Before Australia could hope to take a large part of Great Britain's egg pulp trade it would be necessary that both quality and method of packing should be made uniform. Mr. Jennings said that a trial shipment of half a ton was distributed by his company, and all users were very satisfied. One large buyer was prepared to cancel his orders for Chinese pulp and use Australian. A late trial shipment was not so good, as some of it was dirty and contained shell and straw. Provided that these faults could be overcome, by insisting that all pulp for export should be packed under Government control, and that standardised containers were adopted, there was no reason why Australian pulp should not displace the Chinese.

The cutting is from the Brisbane Courier of Friday the 1st of July 1932 in which he announces that he has already bought eggs to the value of £100,000 (almost 5 million pounds today) for shipment to England and goes on to say that if the Australians can get their egg packaging sorted out they could "displace" the Chinese from the market.

perhaps this is the type of dealing that Britain thinks they will be able to do "Post Brexit" but the world of trade is now poles apart from that of 1932, it's a shame that the Brexiteers cannot see that

In 1944 Herman Jennings is recorded as purchasing from Sackville Pelham the 5th Earl of Yarborough, (Who succeeded the title on his father's death in 1936) an area of land to the East of Wales Bar and further extensive land, farms and houses to the west around and including Waleswood. Herman Jennings may well have known the 5th Earl and living locally might just have happened to mention to the Earl that he might be interested in buying any of the Yarborough estate that he may wish to dispose of or, perhaps the Yarborough estate was advertised for sale on the 1944 equivalent of Rightmove, who knows? One thing is for sure, as the year progressed and with D Day changing the course of the war, there must have been a mounting feeling within the British population and the world at large that better days were ahead and optimism for a brighter future.

The purchase amounted to an area covering almost 500 acres including 5 farms, a wood and a village containing 5 houses all for the princely sum of £9000. This purchase took place in the war years when nothing was certain but with an estate such as the size of the Earl of Yarboroughs then it is quite reasonable to assume that he had a good land agent to advise him on the estates value and to agree a realistic market value?

Looking back at historical land prices, in 1926 untenanted agricultural land without buildings was valued at £30 per acre and by the time Herman Jennings did the deal with the Yarboroughs it had risen to around £60 per acre. Of course the land involved in this sale was tenanted so would have been worth

less but at a price tag of £18 per acre including 5 farms and a village it was surely bordering on the deal of the century!
 Perhaps, in addition to the recorded documents of the sale there was also an "under the table" cash transaction? But that we shall never know.
One thing for sure is that when Herman Jennings looked into his crystal ball he could see that times were changing and with the war effort concentrating on boosting agriculture and food production, of which he was one of the big players, then land prices would surely rise.

The sale included:-
Pithouses Farm, tenant Mr Brabbs with 127 acres, annual rent of £178,
Waleswood Farm, tenant Mr J Coulson with112 acres, annual rent of £131,
Waleswood Hall Farm, tenant the executors of R. Munro Smith with 169 acres, annual rent of £97
Wraggs Farm, tenant Mr J Pinder with 43 acres, annual rent of £55,
Bedgreave Farm tenant Mr E Mallender with 36 acres, annual rent of £35,
Bungalow and gardens including old cottage buildings at Waleswood, tenant Mr Edward Mallender with 4 acres, annual rent of £21,
House and croft, Waleswood, tenant Mr Ernest Ross extending to 2 acres at an annual rent of £9,
House and croft, Waleswood, tenant Mr A Harding with 4 acres at an annual rent of £14,
 Lime Tree cottage, Waleswood, tenant Mr George Froggatt with 1 acre and rent of £10 per year

Land around Waleswood colliery tip encroachment including 2 cottages rented to Skinner and Holford of around 4 acres at an annual rent of £37.

Now the mathematicians amongst you will see that for the purchase price of £9000 Herman Jennings was to receive £587 annual rental income providing him with a 6.5% return on his investment. History confirms that interest rates from the mid 1930's, through the war years and into the early 1950's were at a constant low of 2% so for anyone with a sizable sum to invest, such that Herman Jennings had, would have been more than happy with the return on investment.

So now the principal owners of the majority of land and property in Wales Bar and Waleswood in 1944 were Skinner and Holford and Mr Herman Jennings.

On December 18th 1945 Herman Jennings agreed in writing to sell his previous year's acquisition to Skinner and Holford and on that same date he received a deposit of £2600 as part of the agreed sale price of £23550.00!!

On the 21st of December 1945 Herman Jennings died!!!

On the 2nd of July 1946 Gertrude Jennings, the benefactor of her husband's will of £55178 (more than £1.7 million today) along with John Thomas Dobson and Walter Edward Moore, co executors of the will, met and agreed to honour the sale that Herman Jennings had set up on his death bed and the sale of the estate that Herman Jennings bought just 18 months earlier for £9000 was completed the following day the 3rd of July 1946 to Skinner and Holford Ltd for £23550.

Just six months later on the 1st of January 1947 the same estate passed to the National Coal Board by compulsory purchase.

Following centuries of land and buildings at Wales Bar and Waleswood being part of the Yarborough estate, suddenly within the space of barely 2 years the land in question passed from Yarborough to Jennings, from Jennings to Skinner and Holford, and from Skinner and Holford to The National Coal Board.

I am confident that Herman Jennings certainly had no plans to die when he did but with death duties running at rates in excess of 60% at the time then my guess is that on the realisation that his days were numbered he quickly set up the deal with Skinner and Holford so that death duties could be reduced or even avoided?

Furthermore at that same time Skinner and Holford knew that their future business was destined to go to the government at the end of the following year and they no doubt already knew that the level of compensation they would receive for their most recent acquisition would be significantly more than they had just paid to Herman Jennings?

I have just one final observation.

The sale to Skinner and Holford was completed on the 3rd of July 1946.

The Coal Industry Nationalisation Act received Royal Assent on 12 July 1946 and the National Coal Board was formally constituted on 15 July 1946 less than 2 weeks after the sale was complete.

Read into that what you will.

RIP Herman Jennings.

Gertrude Jennings lived on for 18 years and ended her days living in Ashfurlong House which was just a stone's throw from the grand stone pile of Newstead. Ashfurlong House was not on the same scale of grandeur but was still fitting for a woman of her status. She died on 26th January 1963 leaving £41248 in her will (around £600,000 today) to three benefactors, her spinster sister, a married woman (perhaps her cleaner?) and to Walter Edward Moore in equal amounts. You will remember that Walter Moore was an accountant and also executor for Herman Jennings estate and he was certainly good with figures as, not withstanding his legacy from Gertrude, when he passed away on 19th May 1976 he left £221,044 in his will (over £1.1 million today)

***

Skinner & Holford Ltd

The limited Company of Skinner and Holford was formed in
1884 bringing together 2 local families of land and colliery
owners. In 1896 records show that the company owned
Waleswood Colliery and employed 552 below ground miners
and 104 surface workers.

By 1933 they were producing 350,000 tons of coal per year used
primarily for household, making gas and providing power in
manufacturing. The coal was being extracted from 3 different
coal seams named Flockton, High Hazels and Parkgate, which
was later replaced by the Thorncliffe seam, and each seam was
accessed from Waleswood Colliery by a workforce that by that
time had expanded to almost 900 underground mineworkers and
200 above ground workers.

Around this time a certain Mr Albert Edward Bramley appears
on the company record sheets and is listed as both an agent and a
manager of Skinner and Holford with his professional skills as a
mining engineer assuring him of his place within the company.
An associated company is also recorded as Waleswood Coking
Company Ltd of which Mr Skinner is Chairman and Mr Bramley
is listed as managing director and general manager living at
Wallingfield, Waleswood.

Mr Samuel Carr Skinner is shown as living at Throapham Manor
Nr Dinnington which certainly suggests that there was money in
coal but looking further back at the Skinner family history my
research has also revealed that they were undoubtedly in the
right place at the right time.

Samuel Carr Skinner was born into a wealthy family of farmers.
His granddad, Samuel Skinner, was born in 1804 in Whitwell,
Derbyshire, and in his adult life lived at Aston, Sheffield,
overlooking the land on which Waleswood Colliery stands. He is

recorded as owning some 527 acres of land in 8 different lots of which there is no doubt that this land was situated in and around Waleswood and Aston, and more specifically where Waleswood colliery was sunk in the 1850's, as I say right place right time ! No record exists as to how Samuel Skinner acquired the farm and land but again I have no doubt that it had been handed down the generations from previous Samuel Skinners. He lived at Aston along with his wife Mary and in 1841 they produced another Samuel Skinner, Samuel Carr Skinners father.

The sinking of the mine At Waleswood in the 1850's was a turn in fortunes to Samuel Skinner as by the 1870's he is described as a Colliery Proprietor & farmer and his wife Edith Skinner (nee Carr) is described as owning 245 acres and an employer of men and boys. Furthermore they had moved from the farm in Aston and were by then living at Throapham Manor some 5 miles away. Throapham Manor was a fine Country House in rural settings and certainly far enough away from the now scared landscape of Waleswood. The Skinners were busy people and enjoying living with and spending their new found wealth but not too busy to produce 3 offspring, the youngest being Samuel Carr Skinner who was born in 1875 at Throapham manor. Records show that in addition to their family of five Samuel and Edith also had seven servants to look after them, the manor, and the extensive grounds in which the manor stood.

By the turn of the century Edith had died and Samuel Skinner lived out his days with his now grown up family around him and a much reduced entourage of just three domestic servants! Samuel Carr Skinner lived his entire life at Throapham Manor along with his wife Florence whom he married in Paris in 1903. Samuel Carr Skinner was born into farming and mining and by the early 1920's his name appeared on the list of directors of

Skinner and Holford which was presumably after his father
Samuel had died.

A view of Throapham Manor

Are you still with me or have you lost the plot with all the
Samuel's? If not then just to clarify, the three proven generations
were Samuel Skinner born 1804, Samuel Skinner born 1841 and
Samuel Carr Skinner born 1875. There were probably Samuel
Skinners in the 1700's but as far as I can ascertain Samuel Carr
Skinner was the last of the line, having no children and finally
popping his clogs on the 24th February 1942 leaving just £16920
in his will (£550,000 today) to his wife Florence which, in the
grand scheme of the Skinner & Holford company was not a
massive amount.
A sale of assets of Samuel Carr Skinner took place soon
afterwards which makes interesting reading.

Samuel Carr Skinner was just 65 when he died which is certainly not seen as old by today's standards but perhaps it was a blessing that he died when he did before witnessing the heartache of the post war labour government taking from him his family dynasty. I have found no record of Samuel's wife Florence following his death. Perhaps, as they were married in Paris she was French as her Christian name certainly suggests? And there being no record of them having children then perhaps France was where she returned to live out her years.

Samuel Carr Skinner visiting Waleswood Colliery in 1937

Following the death of Samuel Carr Skinner Throapham Manor subsequently passed into the hands of the then West Riding County Council and I am unable to say how this came about. From the turn of the 1950s it was used by the Secondary Modern School and later by Dinnington Comp. as much-needed extra teaching space. A total of eleven classrooms were created within the Manor House, one of which I remember being taught in for a music lesson, it was the bay windowed classroom overlooking the gardens seen in the picture of the Manor House.

I remember a beautiful copper beech in the front garden and in the back garden there was an ancient walnut tree from which the nuts made great projectiles to throw at each other.

Along the lane leading to the Manor was a large glasshouse where grapes, peaches and many other exotic plants were grown and tended to by the School caretaker. The school caretaker's house was just along the lane from the glasshouse and I suspect that tending to the contents of the glasshouse was his hobby as I doubt that the school would have paid him for such a duty.

By the end of 1965 Throapham was no longer used for classrooms as new prefabricated wooden Terrapin classrooms had been built on the school site. Hopes were still alive in 1966 that Throapham Manor would survive as discussions took place to buy the Manor. It had served its purpose as classrooms overspill from the nearby school and it was then suggested that it could be used as a Remedial retreat. Unfortunately that never materialised and Throapham Manor was demolished in the late 1970s. It was a very sad end to a magnificent historic building with a glorious past.

To the side of the Manor was a large wood locally known as Skinners Wood and only now do I see the link to the name of the Skinner family!

There was also a small farm attached to Throapham Manor
which became the School farm where me and my classmates
enjoyed our GCE Agriculture education, remember headless
chickens and scary feet earlier?
Our school cross country runs meant pounding the former estate
of Throapham Manor and surrounding lands following in the
footsteps of Samuel Carr Skinner and his father Samuel who had
no doubt trod a similar path in previous years, but far less
arduously!
Cross Country runs and Throapham Manor was not all bad as I
recall, especially when the teacher taking the lesson chose not to
over police the event. Throapham Manor was some distance
behind the school and accessed by a lane that passed by the
school caretaker's house before disappeared into woodland,
passing the glasshouse and then on to the manor which was all
but surrounded by the thick woodland. Our course was to run
along the lane, past the caretaker's house and glasshouse
and on to the manor where we then ran around the rear of the
manor complex, into Skinners wood and what seemed an eternity
later, reappear in front of the manor house, running across the
lawns past the beech tree and back to the wooded lane where we
would then run past the glasshouse once more and reappear into
daylight and into Mr Billingsly's vision by the caretakers house
and then run the entire perimeter of the school playing fields, all
of which was previously Skinner land.
Mr Billingsly was our favourite PE/cross country teacher as he
was lazy, preferring to have a crafty fag from his vantage point at
the back of the school gym where he could not be seen by the
school hierarchy but could see us running across the manor
lawns by the giant Beech tree on our return from Skinner wood.
It was a good distance between these two points and we could
only be seen as a group of runners in the distance but this was

enough for Mr Billingsly to satisfy himself that the required
course and distance had been run.

The rear wall of the glasshouse was built in brick and supported
the large cast iron pipes that provided the heating for the tender
plants. The boiler room for this heating was a brick built lean too
building behind the glasshouse.

As we disappeared from view, running along the lane and into
the woods, for those of us who's turn it was to "take a rest" from
the Throapham circuit, refuge was sought in the glasshouse
boiler room and then as the runners returned across the Manor
lawn and back into the woods we would rejoin them as they past
the glasshouse and back into daylight by the caretakers house to
continue the gruelling run around the sports field. Of course we
would always join the rear runners as those at the front prided
themselves in winning and not cheating, but I very much doubt
that even without the exhaustion of the Throapham leg of the run
in our favour that we could have kept up with the front runners
for long.

 Funnily enough throughout the companies existence there are
generations of Skinners that appear as directors of the company
but no record exists that a Mr Holford was ever involved with
the company but that is not to say they were not active in the
companies increasing prosperity.

In 1796 a gentleman called Joseph Holford was born. Not in
Yorkshire but over the hill in Haughton, Lancashire. In 1841 he
and his wife Betty had a family of 6 children, 3 boys and 3 girls.
James was the eldest boy with Henry 4 years younger and James
was 13 years senior to his youngest brother William Daniel. By
the 1840's the principal employers around Haughton were cotton
mills together with fledgling coal mines and other lines of work
that supported these industries and their workers. Coal miners,
power loom weavers, spinners, twisters and winders are listed as

the Holfords near neighbours together with a Butcher, Saddler, Farmer, Beer Seller, an Engineer and even a Hatter which certainly suggests that there were also neighbours of middle class standing in the area. Joseph Holford was a book keeper, or an accountant as we would describe him today. James Holford was 20 years old and was also described as a book keeper so following on in his father's footsteps, while younger brother Henry at the tender age of 16 was described as an engineer which at such a young age was some achievement! The youngest brother William had still to find his way in life which we shall see shortly. Book keeping was certainly a good profession to follow as by 1860 James Holford had moved over the Pennines to Gods own county of Yorkshire, being described in local records as a Colliery Master and Partner. By 1880 he was listed as the owner of Grange Farm in Aston with 350 acres of land and a colliery proprietor and employer of 380 men and a boy. Whilst his book keeping skills were no longer mentioned it leaves little doubt in my mind that his training in this profession was a major factor in his growing wealth.

Henry Holford was not as adventurous as his older brother and stayed in Lancashire but was still successful in his own right as by 1860 he was an Engineer and employer of 5 men and 4 boys. William, the baby of the family was obviously impressed by big brother James success as by 1880 he too had crossed the Pennines to the land of opportunity and was described as a mining engineer and colliery mine manager which was as likely as not to be Waleswood Colliery.

The company of Skinner and Holford was formed in 1884 to consolidate the activities of 2 local land owners who, by luck or by judgement had already discovered rich seams of coal beneath their lands.

At last the war of the white and red roses was settled and the amalgamation of the Skinner and Holford families in both farming and mining produced black gold with great success and financial gain. The integration of their resources was the obvious way forward but just 2 years earlier James Holford had died at just 60 years of age leaving his baby brother William as the only Holford working for the company. The fortune that James had amassed working alongside Samuel Skinner, his farming neighbour and fellow colliery owner, was left to his widow Emily Holford who was a mere 45 years young. She inherited almost £16,000 from her husband James which today would equate to 1.8 million pounds!

Following her husband's death she most probably kept her interests in the company and perhaps it was the death of James that forced the business relationship of Skinner and Holford to be formalised into the company of Skinner and Holford limited. Emily didn't remarry and moved to Sparken Hill in nearby Worksop to a house called White gates. Sparken Hill was the place to live in Worksop and to this day many think the same. The houses that occupied Sparken Hill were Victorian mansions of great size and splendour and while a few still exist today many have disappeared in favour of progress and smaller more manageable houses, yet still on a grand scale when compared to a standard family home of the 21st century. Emily lived to the ripe old age of 90 and left almost £21,000 in her will (£1.2 million today).

By the turn of the century William Holford was a director of the company along with Samuel Skinner senior but by the time Samuel Carr Skinner was on the board of directors the Holford name had gone in all but in the companies' title. That is not to say that the share holding of Emily Holford still held a big stake in the company and also received rich dividends as her legacy testifies too.

William Holford took a sideways step as Samuel Carr Skinner played an increasingly dominant role within the company and William is later recorded as being the Chairman of Sheffield Iron foundry company William Cook and Co, manufacturers of Steel, iron, horse shoes, iron bars, steel wire rods, channel steel for rubber tyres and wire ropes of every description all with a workforce of almost 1000. All the products that the mining industry used at that time on a daily basis so Skinner and Holford, along with many other local and national mining companies continued to feather the nest of the truly entrepreneurial family of Holfords.

By 1947 and Vesting Day a Major Sir A.N.Braithwaite D.S.O., M.C. was listed as chairman of Skinner &Holford Co Ltd (He was chairman of many companies at that time and was a serving conservative MP which suggests that he was a very useful individual to have on the board of directors) with Mr Albert Edward Bramley as managing director overseeing a workforce now reduced to 473 underground miners and 200 surface workers.

The 1st of January 1947 finally brought to an end almost a century of profitable private mining when a labour government, thinking that they were taking on rich pickings from wealthy land and mine owners, nationalised the industry. Time has proved that nationalised industries do not work as there are always more chiefs than Indians and as a consequence profits disappear. Private enterprise is lean and mean as I have proved by documenting the fortunes of the Skinners, the Holfords, Herman Jennings and all those who choose to serve with them. They are my heroes; long live the mavericks, the entrepreneurs and captains of industry who shape the world we live in.

Wallingfield the Early Years

Wallingfield was built by Skinner and Holford as a grace and favour residence for the colliery manager. This was common practice although I doubt that many such houses were built to the size and standard of Wallingfields as I will describe to you shortly. Perhaps Samuel Skinner thought he might one day live there himself but that we shall never know and its certainly not how things worked out.

The owners of Skinner and Holfords had one objective which was for the company that they had created to keep them in the manner in which they were accustomed. While the Skinners were active members of the company they needed reliable and qualified people around them to manage a workforce of close on a thousand and by providing a residence of the size and grandeur of Wallingfield this assured loyalty from the occupant.

The first manager and later director of the company to occupy Wallingfield was Mr J H Ashton who is recorded as manager of Waleswood colliery in 1896 and went on to be a director of the company in the following 25 years. It is most probable that Wallingfield was designed by Mr Ashton and Samuel Carr's father. What they produced was a house that certainly stood out as a fine residence fit for any well to do family to live in.

When Samuel Carr Skinner came of age and took to the helm, new names began to appear as rising stars within the company and the most prolific of these was Albert Edward Bramley. He had a number of positions attributed to him rising from Manager to Agent then Director to Managing Director.

Albert Bramley became a key player in the company and he needed to live close to the action of Waleswood Colliery and Waleswood Coking Plant as he was now the manager of them both so Wallingfield became his home in the mid 1920,s.

Wallingfield was a lively household with Albert and his wife
Ann enjoying family life with their 4 children, Martha aged 10,
Margaret aged 8, Dorothy aged 6 and William aged 4.
Albert and his family lived at Wallingfield until the nationisation
of the coal industry in 1947 and perhaps for a year or two longer.
The years between the two world wars were halcyon days in the
fortunes of Skinner and Holford together with Albert Bramley
and his family. 1941 brought the unexpected death of Samuel
Carr Skinner which left Albert Bramley in a commanding
position within the company's of both Skinner and Holford and
Waleswood Coking company, the latter of which had been very
much Albert's own project.
I have done extensive research on various ancestry web sites into
official records to chart the families already mentioned and the
original documents I have studied prove their history.
Some of the information relating to the Bramley family has been
sourced from what is generally described as the 1939 Census
which is in fact is not what it seems. The official description of
this survey of the population is the 1939 Register. The
government at that time knew that there would be little chance of
the next official census due in 1941 actually taking place so on
the 29th of September 1939, just 26 days after the Second World
War officially broke out 65,000 census enumerators descended
on every household in England and Wales to count the
population. Rationing had not yet begun and there was a feeling
of both excitement and fear within the British population of what
the war might bring.
This mammoth task of taking stock of the population had long
been planned by the Government who knew that war might come
and they needed to identify the trades and skills that would be
useful to them in the war effort which the previous census of

1931 would not reveal. It also enabled the Government to issue identity cards, ration books and to plan for mass evacuations.

Subsequently the 1931 census was accidentally destroyed by fire unrelated to enemy action during the Second World War and with no 1941 census the 1939 Register is now the only surviving record of the population between 1921 and 1951 when the next official census took place. Fortunately as the 1939 register does not fall under the rules and laws of a census it is now in the public domain whereas government legislation dictates that a proper census cannot be released until 100 years have passed. For the geeks among us we shall have to wait until 1st of January 2022 for the release of the 1921 census which I am sure is already in the process of being digitised in preparation of its release. I cannot wait as it will finally reveal and confirm who was resident at Wallingfield at that time

On the 29th of September 1939 Albert Edward Bramley completed the required paperwork listing the members of his Wallingfield household.
Albert E Bramley born 14th June 1887 status married
Mining Engineer Director & Agent of Colliery & Coking Company.
Ann E Bramley born 1st September 1890 status married
Unpaid Domestic Duties.
Margaret A Brooksbank (Bramley) born 24th January 1917 status single
Unpaid Domestic Duties.
Dorothy A McGhee (Bramley) born 12th November 1919 status single
Secretary to Doctor.
William E Bramley born 3rd March 1921 status single

Apprentice Mining Engineer.

There were also 2 young ladies registered as being in domestic service.

On first reading all seems fine. Their eldest daughter Martha E Bramley had married on the 12th of August just 6 weeks earlier so had moved to her new marital home. However her 2 sisters are recorded as single and living at Wallingfield but with different names and a suggestion that Bramley is their maiden name. This turns out to be quite normal when reading the original documents as many have been amended to show married names. Had these documents been from a census and not a register then these amendments would certainly not have been allowed to happen however it has proved to have been very helpful in finding out the Bramley family history.

Margaret was married to Edward J H Brooksbank in the Spring of 1941 and Dorothy married Richard P J McGhee in the Spring of 1942.

One final twist shows that following Margaret's marriage to Edward Brooksbank he became the manager of Waleswood Colliery and they moved into Waleswood villas, the grace and favour houses owned by Skinner and Holford and reserved for the company's hierarchy. It certainly looks that following the death of Samuel Carr Skinner in 1941 Albert Bramley took a firm hold on both the colliery and the coking business and made sure that control stayed within his family, with his daughter and new son in law not only getting their own house but also his son in law getting a key role within the company, nice move Mr Bramley!

It is probable that immediately following nationalisation in 1947 that the Bramleys and Brooksbank's continued to live at Wales Bar and manage the colliery and coking plant but the writing was on the wall for both operations. The closure of Waleswood

Colliery in 1948 brought to an end Mr Brooksbank's fledgling career as a it's manager and by the early 1950's Wallingfield and the 6 Villas that had been the homes of those associated with Skinner and Holford was to undergo a transformation.

The Waleswood Coking Plant had been established in the 1920's as Albert Bramleys pet project and of course with Skinner and Holfords money. It was rebuilt in 1938 with a state of the art plant installed which was the most up to date of all the coking plants in the area. Unfortunately the new plant proved to be too small to cope with the increasing production required as demands for coke grew. The plant was badly damaged by fire in 1952 and with the closure of Waleswood Colliery four years earlier the coking plants future was in doubt. The plant was repaired following the fire and continued to produce coke but in 1954 the plant went into receivership and by 1956 the plant was closed and so ended the Bramley Families association with Coal and Coke.

Fire raging at the coking plant in 1952

On the plus side and perhaps because of its small size the plant was free from labour troubles. It was also untypical in that it had its own sports facilities and welfare ground situated across from nearby Pigeon Row that I took you around earlier. Albert Bramleys son in law Edward J H Brooksbank was the plant manager post nationisation and together with another nominee from management and two workmen they were trustees of the Sports and Social Club. They even secured grants from the Coal Industry Social Welfare Organisation for repairs to the cricket ground and the pavilion during the 1950s which was a testament to the enthusiasm of Mr Brooksbank. Frequent social events were organised by the plant and held at the Wales Bar Hotel. Waleswood Coking Plant had the best record for sports and social activities of all the coking plants in the area and everyone wanted to be part of the many events that took place.

Waleswood Coking Plant Cricket team in front of the Cricket Pavilion before a Saturday afternoon match

Photos of the Bramley family times at Wallingfield various activities both Waleswood Colliery and the Coking Plant confirm that Albert Edward Bramley and his family enjoyed the good things in life with nice cars, holidays, mixing with the country set and young William Bramleys private education at the public School of Worksop College while his sisters enjoyed a free and easy upbringing.

Bramley Family cars at Wallingfield

Albert Bramleys Rolls Royce is in the background

Albert and Elizabeth relaxing at Worksop College.
A family holiday in Scarborough.
Albert Bramley enjoying a break from a day's shooting.

Albert Edward Bramley with Ann Elizabeth Bramley

Albert Edward Bramley retired to Dore in Sheffield and died on 26th of January 1962 leaving £30418 in his will to his widow (£455,000 at today's value).

No one has a crystal ball or, at least one that works. We plan for the future or sometimes others might plan it for us, but either way it works out or it doesn't to a greater or lesser degree as we meet with and take on all the predicted or unforeseen that invariably comes at us on life's journey.

Albert Edward Bramley worked hard at his life which paid back enormous dividends to him and his family, some of which I have already described and with more to follow. With the arrival of the Bramley family to Wallingfield in the mid 1920's they had their whole life in front of them and for the following 20 some years Wallingfield embraced them. Albert Bramley was a very astute and successful businessman and his hard work meant his close family wanted for nothing and it seems there was nothing that they didn't have, unlike the 1000 or so workforce that he controlled. His employees worked their fingers to the bone just to feed their own family but in doing so would have surely respected their employer's hard work in providing them with a job and a roof above their heads although I also suspect that then, as now there were those who despised their task masters success and accredited it their own input rather than his. As is often said "that's life".

With WWI commonly understood to be the war to end all wars the future was for there for the taking and Albert Bramley certainly did that. The idea that a government would eventually take from him both his, and his families opulent life style was a ridiculous notion but with another World War and government nationalisation some years down the line that is exactly what did to happen. However, when the coal industry was nationalised Albert Edward Bramley was 60 years old and ready to retire, by that time he knew what was coming and had made his preparations as I eluded too earlier, remember the Herman Jennings transaction? Albert Edward Bramley had prepared for his retirement and was ready to walk away a very rich man.

***

A New Era

On the 1st of January 1947 Wallingfield was sold to the newly formed National Coal Board. In the grand scheme of things Wallingfields, along with numerous other houses, farms and none coal industries that happened to belong to the companies that owned the pits were surplus to requirements but everything came as a job lot!

For a short time nothing really changed as the pits still had to be managed. Gradually as new management was brought into the National Coal Board, together with new ideas as to how this giant industry that the government had bought was going to work, slowly but surely changes did happen.

On the 19th of January 1946 a young man of just 22 graduated from Sheffield University as a Bachelor of Engineering, his name was Raymond Hall. He was one of the many fresh faces that just a few short months later in 1947 became a mining engineer with The National Coal Board (NCB) becoming a key player within the newly formed and soon to be restructured industry.

The same year marked another major milestone as on the 6th of September 1947 Raymond Hall married my mum, Nora Evelyn Hall (nee) Knight.

Mum & Dad on their wedding day and later on their honeymoon

Our home was in Mansfield and within easy reach of the offices of No 1 Area East Midlands District of the National Coal Board where dad was based. During the next 7 years the NCB took on its own identity and dad did his bit in this process. At the same time he worked hard to improve his qualifications becoming a Chartered Engineer and was able to boast the title of Raymond Hall B.Eng. C.Eng. Well done dad.

Our Mansfield home, Stourton, High Oakham Hill, Then & Now

In 1949, dad and a small group of mining engineers were sent by the NCB on a fact finding mission to a bomb ravaged Germany as part of the process of rebuilding the mining industry there and also to find how German ideas could be used to improve the British mining industry. Many years later I did ask questions of my father's visit, however it was more out of interest to the damage caused by war than about his visit so those details remain a mystery to me. That same year mum and dad became three with the arrival of my eldest sister Jane followed in 1952 by my second sister Diane.

In November 1953 dad was given the news that, following a recent job application he had been accepted to take up the post of Planning and Mining Engineer in the neighbouring NCB department of South Yorkshire No 1 area the following year. Great news but his new base was to be Todwick Grange, a beautiful country house between Sheffield and Worksop originally built in 1865 for a wealthy land owner and which the NCB had bought in 1947 as a new HQ for the South Yorkshire Area. Following the purchase a large extension was added mainly of glass so that the planners had plenty of natural light in which to draw their plans.

What a magnificent setting in which to work, the gardens surrounding the grange were beautifully kept and the two entrances to Todwick Grange were both guarded by a lodge that stood by the private roads that led to the Grange. The Grange even had its own cricket field and pavilion!

1954 was a new beginning for the growing Hall family, first with a new job and on 2nd March I arrived!! Travelling everyday from Mansfield to work at Todwick Grange was not the traffic thronged journey that it would be today but back then, making the daily return journey in a Ford Popular on winding country roads would have been no less arduous. It was time to think about a home closer to work.

Todwick Grange

Within a few short months of nationalisation Mr & Mrs Bramley had willingly taken the proceeds of compulsory purchase, packed their bags and said goodbye to Wallingfield with a new life of retirement beckoning in Dore, Sheffield. Also their son in law and daughter were destined to leave their Waleswood Villa when the Colliery at Waleswood closed in 1948 along with the rest of the old guard of Skinner and Holford who no longer qualified for their grace and favour home in the villas.

Gradually as the NCB's restructuring of the industry took hold the New Order arrived to the villas, senior management from various newly created departments moved in but this time as rent payers. There was no need for the NCB to concern themselves with the terraces at Waleswood and Wales Bar as the miners who occupied them continued to pay their rents and ply their trade, it was just their employer and landlord which has changed.

But what could the NCB do with a house like Wallingfield? The house and grounds were simply too big to justify renting as one home to senior management so in 1948 a plan was put forward to turn the house into 2 flats, one upstairs and one down. Thankfully the plan didn't massively change the external appearance of Wallingfield and the inside changes too were not as drastic as to change the houses character but nevertheless one house became two. The planned conversion finally took place during 1952 and was ready for 2 new tenant families the following year.

It was the NCB that made the decisions as to who should be offered accommodation as part of their employment package and following dad's arrival at Todwick Grange, Wallingfield was suggested as a new home for the Hall family.

Following the conversion of Wallingfield to flats my parents were given the choice of which of the two they preferred. The division of upstairs and downstairs had been relatively easy to achieve. The inner porch had been rearranged with an extra door that now led to the staircase that in turn had been separated from the ground floor by a new wall and a new rear entrance and external staircase had been installed at the back of Wallingfield and accessed from the rear yard.

As there were already 2 garages the left hand garage was allocated to the first floor flat with the other that adjoined the ground floor allocated to the ground floor flat. For obvious reasons the drive was common ground but in reality other than the coming and going of the first floor tenant's car the drive was a natural extension of the ground floor and from there on the lines were drawn. The first floor flat was given the rear yard and the kitchen garden behind Wallingfield and the ground floor flat got the rest.

The tennis court, greenhouse, summerhouse, orchard, rose garden, the lily pond, the air raid shelter (which was hopefully now redundant), the inner yard, coal house, workshop, washhouse and billiard room all belonged to number 1a Wallingfield.

My parent's choice was easy, we moved in to 1a.

I don't know what mum and dad thought of the idea of moving from their own home in Mansfield to a ground floor rented flat at Wales Bar but the offer was taken up to move home. It was the summer of 1954 when I arrived at Wallingfield along with mum dad and my two sisters and as they say, the rest is history! Some of which I have already shared with you with much more to follow.

Our family car in 1954 was a grey Ford Pop

I shall always remember the story told by my parents of our arrival at Wallingfields on a hot August afternoon. On our journey from Mansfield it seems that I had filled my nappy and the resulting smell got worse and worse towards journeys end, even with the car windows open! An experience I can relate too as it has happened so many times with our own children.

Nappy washed and clean and ready for the washing line

Our upstairs neighbours became good friends and had their first child around the same time that my kid brother Andrew arrived in 1959, suddenly I was a grown up and no longer the baby of the family! Our neighbours moved on shortly afterwards and new ones arrived within days. Mr & Mrs Gray with sons David & Brian stayed for about 7 years before moving to a new bungalow that they had built just 100 yards further up Mansfield Road. In keeping with Wallingfield and the villas, all of which had house names rather than numbers they too gave their new home a name, "Grayways", I ask you, a name that's up there with Dunroamin, Clouds End or Dingley Dell, there's nowt as strange as folk!

The upstairs of Wallingfield stayed empty for a year or two and peace and quiet reigned as, although the house was now 2 flats it had never been meant to be that way and living on the ground floor we could always hear the first floor tenants walking and talking. Thoughts began to surface of the possibility of buying Wallingfield in its entirety but dad was not keen. Then, new tenants arrived and any thoughts of buying Wallingfields faded. We had become used to being on our own with no footsteps or

voices above us but now we were back to square one, we hated
it. In 1970 two very significant events happened.
 Firstly our neighbours moved out and secondly I left school to
start my new job as an apprentice joiner at Sheffield Corporation
Public Works Department (read Bricks & Mortar). I had already
shown my hand at all things practical with the construction of a
tree house a year or two previously and even before I left school
I was doing odd jobs for people, complete with my every
growing set of tools. These two events coupled with the thought
that new neighbours might soon arrive, prompted dad to bow to
pressure from mum and to approach the NCB with a view to
buying Wallingfield. So it came to pass that in 1971 Wallingfield
in its entirety became our family home and with my developing
skills within the building industry I became our resident in house
builder.
We soon expanded our lives into the whole house by reversing
the alterations previously carried out to create the two flats and
returned Wallingfield back to its former glory. Work proceeded
at great pace almost every night after work and weekends too.

* My parents decided not to buy the kitchen garden behind
Wallingfield at that time but it doesn't end there, it has a tale to
tell all of its own but that's for another time*

I can only imagine how much pleasure Wallingfield gave to the
Bramleys during their time there however, I do know that over
the 60 years that Wallingfield was our home it gave us pleasures
in immeasurable amounts and more besides, of that I am sure.
Myself and my 3 siblings have lived with Wallingfield almost
our entire lives and we each hold our own treasured memories of
all that 60 years can bring. Just some I will now recall which I

hope will entertain you. There are so many more but that would take me another 60 years to recall!

Wallingfield stood for the best part of 100 years and is now resigned to the history books. To those who now pass along Mansfield Road they see today's Wales Bar, but not me. Nothing remains of Wallingfield and the rolling landscape of green fields extending to Waleswood and the former colliery when Wallingfield was built almost a century ago and when I arrived in 1954. Now the landscape is alien to those times but in my memory Wallingfield and its thereabouts is still there, as clear now as it was then and for those of you who have forgotten, or perhaps never even knew of this all so typical yet unique south Yorkshire village that shaped my life, I hope that you enjoy my guided tour.

Going, Going, Gone

But wait, let's not finish my story here, what follows is my view of Wallingfields in the Bramley days with later recollections of my own time thrown in for good measure.

Welcome to Wallingfield, come in and I will show you around.

The simplest explanation to the name of Wallingfield is that before Skinner and Holford bought the land on which the house was built it was a field. When the house was complete it stood in an acre of beautifully landscaped gardens surrounded on all four boundaries by 6ft high brick walls topped with ornate terracotta apex coping stones between regular brick pillars that rose above the walls height and crowned by a stone capping sat on a square plinth with four triangular sides coming to a point at the top. A field within a wall or a Wallingfield!

The entrance gate was to one side of the perimeter wall that faced onto Mansfield Road so that the long flowing driveway that swept down to the house didn't dissect the landscaped gardens. The house sat in the rear quarter of the walled acre allowing all the principal windows a view over the lawned gardens with its many features and stunning tennis court.

The walls swept down gracefully to each side of the entrance gate where they met with and blended perfectly into large rectangular stone pillars with carved tops that matched the stone pillar caps that graced the walls. The gate was no less striking, it was a single gate made of oak with integrated vertical iron spindles of various designs that fitted vertically between two horizontal mid rails and the gates principal framework with the top most rail supporting the name Wallingfield, made from individually cast letters. I remember well as a child, standing on the rails of the gate and holding tight while it was swung open to get in or out but, the gate was showing its age by then and the toe of the gate progressively gouged an arc in the tarmac driveway as it dragged along the ground. We still rode the gate but our parents had to push so much harder. In the early 70's as I honed my skills as a carpenter the gate was replaced by a new one of my own making.

The wall was 6 feet tall and in places even more, it seemed taller still when I had scrambled up onto the intermediate pillars with the aid of the trees that grew along the inside of the wall and then looked downwards. It was quite a dare to balance on the sloping stone pillar and take a leap of faith onto the ground below.

The alternative to jumping was to walk along the top of the wall which had its own problems as the apex terracotta copings fell away at a 30 degree angle to each side of the centre ridge meaning that the left and right feet were at an unnatural angle to each other when walking and of course it put considerable strain on the ankle joints. Practice made perfect but only when plimsolls were worn and the wall dry!

The driveway curved gently as it descended to the house. The curve was no more than the width of the drive but with this geometry it meant that it was not possible to see the house from the entrance gate and vice versa. The drive then swept across the front of the house and after circumnavigating an ornate stone Lilly pond around which were planted flowerbeds and a crescent shaped dwarf dry stone wall supporting a bank and manicured privet hedge, the drive then turned left to rejoin the driveway to the entrance gate or, if turning right you could go round and round the drive in circles.

Of course this was the perfect playground for us with our bikes, trolleys and scooters. We would race round and round and up and down the drive for hours and hours having endless fun but, not before school with no brakes and new school shoes!!!

Young William Bramley on his bike with his sister hitching a ride as they appear from the passageway by the two garages leading to the yard by the kitchen door where I had my unfortunate collision with a milk crate after losing control of my bike

Looking towards the house as the drive curves to the left and then to the right past the front of the house and the Lilly pond before returning to merge with the drive and back to the entrance gate.

To the left of the driveway as it descended to the house and garages were wide flower boarders and a series of poplar trees along the inside of the perimeter wall. I have designed a number of large gardens over the years both for clients and for various homes that we have lived in and there is always an eagerness to establish a garden as quickly as possible. This desire may well be achieved in the short term by overplanting or planting fast growers but over time the error of such ways are realised. When saplings become giants and are too close together or too near a wall or a house and as a consequence cause structural damage. Such was the case at Wallingfield as the poplars by the walls eventually grew to enormous heights, disturbing the boundary walls. There was a magnificent plane tree planted as an ornate sapling in the Bramleys time that grew into the most magnificent specimen of a tree but it was barely 6 feet from the house and eventually had to go as the house foundations began to suffer. Of course in the Bramley days the trees grew in young isolated splendour but as the saying goes "Mighty oaks from acorns grow". The poplar trees did provide the Hall children with great fun and entertainment with a Tarzan rope that was fastened high in the poplar tree branches and the tree house I built in another poplar tree by the garage.

The Plane tree that was planted by the house in the early years was an ornate sapling which hardly reached the first floor windows but 40 years later it was a monster reaching over twice the height of the house

The small tree on the skyline above the hedge in the centre of the picture on the left is the same tree 40 years later where I built my tree house

Our Tarzan rope gave us hours of endless fun and what started out as a rope tied to a lower branch of the giant poplar tree close to the entrance gate to Wallingfield became more and more sophisticated and daring. A new rope was given to us by Charlie

Coulson our friendly farmer, it was a thick, strong, traditional rope made from natural fibres and unlike synthetic ropes of today it provided a much better grip for hands and feet as we swung back and forth. Charlie had seen our antics of trying to set up a Tarzan swing as he and his tractor Alice had passed by the lane that ran alongside the entire length of the North wall of Wallingfield as he took the Alice and her dray into the fields beyond to collect the harvest straw. The carefully wound ropes used to secure his load were hung onto the rear framework of the dray and would swing from side to side as the empty trailer rattled along the uneven lane and it was one of these that he gave us when stopping one day to watch our less than successful efforts with the swing.

Eearr, thad be better wi one ur these big uns to swing wi, he said, as he climbed down from Alice and unhooked an enormous coil of rope from the dray. Mine thee thal ave to string it rate up thea in them top branches and then thal get a rate good swing but be sure to tie it good and tight nar, al be watchin the next time a se thee.

Following Charlie's instructions to the letter I climbed high into the poplar branches and secured the rope as high as I dare go. I even cut a large branch off from further down the tree so that the travel of the rope from North to South would extend from 8 o'clock to 4 o'clock. At first, to launch ourselves we would stand on a tree stump by the wall and swing out towards the bordering privet hedge of the drive but it was not long before we were in trouble for trashing the hedge as our feet used the hedge as a brake. We needed to get higher up the rope so that its pendulum motion would leave us free to reach out over the driveway at 4 o'clock and beyond the boundary wall and over the lane at 8 o'clock. Our Tarzan antics became more and more daring and as the knots tied in the rope to ensure a good grip got higher and higher the privet hedge was no longer an obstacle as we flew high above it. The final and most daring improvement was to use the boundary wall as our launch pad and to fix a stout branch of about 2 feet long onto the rope as a seat. The position of this improvised seat was critical, it was in just the right place to be able to clamber onto the wall, balance on the apex copings, lean back with the rope between our legs and tuck the branch neatly under our bum cheeks and then with a push of the feet from the angled wall coping we really did "fly through the air with the greatest of ease, those daring young kids on the flying trapeze". The momentum was amazing, flying high over the driveway and then back over the boundary wall and above the farmer's lane and, with some skilful legwork it was even possible to land back onto the wall before the momentum propelled the Tarzan rope and its passenger once more towards the driveway.

Brother Andrew posing for the camera with an early version of our Tarzan swing

There was one hazard that we had to be mindful of as we swung back and forth on the rope which occurred every spring at nesting time. Birds generally keep themselves to themselves while building their nests, laying eggs or ferrying back and forth with food for their young chicks. We had blackbirds, sparrows, starlings, jenny wrens and song thrushes and even the occasional magpie nesting in the garden and they never bothered us but the mistle thrush was an angry bird. They were very protective of their territory and if one of them had decided to set up home close by our Tarzan swing then we knew about it. They would constantly dive at us and miss by just inches, screeching as they plummeted towards us. Mistle thrushes were a force to be reckoned with.

I described earlier of my many jaunts around the old shunting yard at Waleswood Colliery and the offices and stores area abandoned by the builders of the M1 motorway which was a magnet for exploration. Well, already being into all things practical and constructive (some might say that I was destructive or, was it distracted?) I loved to bring home pieces of plywood that were laying around, either offcuts from larger pieces or larger pieces that had been used as concrete shuttering for the numerous concrete forms that had been cast on the motorway site to make bridges, culverts, manholes and many other civil engineering structures. There were nails too, rusting in boxes and buckets and an abundance of timber in all shapes, lengths and sizes. Looking back I am not sure what came first, to build a tree house or, to collect all the lovely bounty of plywood nails and wood and then think, what can I build with this lot? Either way, gradually the tree house began to take shape, first a platform then some sides and eventually a roof; I even built an extension sometime later that stretched out along the supporting branch as a bedroom. Surely these were the foundations of my future career path!!

The tree house was my long term project in the 1960's and didn't go unnoticed. One summer's day a lady called at Wallingfield and introduced herself as a reporter from the Sheffield Star. She explained that she had watched the tree house project evolve as she passed to and from work on the no.6 bus and would like to take some photos and do an interview with the builder! Wow, fame and at such a tender age! She returned a few days later with a photographer and a number of pictures were taken in various poses and positions of me and my brother Andrew "hanging about" in the tree.

A few notes were made by our roving reporter with an assurance that the write up would be true to my words and would appear in the newspaper in the next few days. Well, for the next few days as soon as I had collected the Stars from Harold Prestige to do my evening paper round I would leave the shop at Wales, run around the corner from Wales Square onto School road and as soon as I was out of sight of the shop whip out a Star and pull the pages apart one by one in the hope that I would be looking out at me. On the 14th of August 1968 I appeared!

"It looks a bit rickety, but the house that John built is as stable as any that Tarzan swung from on his jungle adventures.

Perched high in the treetops in the front garden of his home in Mansfield Road, Wales Bar, 14 year old John Hall shares his adventures with eight year old brother Andrew.

John spent 6 months building a "penthouse" from old boxes in a favourite tree. It has already survived gale force winds.

Andrew has his own den a few branches below.

Said John: "It keeps us out of mischief, and it's a good place to hide!"

One of their favourite TV films is Tarzan.
If they don't like it, the boys just swing back into the tree tops.
The brothers are pictured outside their den."

I cringed when I first read the reporters scoop and 50 years later as I retype her report I am cringing again. For the record I have never watched a Tarzan film in my life and still have no desire to do so and while the report suggests that my "penthouse" survived gale force winds unfortunately the following year it didn't which was probably due as much to the sheer size and weight of the construction as it was to the wind.
The following plans drawn in 1948 show the original layout of Wallingfield before the National Coal Board decided to rearrange the accommodation into one upstairs and one downstairs flat. The plans were found in the loft of the garage at Wallingfield, inside an old leather suitcase and then later stored in an antique oak writing bureau that was passed down from my granddad to my father and arrived at Wallingfield with me and my family in the summer of 1954 where it has been in daily use through the 60 years we and it lived there. The bureau now lives with me and I am its current custodian, it is a cherished family heirloom which continues to be used daily. The thinking, researching, writing, editing and rewriting of this book have all been done while sat at the bureau. Unfortunately the plans have suffered considerable wear and tear over the years and at some point were the object of a colouring in session with wax crayons but I put that down to my siblings as I don't remember doing such an unthinkable mischief! I have also found it necessary to add back some parts of the plan that were missing but rest assured that any touching up is completely accurate.

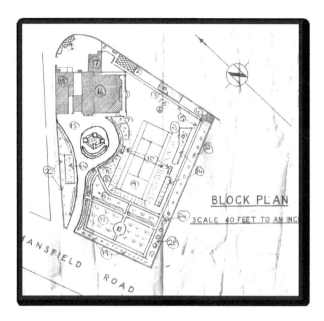

The plan of the garden is numbered for identification

Wallingfield had a total of three greenhouses, two within the grounds and a third that was larger than these two put together which was situated in the kitchen garden that I will come too later. The greenhouse(1) in the rear yard was the smallest of the three but just like the other two it had its own coal fired boiler and cast iron pipework heating system. It faced south and like all three greenhouses leant against a high whitewashed brick wall that provided the support for numerous levels of shelving and the cast iron heating pipes that ran beneath them. An internal pathway of polished terracotta tiles set within ornate concrete kerbstones provided for easy movement from one end to the other while tending to the plants on the shelving or on the full length slatted benching traditional to all greenhouses. Water was cleverly harvested as it rolled down the sloping glass but not into

a suspended gutter as you would expect. As the water fell from
the roof it landed in a perfectly positioned and shaped concrete
gulley cast on the ground and then running along the entire
length of the greenhouse exterior with just enough downward
slope to carry the water to a large concrete sump positioned
within the greenhouse. Consequently the sump water was
available at all times and couldn't have been closer to where it
was needed. I suspect that this greenhouse served as a halfway
house to the much larger kitchen garden greenhouse which was
some distance from Wallingfield and where the resident gardener
"George" would leave produce ready to be selected by the
domestic staff to prepare and feed the Bramley family.

*George was the Bramleys resident gardener for many years and
when we arrived in 1954 he was still there. For a year or two
following our arrival George remained a fixture of Wallingfield
as did the Wallingfield cat with the amusing name of "Tiddles",
neither of which were paid as staff by mum and dad I hasten to
add.*

 Wallingfield and its gardens belonged to George and George
belonged to the gardens, he had always been there and wanted it
to continue that way and my parents were to indulge him.
The second greenhouse(2) was used specifically to rear the
numerous bedding plants that adorned the flower beds around the
garden and no doubt also to rear the abundance of roses that
formed the rose garden and trelliswork on which the climbing
roses flourished. (12). This greenhouse was in two sections with
a partition door midway along the internal terracotta path. The
first half of the greenhouse was the plant preparation section and
where numerous terracotta plant pots were stored along with the
tools of George's trade. An enormous grape vine in the second

half of the greenhouse intertwined along the underside of the glass roof supported by sturdy wires strapped to the roofs structure. Looking back I now realise that this vine was at least 30 years old when we first arrived and had developed a generous root table as by the 1980's when the greenhouse had long since succumbed to the ravages of decay and gales the grapevine continued to flourish on the tall whitewashed wall that was the only survivor of this magnificent greenhouse and surely every horticulturists dream. The grapes were small, red and full of pips!!

From left to right, the 1930's greenhouse in its prime.
1954 my sisters relaxing in the garden
circa 1965 when the greenhouse had seen better days.

The Bramleys were very keen aviculturists as their aviary (3) contained many non native birds. The aviary was a good size and had an open framework clad in chicken wire so that at a distance the birds within looked to be free but sadly they were not. It is only now when studying the information of Wallingfields past that I realise the large concrete base and ornate upright bird table on which we would stand to pull the conkers from the overhanging chestnut tree was the site of the aviary. I distinctly remember that the conkers from this tree were not the best, the outer casing was smooth and the conkers inside were full of water but the white spring blossom that this tree produced was spectacular.

I am perhaps being too kind to the Bramleys by suggesting their interest was in living birds as, whilst they were keen breeders of birds they were also just as enthusiastic in their slaughter. Albert Bramley was a keen member of the hunting fraternity and in a large compound to the rear of Wallingfield were many sheds and rearing pens where pheasants and partridges were given a short but wonderful life, they fed themselves at will from the grain that was thrown into their pens on a regular basis in preparation of their controlled release as live targets For Albert Bramley and his cohorts to slaughter at a weekend shoot.

There were chicken coops too, providing eggs and of course roast chicken which was always available for the Bramley dining table.

The breeding pens and chicken coops on a snow covered winters day with Waleswood Colliery tip in the background and the aviary and bird table which we later stood on to reach the conkers on the chestnut tree

What an indulgence the summer house was (4) although I question its orientation as it faced almost directly north and only in the height of summer was it possible to catch the setting sun as it disappeared over the roof tops of Wallingfield. Still, it would have been a peaceful place to sit to while away a sunny summer afternoon as the more energetic of the Bramley family played a game or two of tennis.

Who's for tennis? The summerhouse in the background in all its splendour circa 1935.
By the time I had turned the tennis court into a race track circa 1955 the summerhouse had already lost its roof and was gradually returning to nature.

The paths and walkways around the garden were plentiful and well thought out as is the way with any successful garden design. The whole plot that Wallingfield stood on sloped gently downwards from Mansfield Road and the need for the tennis court to stand on level ground meant that gradually increasing slops along the sides and to the top of the tennis court area made for extremely interesting landscaping opportunities which had been seized upon with impressive results.

Come on, let me take you for a garden stroll on a typical warm summers evening in the 1930's and then take a look inside the house. At the same time I'll take you forward to my time at Wallingfield and the memories the following tour bring to mind. We start at the front door of Wallingfield, by the oval window and the plane tree (7) and pass along the side of the house with the red brick dwarf walls on the right and the Hydrangeas that adorn the flower beds beyond showing their snowball shaped coloured heads above the wall, some are even resting gently on the wide coping stones that cap the wall. They are in full bloom and moving gently in the breeze. Passing by the reading room window the semi circular herringbone pattern brick steps lead down to the lawn between the central opening in the dwarf wall. The brick pillars to each side of the opening match exactly the pillars that mark the start and finish of the wall from the front and back of the house.

A favourite game of ours was to run along the wall and leap the gap above the steps by launching ourselves skyward from one pillar and hopefully landing on the other. It was quite a dare and seemed like we were attempting the world long jump record when the penalty for failure would have meant blood and broken bones. I don't recall any mishaps and as we got older the gap seemed to get narrower!

The dwarf wall where we practiced our long jump

Now we are by steps that take us onto the path by the greenhouse, let's go inside and see what George has been busy with today. The coal store by the greenhouse door is empty but in a few weeks time George will have filled it again ready to generate the winter heat required to nurture the tender plants that he will be growing in the colder months. The entrance door and middle door are open and all the roof windows too, allowing the warm summer heat to escape. Even though all the bedding plants are long gone and now at their best in the garden the grape vine and other more exotic plants which George grows specifically to brighten the many rooms inside the house still need fresh air, or they will wilt under the heat from the glass as the thermometer is showing almost 90 degrees Fahrenheit.

The well stocked greenhouse, through the glass you can the summerhouse in the distance.

It's too hot in here, let's walk to the shade of the chestnut tree (6) and throw some seed in to the aviary (3) for the birds. As we leave the greenhouse I unhook the watering can from the tool rack and plunge it into the water sump by the door so that I can fill the bird bath in the aviary. The birds seem happy but surely dream of freedom.

We make our way to the corner of the garden and the summerhouse (4) where a table and chairs on the veranda welcome us.

Where the side and rear perimeter walls meet they make two readymade walls of the summerhouse and the twisted, bark covered, stout tree branches that the summer house is made from provide a truly rustic feel to the building. The floor is made of boarding laid over a concrete base which gives the whole place a warm feeling and the sun that has shone on the brick walls from behind throughout the day has now warmed them with the heat now radiating into the summerhouse. Perhaps it was the right place to build it after all?

From the summerhouse the long straight path (5) takes us all the way to the top corner of the garden which is out of sight at our current vantage point as laurel bushes and privet hedges have been strategically placed to break the sightline. Let's not rush as there are lots of things to see along the way. Next to the wall to the left of us are a line mulberry trees (21) that do enough to take out the starkness of the brick wall although the wall in itself is a work of art with its terracotta apex copings that step up at each brick buttress to ensure that the wall maintains its height as the ground level rises. Providing an added screen is a continuous trellis that sits above the wall, discreetly supported on timber posts. During the height of the day the sun's rays make patterns through the multiple diamond shaped holes in the framework as they play on the flower borders. To our right is a copper beech tree (23) standing alone and dominating the flower border that surrounds it. George has excelled himself again this year with bedding plants of all colours adorning the borders and as usual, there is not a weed in sight.

George is a permanent fixture in the garden and although he is paid for his labours he does the work of three men and should be paid accordingly.

The tennis court is looking at its best with the striped lines of grass where George has cut the grass earlier running in perfect alignment with the whitewashed lines of the court. Also, look at the high netting around the court that stops any wayward balls straying onto the flower beds, George would not be pleased and nor would Mr and Mrs Bramley if their showpiece garden was disturbed.

As we draw parallel to the centre line of the court where the net is strung tightly between its two supporting posts there is a gap in the flower border. Let's sit for a while on one of the matching benches (10) which are precisely positioned at each side of the court so that spectators can watch the players and also double up as court umpires. Looking across the court and to the top of the lawned bank two more decorative planted flower and shrub borders mirror the ones at each side of us.

Mrs Bramley enjoying the flower borders as she makes her way past the willow tree (8) and towards the umpires bench (10)

Towards the back of flower borders opposite us, where they meet with the privet hedge that hides the driveway beyond, there are shrubs of medium height which have the desired effect of creating an upward flowing line of summer colours from the marigolds, asters and lupines, to the cornflowers, moon penny daisies and finally the beautiful peony bushes with rose like dense red blooms that contrast perfectly with the variegated green and yellow leaves of the immaculately manicured privet hedge that they stand against..
You have to agree that George is a master of his trade.
Diagonally opposite the beech tree (23) is a weeping willow (8) which in turn dominates the border in which it stands. In later years the willow tree grew thick and solid and its weeping

branches that touched the floor created the perfect den for us to hide. We called it the London tree but I don't remember why. We get up from our umpires seat and walk on, past the second flower border where we have a choice of route, either straight on or, to the right where the path trials along the top of the lawn, banking down on the right to the tennis court with a rockery bank on the left retaining the orchard above, then on past the willow tree to a wooden paling gate that gives access to the drive. We walk straight on as our garden stroll will bring us onto the other path later. As we get closer to the still obscured top most garden (12) the sweet smell of roses becomes more and more intense as the warm south westerly evening breeze carries the rose scents in the warm air. To our right is an orchard (11) where the grass grows longer. It's not a big orchard; in fact it's more for show as the kitchen garden that we will visit later is where the serious fruit trees grow. There are two pear trees and four desert apple trees, the kind of fruit that you can pick and eat at will but they are not quite ready so let's move on. On our left the end of the row of mulberry trees and the start of a row of Laurel bushes (20) are marked by one large horse chestnut tree (24) that dominates the tee junction of the pathways.

Unlike the chestnut tree by the aviary this tree produced deep pink spring blossom in equal abundance which signified the start of what we always hoped would be a good crop of conkers. The conker yield from this tree in terms of quantity was always a disappointment but this was easily made up for with the fruits quality. This tree produced conkers that could stand any amount of playground competition in a game of conkers.

As we pass the privet hedge that breaks the sightline between the orchard and the topmost garden the true splendour of the rose garden whose scent has been teasing our nostrils is revealed. Look, how can you fail to be impressed with such a magnificent display of roses?

The perimeter paths of the rose garden are surfaced with red shale and a border of concrete kerbs like all the other garden paths but the path that divides the rose garden in the centre is different. We walk along the top most paths that run parallel with the brick boundary wall that I described earlier. There is a dry stone wall retaining raised ground between the path and the wall which contains a row of soldier like, tall, thin, Lombardy poplar trees (19) and at this point the central paths surface is revealed.

The rose garden, in the background the boundary wall with the Lombardy poplar trees in front standing to attention like soldiers in a row

On each side and high over the top of this area is a trellis of cut branches that have been skilfully fashioned into an ornate passageway. Look how the climbing roses have filled the trellis. We walk beneath the roof of roses where it's cool and shaded. The pathway opens out in the centre of the rose garden into a large circular area that is crowned in the middle by an ornate birdbath and the entire pathways surface is paved in natural stone. What a finale to our stroll I here you say, I agree but let's walk a little further. The natural stone pathway continues back towards the orchard and where we pass through the opening in the privet hedge and into the orchard the path turns to the left and the right where the red shale surface returns. Turning left takes us on a journey back towards the laurel bushes, the chestnut tree and the long line of mulberry trees and to the right takes us to another wooden paling gate that gives access between the privet hedge and onto the driveway beyond.

A section of Trelliswork in the garden waiting for the summer months when the climbing roses almost totally cover them

Just a few more strides and we are standing at my most favourite place of the entire garden.

The natural stone path ends where it meets with the path that links the chestnut tree (24) with the willow tree (8) and at this point three wide stone steps descend to the path below.

No, don't take the steps, stop and look around. In front of us the expanse of the tennis court with the flower borders to the sides and the lawn and garden buildings beyond seem to go on forever. A glance to the left and we can see the first floor windows and the slate roof of Wallingfield with its many chimneys reaching skyward above Georges perfectly manicured privet hedge, further left is the willow tree and the orchard separated by the sunken path that leads to the wooden paling gate and the drive and finally, by turning our backs to the tennis court there is the rose garden with the bird table framed between two ends of the privet hedge and the roof of roses that flows all the way to the towering Lombardy poplars swaying gently in the warm evening breeze. The secret of a successful garden is to create different areas that provide an element of surprise around every corner and our walk around this garden has done just that. I ask you, where else in the world would you rather be? Wallingfield will do for me.

*The rose garden was the subject of a thorny altercation between me and my dad that lasted for two years or thereabouts. Mum became ill in the late 1970's and despite her valiant fight for life she lost her battle with cancer and passed away in 1983 at the age of just 57. When someone close to you becomes ill you sometimes fear the worst but don't necessarily share your fears. We all believed that the worst would not happen as first one year and then another year past and mum was still with us, putting on a brave smile and always thinking of our welfare and not her own. Our mum was selfless to the end. I hold a letter that she wrote in 1980, at a time when she knew the worst and we were hoping for the best. I have read this letter many times and each time it brings tears to my eyes. It sums up completely her love and thought for others above anything else. As she became weaker and took to her bed I visited daily to spend a few precious minutes just talking about the events of my day and I will always remember her words on one of those days when she said "you should not waste time with your daily visits as you must have better things to do and furthermore when I die don't take time off for my funeral as you will have more important things to do" which surely speaks volumes of her humble selflessness. While writing these few words in tribute to our dearly loved mother I have read her letter once more and although it is very private I feel now, all these years later that it should be shared to show you what a wonderful mum and human being she was. In her words she asked that we look after our father who had cared for her so well. Dad had taken retirement when mum became ill and he transformed himself overnight from dedication of his work to giving himself totally to the welfare of our mum, taking the place that our mum had filled throughout our family life and their life together.

As time passed we all adjusted to life without our mum and thoughts began to surface in my mind that Wallingfield was simply too big for just one person to live and I floated the idea of building a bungalow in what had been the rose garden, for dad to live in and to sell the big house. His reaction was less than positive but I put this down to nostalgia getting the better of common sense.

The planning laws in England allow for anyone to make a planning application even if they do not own the land on which the application is made so with this in mind together with my firm belief that my idea was in dad's best interest I went ahead with the application without his knowledge. My thinking was that if my application was successful then more time would have past to soften his current thinking and by then he would warm to the idea. Wrong. Approval was granted for a bungalow in the garden at Wallingfield and subsequently I revealed my plans and the reaction I received was less than favourable. I can't repeat what was said as the full text has long since been erased from my memory as a bad dream, least to say the bungalow idea never happened, nor did any further meaningful conversation between us for the next two years or so!

Thankfully interaction with Pamela and our children Sarah, Becky and Tom didn't falter and life continued normally and by the time baby Luke arrived normal service had resumed.

Never underestimate the strength of someone else's resolve no matter how much you feel that you are doing right by them!*

12.11.80.

I hope the university can find me of some use & help to others.

If ~~so~~, my wish is that there is no service or mourning.

If not, my wish is that there is the least possible fuss — no letters, no flowers, no mourning & no funeral tea! Just a contribution to cancer research if anyone wants.

Hymn :- Through the night of doubt & sorrow.

Thank-you all for the pleasures & help I have had.

Enjoy life whilst you can, & help one another. Look after Dadan who has cared for me so well.

My love to you all, Nora, Mum, Grandma.

**Dear old dad sat in the garden of his beloved Wallingfield.
He survived our mum by 33 years.**

Looking from the rose garden and the bird table along the trellis tunnel covered in climbing roses that lead to the steps where the expanse of the tennis court and all the glory of Wallingfields gardens are revealed.

From the foot of the steps we turn left and walk along the sunken path with the orchard to the left and willow tree to the right and arrive at the gateway with the driveway beyond. In front of us is another of George's design masterpieces in the form of a planting bed (14) with a difference. Here the area is always damp and in shade for most of the day due to the large poplar trees (22) that surround it and the heavy clay soil beneath for some reason holds the water particularly well. The hydrangeas love it here where they benefit from the sodden ground and partial shade, as do the hosta's that provide the ground cover. The fox gloves and cornflowers with their purple and blue flowers match perfectly with the blue, violet and pink blooms of the hydrangeas, all thanks to George's green fingers. Walking on towards the garages (13) and house (16) the privet hedge on our right gives way to the centre piece that is the lily pond (15) and all that surrounds it. This area offers itself to the house alone as it is only by standing at the front door of Wallingfield or peering from the front elevation windows of the dining room, Bedroom or landing that this pleasure on the eye is experienced.

Mrs Bramley tending to the many flowers around the lily pond to her left where the lilies are in full flower (right) and the front door to Wallingfield, ajar and beckoning us to explore the house.

So now we are back to where we started by the front door, the oval window and the plane tree, having taken an hour or more on our evening stroll around the garden which I am sure you will agree was a walk well worth taking.

Wallingfield was certainly a design of its time. As I mentioned earlier it was built in the First World War years and very much in the Edwardian style and although Edward VII's reign was relatively short (1901-1910), the style of housing being built still continued to bear the hallmarks of the period which was generally seen as a progression of the Victorian era. The Victorian era had seen mass production of so many materials which is reflected by the sheer volume of building stock that still survives today however the Edwardian period also saw a return of styles influenced by the Arts and Crafts Movement of the late Victorian period with a return to the use of well-made handcrafted goods. The use of ornate windows and doors were a particular example of this influence and there was much of this in the character of Wallingfield.

Edwardian building standards were a great improvement on those of previous generations and the quality of materials that were used have rarely been surpassed.

The bricks were dense and durable, the timber of high quality and windows and doors, although far from being draught proof by today's standards, certainly stood the test of time. Sash windows often had the upper section divided with glazing bars or, as was the case at Wallingfield handcrafted leaded lights, while the lower part was left plain. This gave the facade an appropriate rustic appearance while the clear pane below allowed an unobstructed view for residents. Their appearance is timeless as even today the styles are replicated, albeit using much more modern materials and construction methods. The architect responsible for Wallingfields design used mock Tudor timber panelling on the gable walls of both the garages and the billiard room which again was inspired by the Arts, Crafts and Neo-Georgian style of properties. There are so many characteristics of the Edwardian period built in to Wallingfield which are undoubtedly a credit to a building of its time. Such features as chimneys sited halfway down the slope of the roof so they stood directly above the fireplace. Roofs with a steep pitch and gable end. Roof slates with terracotta ridge tiles and ornate ridge end finials comparable to earlier Victorian types.

Victorians walls were of solid construction but the Edwardian period saw the introduction of cavity walls particularly for the more bespoke higher end houses of which Wallingfield most certainly qualified. This new method of construction proved to provide much better protection against penetrating dampness and also an improvement in thermal insulation. Builders used various methods to tie the two leaves of masonry together, but by far the most common was the iron tie. Unfortunately while the iron ties were a great idea, over time these ties corroded and left the inner and outer brickwork skins unattached and with widespread use of "black "mortar, which had a corrosive effect on the iron ties, many houses suffered structural failure but thankfully Wallingfield was not one of them.

The following plans of the front and side elevation of Wallingfield reveal just how many chimneys there were. The house didn't have central heating which was in common with most houses of that era (it could be argued that the Wallingfield greenhouses had better heating systems!) but as it was in the ownership of a colliery company there was an unlimited supply of coal which was certainly needed as Wallingfield had fourteen open fires in and around the various rooms with a further 3 greenhouse heating systems each with its own cast iron coal fired boiler.

The chimneys at Wallingfield were obviously necessary and were very much celebrated in their design and appearance with feature brickwork and tall handcrafted terracotta chimney pots. Rising damp was a major problem in houses of Victorian construction and by the time Wallingfield was becoming a reality so were damp proof courses and this was incorporated into its construction together with timber floors to aid ventilation. Quarry tile floors were commonplace in many houses both inside and outside, together with high quality terracotta tiles and Wallingfield was no exception to this trend which I will show you as we take our tour around Wallingfield.

Ceilings of this period tended to be very high with the height of the walls broken with a picture rail or other feature allowing the area between this rail and the ceiling to be filled with a decorative frieze. Ornate covings and decorative ceiling roses also complimented this style of decor.

Wallingfield Front Elevation

Wallingfield Side Elevation

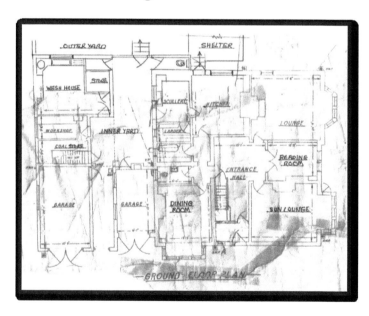

Wallingfield Ground Floor Plan

Inside Wallingfield.

Wallingfield has many architectural characteristics of its time but it also has so much more.
The enormous solid front door is much wider and taller than a normal door with panels formed in the door with raised mouldings to give an appearance of added depth and the semi circular leaded window above and the stone surround that encompasses both the door and window makes for the perfect entrance. Even though the entrance on such a grand scale it is perfectly in proportion with the house facade of red brick which is complemented around the windows with stone sills, mullions and heads. Plinth bricks around the lower lines of the house further enhance the architecture and although the oval window to the sun lounge may be at odds to the general theme of the design its position and style really is a master stroke from the architect's pen.

*In advance of the purchase of Wallingfield in 1971 and my improving skills in joinery I could not wait to get started on home improvements. I had by now established a workshop in what had originally been the billiard room, My workshop was complete with circular saw, mortising machine, workbench, vice and numerous hand tools and accessories found in all good workshops which I had bought from a retiring builder from Norton, Sheffield. I had seen an advert in the Sheffield Star that the seller had placed and my mum had clinched the deal following a phone call to the advertiser, bought unseen! The builder was certainly surprised that his equipment was going to such a young entrepreneur but was happy that the deal was done however he warned that a lorry would be required to move my purchases. That problem was quickly resolved with a further phone call, this time to our old friend Mr Norman Horsley! The following evening Mr Horsley arrived in his green Commer lorry which was so much bigger than I had realised as I climbed up into the cab beside him. I remember the journey well to Norton, full of excitement and anticipation as to see what I had bought for £20 and thrilled too with the commanding view and feeling of importance sat high above the road and bouncing along in the cab of the lorry. It was a journey just as memorable as all those years earlier when Mr Horsley had driven us to the Royal Infirmary but this journey was much more exciting. We arrived to find the retiring builder waiting for us outside his workshop and he invited in. What an Aladdin's cave! By this time I had already experienced the contents of a good workshop with the one at my place of work and also at Shirecliffe College where my employers had sent me for technical training and what lay before me was a match for both. Mr Horsley was as keen as me was to look around, not only to see what my £20 had bought but also to see the rest of the equipment that was still for sale. I followed Mr Horsley and the vendor around the workshop as they chatted to each other and could not help thinking what it would be like to own so much useful equipment. Following our tour Mr Horsley turned to me and with a wink of his eye said that I should consider buying one or two more useful items that were on offer "but" he stopped me right there and said "leave it to me", "but" I said, I only have £20, "leave it to me" he repeated, so I did. We loaded up the lorry with so much equipment that I could not believe my eyes, but how can I pay for it all? I said.

Give me your £20 and I'll cover the rest, you can pay me back later "but", its fine he said, you now have a great start for your workshop and that's what matters.

Just like Mr Horsley's lorry

We drove back to Wallingfield with our load where Mr Horsley, me, mum and dad unloaded the newly acquired purchases onto the drive. My mum and dad were impressed with just how much I had bought for my £20 and before I had chance to open my mouth Mr Horsley stepped in to explain all. Mr Horsley's judgement was given the full respect that it deserved from my parents and the following weekend I made the journey to Wales and the top of Church Street to Mr Horsley's to settle my debt to him of £20. You have a good deal there he said, make it work for you, and I did. I repaid my parents at £5 per month and without doubt it was the best £40 I have ever spent in my life, I was on my way.

The first item I made in my workshop was a new front door for Wallingfield so that as soon as my parents had completed the business of changing from tenants to owners of Wallingfield I could give the house a new identity with a brand new front door. The new front door was ready in advance of the purchase completion and on Christmas Day 1971 I started to fit the new door. Christmas's back then were boring after the turkey had been devoured so what better to do on Christmas day afternoon than a bit of joinery?*

The new front door and a new entrance gate soon followed

Beyond the outer entrance door is an inner porch with a half glazed partition of hammered glass that obscures the sight of what lies beyond but allows the light to flood the inner hall from the semi circular leaded glass above the entrance door and the window to the side.

The porch floor has a large recessed mat well where a thick brown coir entrance mat fits and the red terracotta tiles of the inner porch floor are highly polished. We open the inner porch door to reveal an enormous entrance hall.

The floor is of wood with a long narrow carpet running parallel to the stairs where it meets a larger rectangular carpet of matching design where the hall opens out to reveal doors to various rooms. Where the wooden floor is not covered by the carpets it has been painted black giving the affect of focusing the eye to the patterned carpets. The inner area of the entrance hall has ample natural light which floods through the double glass doors of the reading room which we shall visit shortly.

The walls of the hallway are stunning. A picture rail runs around the entire perimeter of the hall with a beautifully detailed moulded cornice at the junction of the wall and ceiling that is complimented with two matching ceiling roses where the chandeliers hang, one in the centre of the inner hall and the other in perfect alignment closer to the inner porch door.

The skirting boards, doors, door surrounds, picture rails and all other timber mouldings throughout the house are the same. They are made of pitch pine but have the look of oak which has been achieved by a form of decoration popular of the time when money was saved by using a cheaper timber. The technique is called graining, where a tradesman applies imitation grain patterns over a darker previously dried base coat that gives the impression of a more exotic timber. This technique is used throughout Wallingfields to produce what looked like oak, and to great effect. The crowning glory of the wall and ceiling design is the real oak panelling, a theme that extends throughout the ground floor rooms habited by the Bramleys, two lounges, the dining room and the reading room. Between the 15 inch high skirting board and the door height picture rail are vertical oak strips of oak some 4 inches in width that dovetail neatly into a similar sized piece of oak running horizontally directly above and below the skirting and picture rails which together create individual plasterwork panels of 6 feet high and 3 feet wide. Each of these panels are decorated in the oak graining style to produce the look of continuous oak panelling which it has been done to great effect.

This is not a photo of Wallingfield but is an excellent example of the interior decor I have described.

*The hall was a great place to play when the weather was not favourable for outside activities although ball games were frowned upon indoors. "Use a soft ball and throw it gently" was the constant instruction from our parents but while the cats away the mice will play or something like that! One afternoon with our parents out my brother and me started up a game of football in the hall. The oak panelling made for perfect goal posts with the picture rail as a crossbar. I was in goal while Andrew lined up the ball from the penalty spot down by the porch door. All went well for a while until the ball came hurtling towards me at some speed and as I reached with my left hand to tip it over the crossbar the ball trapped my arm between it and the wall. I felt a sharp pain but unlike the pansy footballers of today, I played on. With the game over we moved on to other entertainment but all the time I felt my arm aching. Eventually I had to come clean as to how I had sustained such an injury but my parents still found it hard to believe how playing catch with a soft tennis ball could result in such pain and suffering!

I soldiered on for a few days but by the following Friday and a visit to the doctors I found myself sat in the hospital x-ray department waiting room. X-rays revealed no breaks and a stiff bandage was applied with the instruction to rest it and come back if the pain continued. Well, the pain did continue and a second set of x-rays revealed a broken wrist! My left forearm and wrist spent the next three weeks in a plaster cast which turned out to be quite a crowd puller. I was 13 and in my second year at Dinnington Comprehensive and by the end of the first week of wearing my solid white cast it was covered in the names of everyone in my class and a few more besides. The pain eventually subsided and four weeks of a bandaged and plaster cast arm came to an end, as did the best four weeks of my school life, why? I here you ask, well that's easy to answer, I am one of the estimated 10% of the population that are left handed and trying to write with a plaster cast around your hand is impossible! *

Leading directly off the entrance hall is the lounge, reading room and sun lounge of which I am sure you get the flavour of from my description and photo above. In all 3 rooms the fireplace and surround are integrated into the theme of the oak panelling and are the room's focal point. Of the three rooms the sun lounge is my favourite.

Without doubt the sunrise and sunset has dictated the orientation of the house. The east facing window in the lounge catches the early sun's rays as it rises above the fields that obscure Wales and Kiveton beyond, while the expansive bay window that faces south captures most of the morning and afternoon sun thanks to the thoughtfully splayed sides of the window that take full advantage of the suns arc as it travels from East to West. The reading room windows also face south but thanks to the canopy roof that sits over the bay windows of both lounges and spans the two above the reading room window, this canopy provides a welcome shade to the room in the summer months where quite time is enjoyed in the indulgence of a good book. Only in the winter when the sun skims low above the horizon does it cast its weak rays into the reading room.

*In our early years at Wallingfield the former reading room was mine and my brother's bedroom and then later an office. It was also the scene of an incident I recalled earlier when I had the misfortune of trapping my fingers in a sliding sash window one Saturday afternoon while at home. It was very painful and all the more so as I was unable to free my fingers on my own. It took more than 15 minutes to attract my parent's attention of my predicament. There was no thought of the possibility of further injury to my fingers when my father finally arrived as, grasping the sliding sash window he thrust it upwards to release my trapped digits. The sight of my released hand suggested that my tears were real and to this day my left hand index finger has never fully recovered.

We slept in bunk beds, me on the bottom bunk and my brother on the top bunk. My brother is 5 years younger than me so perhaps that was the thinking behind our bed allocation or, perhaps because his bedtime was earlier than mine it was thought that I would not disturb him when slipping into the lower bunk? What I do know is that my bed gave me one big advantage. If my brother was snoring or just maybe annoying me by his mere existence, as younger brothers do, then I would pull my knees up to my chest, place the soles of my feet underneath the mattress directly above me and then push the mattress, and my brother, as hard as I could. He would soon stop snoring after a kick or two but sometimes the sheer joy of my actions continued to a point when snoring gave way to tears and then it was trouble for me. Why can't younger siblings just take their punishment without whining?*

The sun lounge is also the garden room as the bay window incorporates a door leading out to the shaded canopy in front of the reading room which is the perfect sheltered place to sit to enjoy the sun and also to wander into the garden via the semi circular herringbone pattern brick steps or to set off on the garden walk that we went on earlier.
 When the afternoon sun has past the bay window its evening rays shine on the front of the house and thanks to the thought in design the suns evening rays pass through the oval window and cast light onto the fireplace and surround on the opposite wall. To take full advantage of this the inset panels within the oak surround of the fireplace opening are of bright stainless steel, the sides of which are concave in shape and deflect the sun's rays in all directions creating shimmering lights across the room onto the floor, walls and ceiling making the room live up to its name until the sun finally set over the hills towards Sheffield.

in our time this was our favourite room too but the position of the oval window and the advent of television proved to be incompatible due to the badly positioned TV ariel socket by the fire surround that dictated the position of the television. The sun shining on the TV meant that the curtains to the oval window were permanently closed when watching Chris & Val on Blue Peter and other children's hour TV following a day's school and before the arduous task of homework.

The dining room is the perfect size for formal family dining and entertainment with the large dining table providing amble space for 12 or more diners and the fixed window seat that runs around all three sides of the bay window extending a welcome to after diner relaxation and the view to the lily pond just a few feet away.

During our early years at Wallingfield this room served as a bedroom for my 2 older sisters so was a no go area for me and my brother!

Looking at the plans you will see that Wallingfield boasted a bathroom and toilet on both floors but only the two toilets and the upstairs bathroom were intended for the Bramleys use. The downstairs bathroom and outside toilet in the inner yard by the scullery were for servant or domestic help use..
For diners caught short and for general convenience (excuse the pun!) the family toilet by the dining room is well placed. Like the rooms we have visited so far there is great attention to detail in this room too. The theme is pink. From floor to ceiling the walls are clad in coloured vitreous glass tiles in the art nouveau style and the toilet and washbasin are pink too, square, bold and chunky with chrome taps and towel rails to the washbasin supported on a solid, square pedestal continuing the chunky theme. Above the washbasin is an over mirror in a chrome frame with 2 glass shelves supported on chrome brackets that seem to float on the mirrors glass surface. The toilet too follows the same solid lines and unlike the toilets of a few years earlier the pink cistern sits neatly behind the toilet base with a convenient chrome handle for flushing rather than a chain hanging from an overhead box which, while performing the same function would

not look right in this setting. The pink of the glass wall tiles is barely distinguishable from the pink sanitary ware and makes the room look more spacious as a result. At about 4 feet high there is a border of pure black vitreous glass tiles some 6 inches wide and a further border 4 feet higher still, a subtle statement and so art nouveau. For the smallest room in the house it certainly has the biggest ego.

*A strange feature of the art nouveau cloakroom and toilet was the window. Well, not the window as such as you would naturally expect a window in this room but the strange thing was that this window didn't look to the outside but into the garage that was immediately beyond it. I am only now able to continue with this little story, safe in the knowledge that if some less than honest person were to read it that nothing would be gained by thinking they could follow my lead and enter Wallingfield without permission!!
The window was a sash style window like all the others at Wallingfield which were not the most draught proof or burglar proof of windows but as long as the window catch was fastened then it did offer some level of security, but this window never was. On the rare occasion that we might return home to an empty and locked house when the last person to leave had forgotten to leave the back door key in the tobacco tin, in the unlocked cupboard, inside the unlocked workshop, but instead had put it their pocket, then the toilet window was our point of entry. Although there were many tools to choose from in the workshop a garden spade was the best choice. The sharp edge belonging to the business end of the spade easily slide into the gap where the bottom rail of the sash window rested on the window sill and with a bit of leverage the window would slide

upwards and an extra push would open the window wide enough to climb in.
We would then balance one foot on the outside drain that doubled up as a step while the other foot swung through the window and over the toilet cistern rather like mounting a horse, but without the danger of one foot disappearing into the toilet if the seat was not down. It is not strictly true to say that this toilet window was never fastened securely as I distinctly recall the last words spoken before leaving home on our holidays, "has someone locked the toilet window?"*

Before we look around the engine room of the house where the domestic staff attend to the Bramleys every need let's have a look upstairs. Walking back through the arched passageway that links the dining room and the entrance hall we turn right and meet with the staircase climbing to the first floor. The bottom bull nosed step and the robust turned oak newel post carries the matching balustrade up the open side of the stairs and on reaching the first floor landing continues around the open stairwell in the same style. The first floor hall and landing is expansive to say the least with plenty of room for the two easy chairs that are by the open fire beyond is the landing window providing a view to the lily pond and beyond. The interior design has changed. There are still picture rails, cornices, centre ceiling roses, skirting's, with doors and their surrounds that continue the theme of the ground floor to all rooms but the decor to the walls between the skirting and picture rail has changed. The walls are covered in patterned wallpaper typical of the period and the wooden floors are painted black in the area not covered by the loose carpets.

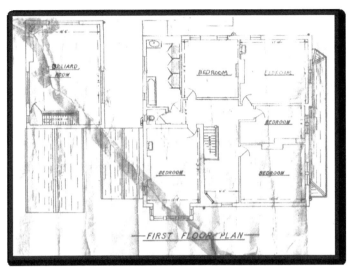

Wallingfield First Floor Plan

There are five bedrooms, four of which are big enough to have at least two double beds, two wardrobes, two dressing tables, easy chairs and a settee with ample room to spare but they have just one bedroom furniture set in each so are extremely spacious. The fifth bedroom is of a more modest size but still big enough for a double bedroom furniture set. Each bedroom has its own fireplace for winter comfort.

The toilet and bathroom are a rare luxury and nonexistent in the lesser houses of Wales Bar where the sanitary facilities consist of a tin bath hung by the back door for a once a week bath in front of the blazing living room fire and outside toilet at the bottom of the yard with a "guzunder" under the bed for the overnight call of nature.

guzunder is a Yorkshire term for what non Yorkshire folk would refer to as a chamber pot, kept under the bed and used to avoid a long and perilous middle of the night trek from the bedroom, down the stairs and to the outside toilet at the bottom of the back yard. Still confused? Guz (goes) under, goes under the bed, got it?

Back on the ground floor we enter the kitchen via the door that is perfectly placed to ferry back and forth all the food and drink that is consumed by the Bramleys in their spacious dining room just a few feet away. As I referred to earlier we are now entering the engine rooms of Wallingfield.

The Bramleys enjoyed a good life which was only possible because of the services of their two servants (domestic help) and of course George the gardener who, if truth were known was the key figure in keeping Wallingfield running seamlessly. George was given due credit for his efforts in the gardens because everyone could see the results of his hard work but there were so many unseen chores that he carried out without complaint. Never mind how much coal and attention was needed to keep 3 greenhouse heating systems working through the winter months, there was also 14 house fires, or 15 if we include the fire beneath the wash house boiler, each of which required a constant supply of coal. Cars too were always clean polished and gleaming and unlike cars today the mechanics needed weekly checks to ensure all was as it should be. Repairs and maintenance around the house was another string to Georges bow. The workshop by the inner yard was George's domain, not a place where he could hide for a quick smoke and forty winks, he had no time for the latter but always had a woodbine hanging from the side of his mouth or nipped between two yellow nicotine stained fingers as he went about his busy day.

Now that we are in the kitchen area the emphasis is on practical things. Gone are the timber floors and decorative wall finishes, we are now standing on red and black quarry tiles laid diagonally across the kitchen, scullery and larder with the tiled surface shining from its daily mopping and scrubbing. The walls are plastered and painted with a high gloss cream finish so that they are easily wiped clean. Dominant in the room is the Yorkshire Range and unlike a similar black coloured range in the wash house across the inner yard this range has a light fawn enamel finish and chrome handles with all the bells and whistles of the latest design, although it must be said that this Yorkshire range's days are numbered according to George who tells us that the Bramleys are in the process of bringing gas into the house, which puts a smile on his face in the hope that his coal chores will be reduced. Large built in cupboards stretching from floor to ceiling fill the recesses to each side of the chimney breast where the Yorkshire range stands and a huge pine preparation table occupies the middle of the room.

*The Waleswood Coke Company manufactured gas as a by product of the coke making process and with the gasometer tower just along Mansfield Road by the Mission Hall it made perfect sense to bring this much cleaner and more efficient fuel into Wallingfield *

In our time at Wallingfield this kitchen was our living room and then later the dining room. As our living room it was the hub of family life. The dining table was multipurpose, I cannot begin to think how many times our mum would call out "come on, get your things put away, I need to set the table". My homework had to be done sat at the table although I seem to recall my sisters were allowed to do theirs at a desk in the bedroom, obviously I had to be watched!

The Scullery next door has a white porcelain sink of huge proportions and sits directly under the scullery window that looks out to the inner yard. The window looks abnormally large for the size of the room but it does make the chore of washing pots and pans more bearable in the natural light it casts over the room. In the corner of the room beneath a large metal canopy there are 2 appliances which really are state of the art. The Bramleys have installed a water heater and an oven to make things easier for their domestic staff and both run on electric! This means that in the summer they can still have constant hot water without the need for coal fires and to cook without the need of the Yorkshire Range but George still has to keep the range fire burning throughout the year as it heats the water for the bathrooms, George smiles and tells us that the old ways are still the best!

State of the art equipment, you get the idea!

***

Understanding the Generation Gap

*The scullery was our kitchen and it brings to mind an incident
when I was caught red handed so to speak, bear with me here.
Firstly you must understand that in 1973, for my parents there
was still a pretty clearly defined line between being single and
married and at what age this line could be crossed or perhaps
become slightly blurred. This line was about to be tested by
yours truly! It was the spring of 1973; I was 19 and Pamela 18.
We had met the previous summer and were "going steady". We
started to think about summer holidays and together with another
couple we agreed to rent a static caravan in the Dorset resort of
Weymouth. We remained vague with our parents as to exactly
the accommodation we had arranged and all was going well until
our friends pulled out of the planned holiday. By this time the
holiday was paid for so we decided to go it alone but didn't
disclose the fact, who was to know anyway?
We set off on a sunny Saturday for our week in Weymouth.
Weymouth was a resort I had visited many times on day trips as
a child with my grandma so was very familiar to me and was
probably the reason for choosing to holiday there. Our
grandparents lived in Somerset and much of our summer
holidays as children were spent in the beautiful village of Queen
Camel where my grandparents owned a shop, or to give its
correct title a Supply stores. Supermarkets or chains of shops
were around in the larger towns and cities but not on the scale we
see today. The rural backwaters were not yet their domain as
people didn't have the same luxury of car ownership that applies
today and were therefore far more reliant on local shops and
doorstep deliveries. E H Knight Supply Stores provided the
service that Queen Camel, together with the numerous villages
and isolated settlements within the area required. The shop had

customers from the minute it opened until closing time. Customers from further afield would telephone in their requirements or for those without a phone my aunt and uncle, who also worked in the shop, would tour the area each week to call on customers to collect their order. It was a slick operation and with 2 grocery delivery vans it was a very successful business. My granddad was a master grocer having served his apprenticeship in London with Fortnum and Mason. London was also where he had met my grandma who at the time was training as a book keeper. Their qualifications created a dream team in love, marriage and business and of course in creating our dear mum.

We arrived in Weymouth and eventually found our caravan site and home for the week (no satnav to guide us back then) which was just one of many static caravans on a windy hillside a mile or so outside Weymouth. Our first holiday together was off to a great start.

The following day we explored the area and later in the afternoon returned to our caravan where we ate a feast of fresh local strawberries and Devon clotted cream purchased earlier at a stall by the harbour. We have always put the blame on what happened next to my overindulgence of strawberries and cream that afternoon but perhaps it was simply convenient to do so? That evening and throughout the night I developed really bad stomach pains to such a degree that the following morning we decided that a visit to the local doctors would perhaps be the most sensible thing to do. Following a consultation at the surgery we were sent to Weymouth and district hospital where I had a further examination. Suppositories were dispensed together with a brief explanation of how to administer them which was surely prompted by the vacant expression on my face as I stared quizzically at the mini torpedo's in my hand!

We sat in the hospital waiting room and waited, and then waited some more, but the torpedo's hadn't hit their target. By this time I was starting to feel more comfortable and was convinced that very soon I would be given the all clear and our holiday could continue.

The nurse who had advised how to fire the torpedo's then approached us pushing a wheelchair and asked me to climb aboard, what was going on? She explained that I had a suspected appendicitis and I was to be admitted for further tests. "But I feel much better now" was my response but it fell on deaf ears as she wheeled me away into the warren of hospital corridors with Pamela following on looking as bemused and bewildered as I felt.

That day we decided to wait until we knew exactly what was to happen next. Poor Pamela, left on her own and in a strange place. Our car was of no help neither as Pamela could not drive so the car remained in the hospital car park (back then hospital parking was free, imagine a similar scenario today with the current costs for hospital parking!).

Pamela spent that night alone in our caravan having made it back there by public transport. She told me it was horrible. The following morning we were both full of hope and anticipation that our individual nightmares would be over and normal service would be resumed as soon as possible, but that was not to be.

Mr Hall, We shall be removing your appendix in the morning! The game was up and phone calls home revealed all.

I went under the knife the following day. My everlasting memory was the journey to the operating theatre, still laid on my bed that had suddenly developed wheels, then counting to maybe 3 or 4 out of a possible 10 before I was out of it. I remember waking up some time later back on the ward and thinking, is all this a dream? I gingerly passed my hand across my stomach which revealed a large bandage and the confirmation that it wasn't a dream!

Today hospitalisation following an appendectomy is 2 to 3 days but remember, we are talking 1973 here and my stay in Weymouth and district hospital lasted 2 weeks but it didn't end there. As the end of my 2 week stay approached I was told that my next move would be to a convalescing hospital on the Isle of Portland, "an island but! " Don't worry I was told, we call it an island but there's a road connecting it to the mainland via a strip of land called Chesil Beach and you're going there, tomorrow! On the morning of my transfer I felt ill, I mean really ill, but that didn't deter the hospital from carrying out my transfer, perhaps they thought I simply didn't want to go and was feigning pain and yes, they were half right, I didn't want to go but I can assure you the pain was real. With the move complete I found myself in a room with a view in one of the wings of the old Portland military hospital. My room had a view looking out over Portland harbour however I didn't find that out until later as the rest of my day was spent horizontal in bed with awful pains in my abdomen.

That evening I made the effort to ring Pamela and tell her of my new billet. The only public phone in the entire hospital was miles from my room at the end of a rabbit warren of long winding corridors. I felt so ill but just had to make the call. I spoke with Pamela and could not withhold the feeling of agony that was plaguing me, I feel like I'm dying, I said, over and over which was not the best way to reassure her of my welfare, but I really did think I was.

I managed the long trek back to my room and thankfully survived the night but felt the same the following morning. There was a shift change later that morning and our new minder was a rather old, plump, and gruff nursing sister who stood for no nonsense. She immediately set about getting me out of bed to start my convalescing but I really couldn't. I explained my pain and I was grateful that for the first time in 3 days that someone was actually listening to me. She pulled the curtain around my bed and started her examination; "I think I see your problem" she said "don't go anywhere, I'll be back shortly", I didn't and she was! Now, this might be uncomfortable as I am going to take a stitch out and you might feel something warm on your skin but I can assure you that it's for the best. I was a little concerned to say the least but anything to relieve the pain was fine by me. There we are, you should feel much better now, and I did, almost immediately, as the feeling of warmth spread over my stomach then so did the pain ebb away. Sister cleaned me up and asked if I would like to see what she had in her surgical bowl, one look was enough. The Beatles wrote a line in the lyrics to I am a Walrus which reads "Yellow matter custard "and sister's bowl was brimming. The removal of the abbess was such a relief and it was all thanks to the worldly wise Sister. Within an hour I was enjoying my room with a view and all that was going on out at sea and across the harbour. Within 2 hours I was walking in the hospital grounds and feeling brand new.

What started out as a week's holiday in Weymouth turned out to be 2 weeks at Weymouth and District Hospital and another week convalescing on the Island of Portland, and I lived to tell the tale, but there's more.

3 weeks earlier my car had been left in Weymouth Hospital car park and thankfully, as I was a member of the AA they had arranged for its safe keeping. Not in a compound somewhere though as these were the days when you could put a face to a name, years before such organisations adopted central control rooms and a corporate image making it impossible to break through to a real person. The local AA representative kept my

car safe and sound on their own driveway until I was able to drive it back home.

The phone call home to explain our predicament mobilised my mum immediately to come to Weymouth, not for my sake I hasten to add but to comfort Pamela who was now alone and in need of company and some TLC.

It was the school holidays so my brother came along too and as we still had the caravan for the week that was the obvious place to stay. Now 13 year old brothers are a pain at the best of times and his question to Pamela on arrival at the caravan was typical of a younger brother determined to stir up trouble, "so where did John sleep and which bed did you sleep in?" he asked, which was met with a deaf ear from my mother. Our mum was brought up with old fashioned values which to her credit she always practiced but underneath those values was also an understanding of change and of the generation that her children now lived. Her reaction to my brother's devilment was typical of her understanding.

Pamela stayed until the weekend and then travelled home by train together with my brother while mum stayed on in Weymouth in a B&B which was arranged once again by our local AA representative! When I was finally allowed home my mum and me picked up my car and made our way back home to Wallingfield.

So, why does the scullery bring this little adventure to mind I hear you ask? Bear with me we are nearly there!

Now I was officially "on the sick", meaning I was not yet fit to return to work and certainly didn't feel like it either. As time passed I felt better and with still lots of projects on the go around Wallingfield, as the resident builder these jobs proved to be ideal for my rehabilitation. Now we all know that working in the building industry is a strenuous occupation and no doctor would

consider "signing off" a patient who might risk a setback in recovery by returning to work too soon and my doctor was acutely aware of this. I was in my 12th week of "sickness" and well into improvements in the kitchen (former scullery). One morning while stood on the kitchen sink and reaching up to complete a pipe boxing above the window there was a knock at the door. Mum answered it to Woman who introduced herself as the employment health visitor here to check on the progress of John Hall, is that your son? Is he at home? I climbed down from the sink draining board and made myself known. The lady was extremely pleasant and made notes while we talked.
The following Monday I returned to work!!*

*I must recall here another shining example of my mum's tolerance and understanding of a younger generation. Thwarted by our Weymouth Holiday we decided to try again but this time on our own.
In 1974 we booked a bed and breakfast in Great Yarmouth and even bought a band of gold from Woolworths to convince both the B&B owners and our fellow guests that we were the real deal. We had a great time, the sun shone and at the end of the week we packed our suitcases and headed home. The following Wednesday evening following tea, I was washed and changed and announced my departure to see Pamela for the evening. "Oh, just a minute" mum said, "can you give this to Pamela please?" and she handed me a folded brown paper bag. I walked out of the house and as I was driving to see Pamela curiosity got the better of me. I opened the bag and inside was a pair of Pamela's knickers, washed, ironed, and neatly folded!! *

The larder off the scullery is really cool. Every wall of the room is shelved within a foot of the ceiling and a wooden step ladder is leaning behind the open door in order to reach the less frequently used articles that are stored on the upper shelves. A tall narrow window provides the light. There is a stone shelf some 2 feet wide running the length of the room along one side and returning under the window, all of which is supported on brick pillars. A food safe sits on the stone shelf below the window and its fine mesh covering is the only protection between summer flies and the food contained inside. Fortunately George's 1 acre kitchen garden provides most of the household's fresh daily requirements so fresh food storage is kept to a minimum during the summer months.

***

Take Cover!
Air raid shelters, a short history lesson

*In September 1935, the British prime minister Stanley Baldwin, published a circular entitled Air Raid Precautions, inviting local authorities to make plans to protect their people in event of a war. Some towns responded by arranging the building of public air raid shelters. These shelters were built of brick with roofs of reinforced concrete. However, some local authorities ignored the circular and in April 1937 the government decided to create an Air Raid Wardens' (ARP) Service.

In November 1938, Chamberlain placed Sir John Anderson in charge of the ARP. He immediately commissioned the engineer, William Patterson, to design a small and cheap shelter that could be erected in people's gardens. Within a few months nearly one and a half million of these Anderson Shelters were distributed to people living in areas expected to be bombed by the Luftwaffe. They were made from six curved sheets bolted together at the top, with steel plates at either end. They measured 6ft 6in by 4ft 6in (1.95m by 1.35m) and the shelter could accommodate six people. These shelters were half buried in the ground with earth heaped on top. The entrance was protected by a steel shield and an earth blast wall.

Anderson shelters were given free to poor people. Men who earned more than £5 a week could buy one for £7. Soon after the outbreak of the Second World War in September 1939, over 2 million families had shelters in their garden. By the time of the Blitz this had risen to two and a quarter million. Amusingly, the government of the day passed legislation that attempted to control people's behaviour in air raid shelters. If someone was found to "wilfully disturb other persons in the proper use of an air raid shelter" he could be sent to prison. In

December 1941, fifty-three-year-old George Hall (no relation!) was sent to prison under this legislation. In fact, he was guilty of snoring in a shelter. He had been warned by the shelter marshal but continued to snore and was eventually arrested by the police for the offence. When the judge sentenced him to 14 days in prison he replied "I can't help what I do when I'm asleep".*

In the event of another war and with the advancement of air warfare Albert Bramley knew that Waleswood Colliery and the coal industry at large would be a target for the German Luftwaffe to wreak havoc with their bombs so, taking heed of Stanley Baldwin's 1935 circular he took immediate action to protect both his family and senior workforce. As war drew closer perhaps he also considered some form of protection for his workforce but Sir John Anderson put paid to that with the creation of the "Anderson Shelter" and better still, as The Waleswood miner's weekly wage was barely £4 (on a good week) it meant that they all qualified for a free shelter.

*Ironically in the early 1930's these same miners wages had been more than double but following an agreement that Germany could restart selling their coal to France and the Benelux countries
(Be-Belgium ne-Nederland's/Holland lux- Luxembourg) resulted in British coal being too expensive for these countries to buy and British coal prices slumped, along with the miners wages. Well done Adolf.*

Skinner and Holford set too and constructed an air raid shelter in the field behind the company's six villas to be shared by the families of the company's senior management but the Bramleys had their own and before we venture outside let me take you back into the kitchen and show you around Mr Bramleys latest project.

In the corner of the kitchen by the large window a new door has been fitted and the view from the kitchen window that had previously looked out to the greenhouse and the fields beyond is now partially obscured by a supersized slab of concrete. We open the door and are standing at the top of a flight of concrete stairs that descend into darkness. Turning a light switch the steps are revealed.

All the walls are exposed lime washed brickwork in an attempt to brighten the area but with just a single light bulb and no windows it doesn't help much.

Taking the stairs we descend to a wooden floor which extends throughout the shelter complex. I use the word complex because as you can see the facilities here are like a hotel room but without windows! Before we take the door into the living area take a look at the cupboard in front of you. This is where all the food and provisions will be quickly transferred to from the larder by the scullery.

Through the door to the right takes us into the living area and although very stark with the lime washed walls and concrete ceiling, look, there is a dining table and chairs and built in cupboards to each side of another doorway on the far wall. This doorway leads us into one last room, a bedroom!

In front of us are 2 bunk beds with matching bunk beds to the left and right making 6 in all.

Not the height of comfort but better to be down here in the air raid shelter than up above, if Hitler decides to rain down his bombs on us.

The air raid shelter was a dark dank place in our time at Wallingfield and the wooden floors and fitments were well on the way to total decay due to the lack of ventilation. It was beyond use for its original purpose with Hitler long gone and the cold war with Russia gradually thawing. It seemed a wasted space and with my building equipment rapidly increasing in quantity I needed somewhere for dry storage. The air raid shelter offered a solution but it had no doors or at least not to gain entry from the outside. I spent a whole winter punching an external doorway through the shelter wall with just a lump hammer and cold chisel. The walls were 18 inches thick of solid brickwork which had served well in keeping Hitler and the Bramleys apart.

Leaving the scullery via the door sees us stood in the inner yard, looking from left to right there are 8 doors. From the left the first 2 doors provide rear entry to each garage, we will come back to door 3 shortly.

Door 4 takes us to Georges inner sanctum, the workshop and coal store. His workshop is full of every tool required to keep Wallingfield at its best. George's tatty chair, with an old overcoat thrown over for comfort that once belonged to Mr Bramley is beneath the window that overlooks the farmer's lane. We can see in the far distance the tall chimneys and rooftops of Waleswood Colliery with the pit head winding gear that lowers the miners into the depths of the earth to hew the coal that keeps the Bramleys in the life that they are well accustomed too. George has been in the employment of Skinner and Holford as both man and boy. He is in his late forties now and started working underground at Waleswood alongside his father at the turn of the century. He lives in Pigeon Row with his wife and 5 children, the same house that he and his father were born and grew up in. Both his mother and father are dead, his father's life cut short from hard work underground and his mother from complications in childbirth with his youngest sibling, the last of his 9 brothers and sisters. He speaks fondly of his family and strongly supports the views of his late father that Skinner and Holford are the hand that feeds them and are to be respected and obeyed at all times.

Even though Skinner and Holford, like every coal mining company, pushed their work force to produce coal as cheaply as possible in order to maximise their profits, George was grateful for the food on his families table that his labours produced. A miner was paid according to how much coal he produced, not how many hours he worked and his father would often reminisce to George of past times when some miners would take their whole families underground to try to get as much coal as possible so they could earn more money, with each member of the family having a different job to do which would help the miner to get as much coal as possible. Working conditions had begun to improve for George in his early working life at Waleswood and then, after the First World War when a brighter future was envisaged for all he was offered the job of gardener at Wallingfield.

With a workforce of above 1000 at Waleswood Colliery, taking George from the coalface to the relative utopia of the fresh air at Wallingfield was no hardship for the company but a total life changer for George. His workmates were envious but still held huge respect and comradeship for George, as was the way with miners.

On the bench by the side of his chair is Georges enamel billy can along with a small tin of tea leaves and a medicine bottle half full of milk standing ready for his next tea break. All he needs is some boiling water pouring into his billy can from the water heater in the scullery to mash the tea leaves already in the can and a welcoming cup of tea is ready to drink from the enamel cup that fits neatly on top of his billy can when not in use. Three o'clock in the afternoon is tea time along with his 30th or more woodbine cigarette.

The coalhouse has no windows but there is a small door of about 30 inches square at eye level from the lane side. The coal lorry carrying its numerous 1cwt sacks of coal can park on the lane and conveniently discharge its sacks of coal from the back of the lorry and straight through the hatch into the coalhouse.

Door 5 leads us into the washhouse. The room is very neat and tidy and always kept that way by the Bramleys domestic staff. The floor has red and black quarry tiles laid in exactly the same fashion as the kitchen and adjoining rooms in the house. The walls are exposed brickwork and lime washed giving the room a light and airy feel. The chimney breast on the wall facing us as we walk past a storeroom door on the right is dominated by a beautiful Yorkshire range. It's built to last, a real showpiece and a workhorse. Above the Yorkshire range is a clothes airer suspended on ropes that pass through 2 pulleys secured in the ceiling and then to a hook on the wall from where the rack can be lowered and then raised after filling with wet washing that is then left to dry from the rising heat of the fire.

This Yorkshire range is identical to the one at Wallingfield with the clothes airer overhead

A large window on the east facing wall looks out onto the rear yard, the greenhouse (1) and the fields beyond. The trees that surround the kitchen garden that starts some 20 yards further away from the greenhouse are tall and in full summer leaf which obscure the sight of the colliery tip that is clearly visible in the far distance during the winter months when the trees are bare. Beneath the window in the yard and just out of sight, but not sound, is a brick built kennel and compound where the Bramleys hunting dog lives. He is well looked after and very friendly and really does not understand why most of his life is spent behind bars.

Caged

To the left of the window in the corner of the washhouse is the copper. We call it the copper as earlier versions were made of this heat conducting metal but this one is actually made from cast iron and is no less efficient when the fire is lit beneath to heat the water and boil the washing. The small window directly above the copper with its hinges at the bottom and corkscrew stay at the top is left permanently open to allow the masses of steam generated by the copper to escape. Under the window and almost as wide is long shallow earthenware sink fed by a single cold water tap that sits high above the sink and fastened to the central mullion of the window. Expansive stone work surfaces continue from the sink on both sides.

An example of a copper with the sink on the right being very similar to the one at Wallingfield.

The washhouse was our den; it was like having our own house. We cleaned and decorated the walls and were given a table, chairs and old rugs to lie on the quarry tile floor. Under supervision we were even allowed to have a fire burning in the old Yorkshire range. We had running water and a sink and even ate the occasional meal there, brought over on plates from the kitchen. In the summer the sink became our fish pond, full of sticklebacks caught in the ponds around Waleswood pit tip and carried all the way home in buckets.

We leave the washhouse and return to the inner yard. Door 6 on the left is where the dustbins are kept, door 7 leads to the outer yard where the Bramleys dog is still barking and door 8 is the outside toilet. I've saved the best until last, come on let me show you what lies beyond door 3. The opened door reveals a flight of stairs rising up in front of us with a small window at the head of the stairs lighting our passage as we climb the stairs. A door on the right of the 3 feet square landing is closed and as we open it the true spender of what lies beyond is revealed. We are now in the Billiard room.

There are large windows on 3 sides of the room which flood the room with light. Being upstairs the floor beneath our feet is boarded and polished which enhances the quality of the pitch pine flooring. The skirting's, picture rail and cornices are of the same design and quality as the house that I described earlier and the walls between the skirting's and the picture rail are wallpapered in a fine green and white floral pattern._The fireplace surround is tiled and the open fire sits behind an opening made from the same tiles which are now heavily moulded forming an arched ornate top. Above the billiard table is a large light canopy which helps concentrate electric light on the tables playing surface at all times of the day and night. In the corner of the room by the fireplace is a washbasin built in to a cupboard beneath which is tailored perfectly into the woodwork around it.

In the diagonally opposite corner where the room extends over the stairwell there is a table and seating area where resting players and spectators can enjoy the fun.

Obviously not a scene from the Bramleys Billiard Room but in the winter months when tennis on the lawn was suspended an evening in the Billiard room was definitely where the Bramleys gathered to enjoy an alternative ball game and a few drinks.

*During our early years at Wallingfield and before this room became my workshop it was exactly as it had been in the Bramley days but without the billiard table. The decor was fading but the room still reflected its grandeur of earlier days. Each of the windows had fancy pelmets hiding the brass curtain rails from which the curtains, embroidered with fine silk flowers still hung, although the sun had faded the curtains too. A legacy of the Bramley era was lots of apple storage trays that had been left in the room. Come the autumn we would fill them with cooking apples to store, laid on newspaper and making sure that one apple didn't touch the next because we all know that "**One bad apple** can **spoil the whole bunch**". I will always remember the aroma as we entered the room to later select apples to make a pie or, one of mum's favourite puddings. Her signature dish was to remove the core from 3 or 4 large apples, place the unpeeled apples in a Pyrex dish, fill the holes where the core had been with brown sugar, put about 1 inch of water in the bowl and place in the oven to bake for an hour or two. The result was sweet soft apples in a roasted jacket which tasted perfect when covered in custard made from Birds custard powder and fresh milk, and perhaps a spoon full of sugar added too just for good measure.

When our grandparents came to stay the billiard room became their bedroom. The only facility lacking for them was a toilet but of course there was always the Guzunder!!*

I am sure you will agree that following our walk around the garden and tour of the house that Wallingfield is a very special place and the Bramleys are extremely fortunate to live in such wonderful surroundings.

But wait, we have still to visit the kitchen garden or, better still lets view it from up here in the billiard room as the East facing window will give us a perfect bird's eye view.

The kitchen garden lies to the rear of Wallingfields and its shape and size is similar to the land on which Wallingfield stands. The principal difference being that the kitchen garden is surrounded by trees rather than a wall. At the entrance to the garden there is a dog kennel of considerable size, brick built with a pitched, slated roof and a door to the front. It looks like a house in miniature and has been built to the same exacting standards a Wallingfield. To the front of the kennel is a small concreted yard surrounded by metal bars that are identical to the kennel compound we saw earlier. The kennel is empty now but tonight the Bramleys hunting dog will sleep here. To the right of the kennel is a pair of wide wooden gates standing at least 6 feet high. Beyond the gates a red shale path edged with concrete kerbs leads directly to the biggest of the 3 greenhouses at Wallingfield. It stands towards the rear northern corner of the garden against a large brick wall so that full advantage is drawn from the East, South and West where the glazed elevations face. Between the entrance gates and the greenhouse there are 3 vegetable plots of equal length and the same width as the greenhouse which itself is 50 feet wide. These 3 plots are flanked on the left by one single vegetable plot at one end of which is an elevated water storage tank. In the far right corner of the kitchen garden is an orchard of around 20 trees of various varieties. Hidden behind the greenhouse in the bottom corner of the garden is a filter bed system and self supporting treatment plant that caters for all the unmentionables that Wallingfield and the Bramleys produce. If you look to the side of the kennel by the double gateway the two large poles supporting the large metal box is where all the electricity that Wallingfield needs arrives from cables strung high across the fields and linked to Waleswood Collieries power supply, yet more self sufficiency!

So, what am I bid for this incredible country residence called Wallingfield?
But why would the Bramleys possibly consider moving from a grace and favour residence supported in its entirety by Skinner and Holford's Waleswood Colliery and Waleswood Coking Plant, both of which are controlled by Mr Bramley as managing director of both company's?
Sorry, Wallingfield is not for sale.

Before I come to the end of Yorkshire Bred allow me to share with you just a few more memories and adventures of this Yorkshire Bred lad.

Five Cars & A Van

Like nearly all young lads I was keen to pass my driving test as soon as possible. For my 17th birthday my first driving lesson was booked for the princely sum of £1 with Booth and Fishers driving school, the same Booth and Fisher who ran the bus service to Worksop. The thinking back then was to have 10 to 15 lessons by which time proficiency was usually sufficient to apply for the driving test. Then with maybe another 5 lessons you were deemed ready to take your test. I had competed around 15 lessons and still could not get the coordination of clutch and accelerator control correct and try as I might my instructor's car was always full of kangaroo petrol. In frustration I decided to take a break from lessons for a while.

At work, a plumber was selling his car, a Mk1 Cortina with all the trimmings for £240. I wanted that car but had still to pass my test so what to do? I bought the car with the help of premium bonds that my grandparents had bought for me when I was younger and now all I had to do was to find a qualified driver to sit with me while I perfected my clutch control, but who?

Mum offered to be my qualified driver, "but how can you" I said, you can't even drive. "Maybe" she said but I have a driving license that says I can. She explained that she had obtained a provisional driving licence during WW11 and during the war years driving tests had been suspended. After the war they were reinstated but on 18 February 1947, a period of 1 year was granted for wartime provisional licences to be converted into a full licence without the need to pass the test and that was exactly what she did.

Most evenings and weekends me and mum drove round and round Worksop to improve my driving skills and clutch control while hopefully not picking up any bad habits along the way.

Even If I had there was little chance that my "qualified "license holder would have spotted them!

There were no theory tests back then and no knowledge of the mechanics of the car to remember or demonstrate. We were required to read a number plate at 20 paces then drive around town for 20 to 30 minutes which included an emergency stop (when I clap my hands please bring the car to a stop as quickly as possible in a controlled manner i.e. don't skid!), a 3 point turn (touch the kerb and you have failed!), reversing around a corner (my instructor had a sticker in the rear window that read "this car is fitted with He Man dual controls" and he taught all his pupils to pick out the "H" in He Man and make sure that this letter followed the line of the kerb and in doing so the perfect reverse was achieved!), and to navigate at least 1 roundabout before returning to the test centre to answer 2 or 3 questions about the highway code. If all went well a handshake confirmed that the open road was yours but, don't let my simplistic explanation of the test make you think that it was much easier to take and pass your test back then, it wasn't. We went through just the same rollercoaster of emotions that test takers do today and there was no guarantee of a first time pass.

I will always remember as I was returning to the test centre, having driven my examiner around Worksop on what I felt was not an entirely faultless 25 minutes, my examiner asking me to take the next right turn, which I knew would be the last of my test as the turn was by the side of the test centre. I made the manoeuvre and was immediately confronted with a dustbin lorry that was blocking my path. I have always been convinced that the reflex reactions I displayed to negotiate the predicament that faced me blew away any minor faults that I might have displayed during my drive around town. I passed my test on the first attempt and from then on the highways and byways were mine to explore.

I was a careful young teenage driver, keeping to the speed limits, being courteous to other drivers, always keeping my distance from the car in front and above all respecting the weather and road conditions. Well, if you believe that you'll believe anything!!

One wet summer Saturday morning I had driven to Worksop for some reason or another but more than likely simply because I could. I remember as I drove along Gateford Road leading out of Worksop that I had felt the back end of the car "twitch" following a sudden stop and made a mental note to take heed and slow down on the wet road. As I left Gateford the A57 lay ahead of me and now being beyond the 30mph limit I was able to put my foot down, big mistake.

I approached the sweeping bend by Gateford Toll Bar and glided round, first to the left and then to the right and then left and right again and again. I saw the road in front of me and then the road behind me and no matter what I did with the steering wheel nothing happened, at least anything that I wanted to happen! Fortunately and perhaps miraculously there were no other cars in front or behind me as I performed my stunt routine across both sides of the highway, otherwise I may well have not now been sat here telling the tale!

The car stayed upright and on all 4 wheels, well just, even when she left the road and took flight over the raised bank that separated the road from the field of ready to harvest corn before coming to rest some 50 yards into the field. I sat there, staring through the windscreen for what seemed like an age until there was a tap on the window; I heard a voice asking if I was ok and looking round I saw the friendly face of Alan Worsman, a chap I knew from the next village. He opened the door and as I stepped out into the field and looked around the error of my ways came flooding over me. "I saw it all happen, I was travelling behind you, good job there were no more cars near you, you were bloody lucky" Alan said. "Are you sure you are ok? You're trembling like a leaf, it must be the shock". Yep it was shock, and lots more besides!

We managed to get the car out of the field but not without wrecking a good deal more of the ripe harvest crop that had already been flattened by my initial entry into the field and thankfully before the farmer cast eyes on his devastated crop. Back on the road we examined the car and decided that I would be able to drive it home and make a more in-depth study of any damage there.

I am hopefully going to avoid getting too car mechanical here but you have to know the basics of how the front suspension of the majority of cars from the last century worked to understand the problem I later discovered when looking under the bonnet.

The suspension strut on each side of the car at the front incorporates the front wheels and the suspension spring which is held and bolted in place to the inner wing of the car. This system has been tried and tested over many years but in

older cars including the many rust buckets of last century the inner wing often became weak due to rust and consequently so did the suspension.

Once back home I had a good look around the car and taking into account that the car had driven normally on my journey home I thought a good wash and polish would be the end of it, or so I thought. I spent the afternoon cleaning and polishing and eventually forgiving my car for what she had done to me earlier in the day. As a treat I checked her oil and water and that is when I discovered the damage. I lifted the bonnet and to my horror the suspension struts on each inner wing were almost detached from the body of the car. The force applied on them during takeoff and landing in the field together with a degree of existing corrosion had done its worst and it was only luck and the closed bonnet that had been keeping the suspension more or less in place, so what now?

Fielding's scrap yard was our local graveyard for cars and was the first port of call for all car owners who wished to avoid the cost of new car parts, better still they would also fit them for a small fee. By 4pm I was at the scrap yard and following an inspection of my problem it was decided that a bit of welding here and there would make all my troubles go away, phew! Was I relieved or what.

I left the car with them and waited for a call to say the job was done which came the following week.

I rushed back to collect my now roadworthy car and was told that the work had just been finished and it was good to go.

I drove the mile or so back home, pleased that my near disaster of the previous weekend was now behind me. Parking the car I got out, stood back and felt good and my car looked good too, or did it?

I noticed a burning smell and then blue smoke rising from beneath the bonnet, what the -----?

If you pay peanuts you get monkeys and that is just what I had done. The bunch of monkeys that had welded my car had not removed the soft fibre soundproofing from nearby and it was now alight, no doubt ignited from the increasing rush of air as I accelerated on the way home. Without fear of the flames I pulled and tugged at the burning fabric, for once luck was on my side as I managed to somehow stop the flames. I kept the car for another week or two during which time the feeling grew that it had to go and the best way to do that was to put it in part exchange for a different and hopefully trouble free motor.

The Fiat 500 is one of the most popular cars on the road today following its re-launch in 2007 of its iconic predecessor which first took to the Italian roads and their hearts in the 1950's.

And so it came to pass that my first car was part exchanged for a 1967 Fiat 500 complete with fully opening sunroof, the operation of which was not unlike grasping the ring pull of a sardine can and rolling back the lid, come to think of it there is probably as much room inside a sardine can as there was in my Fiat 500. Surely now I was in for some trouble free motoring with little chance of getting into skids spins or speeding as this car was actually incapable of any of these mishaps with its twin cylinder air cooled engine and 0 to 60 performance data that did not even making an appearance in the owner's manual.

I have already made mention of rust problems on cars of this era and British cars had many but continental cars had more with my Fiat 500 being a case in point. I had owned the Fiat for a few months and it was certainly economical to run which allowed me to save quickly and start thinking about buying a real car one more. In its time with me the Fiat 500 accompanied Pamela and myself to London for the weekend where we took it round all the sites, to Great Yarmouth when knickers got in the wrong suitcase and to Blackpool illuminations where the opened sunroof provided an open top tour of the lights. It was a fun car to drive. One day we took the Fiat 500 to Clumber Park for a picnic (that's us not the car!) and finding a suitable spot we pulled off the road onto a grass verge and immediately heard a crunching sound as the car came to an abrupt halt. The original Fiat 500 was low to the ground, not just in overall height but in ground clearance too and on this occasion I had failed to notice a tree stump lurking in the grass which was now showing itself through a large hole it had made through the floor of the car, whoops! It took some pushing and pulling to release the car but the damage caused proved to be severe. It spent a few days at Fielding's where it was patched up by their team of monkeys, some folk never learn but the price was right, and soon after I began my search for car number 3. You will be pleased to hear that my next purchase provided trouble free motoring and was a great pleasure to drive and stayed with me for 3 years until a change in circumstances forced its sale.

 Pamela and myself were married on 3rd of July 1976 and just a few short weeks after I was made redundant. On the 1st of September 1976 I did my first job as my own boss, and as the saying goes, the rest is history.

We now needed a van so my Mk2 Cortina went to a new owner and my love affair with the Ford transit began as I wrote in Bricks and Mortar:-

"Once again, Jeff came to the rescue, Jeff was impressed with my decision to go it alone and gave me loads of reassurance that it was the right thing to do, you have what it takes, and you can make it, were his words of encouragement. Jeff explained that he would be selling his 2

376

vans as they were surplus to requirements and I could have first choice on one of them. That was all very well but I have no money to buy one I said, I'll tell you what, said Jeff, I will sell you a van for £300 and as long as I have the money within 12 months that's fine, also I have a few jobs in the pipeline where I can use you which might help"

My friends EHE 206C, RWB 918E & NET I42G

I have now maintained unbroken ownership of Ford Transits for 42 years and even though I have a limited need for my current Transit van I could not bear to part with her. She is 14 years old this year with the bodywork and mechanics in better condition than many of half her age.

Whilst I loved my first transit, which was our only form of transport for a year or so following our wedding, Pamela started driving lessons and we wanted a car again which is when our Ford Capri came into our lives. What a great car, it looked quite sporty and was good to drive except for one major design fault with which all one time Capri owners will confirm. The car was a hatchback at a time when hatchbacks were quite a novelty and it broke the mould of the usual bonnet and boot design. The Capri had little boot length but did still have a bonnet and what a bonnet it was, being somewhere around half the length of the entire car. There was even a power bulge moulded into the centre of the bonnet giving the suggestion that there was a large and powerful engine lurking beneath while in reality this was only the case for the top of the range model but still it looked good! I have always found it a comfort when driving to be able to see the bonnet stretching forth beyond the windscreen as it gives a sense of distance between you and the road in front and the Capri certainly provided that. However the problem was when approaching the brow of a hill, as the road ahead fell away and descended then all that was visible through the windscreen for a few short seconds was the Capri's bonnet!

From the day I bought my first car I hoped that one day I would be able to afford a brand new one, a car that I would cherish, clean and polish. In 1978 we part exchanged the Capri for our first brand new car, a Vauxhall Chevette. It good owning a new car and the smell of newness for those first few weeks is unforgettable. We enjoyed the Chevette, on one occasion we drove it to the town of Tour in France for a holiday which was our first visit to France and would turn out not be our last!!

Our brand new car was cleaned and polished rarely as I found it a chore. I suspect that like most car owners it is the spit and polish applied that first time after you have bought it and the last time before selling it that are the only times when real TLC are applied.

Transits are forever!
Our Capri had a brown vinyl roof which was all the rage in the 1970's!
The Vauxhall Chevette, our first brand new car

***

Shit off a shovel

Thinking about new cars we were great friends with Bob and
Wendy. I had met Bob at College and Wendy was his girlfriend.
We enjoyed many nights out and the four of us had our first
foreign adventure together in 1975 on a 2 week package tour to
Lloret de Mar in Spain.
Bob was an only child, his dad was a builder and his parents
bought him everything he wanted.
Was he a spoilt brat I hear you say? Perhaps in some ways but he
was a hard worker and we were the best of buddies and the best
of men too as we were each Best Man at the others wedding. For
Bob's 18th birthday his parents bought him a brand new Cortina
Mk 3 GXL in white with a typical 1970,s black vinyl roof and 2
super large CIBIE spotlights mounted on the front grill, it was a
real head turner! The car lasted a couple of years until one day
Bob was driving through traffic lights on green when a car came
through on red and wiped out his Cortina. Thankfully Bob was
unhurt but the Cortina was a right off and worse still, the driver
of the other car was uninsured so Bob's parents had to foot the
bill.
A few months past during which time Bob drove his dads
Chrysler which was a beautiful car but had no street credibility
for a 20 year old Bob. Ford had recently launched a sports
version of their MK2 Escort called the RS2000 and Bob had seen
a special addition model in British racing green being proudly
displayed in the Ford showroom in Sheffield and he wanted it.
What a car that was, shit off a shovel from a standing start. Shit
off a shovel?

This often used description has its origin in the age of steam trains and means Very Fast. In the days when steam trains had a driver and a fireman to load coal and it was necessary to answer a call of nature you would shit on the coal shovel and then throw it in the fire as quick as possible because of smell and hygiene. As the shovel had coal dust on it, the shit did not stick. Interestingly the same shovel could be cleaned with steam and could then be used to cook bacon and eggs.

Bob and Wendy were married in 1976, the same year as Pamela and me. As a wedding present Bob's parents had already given them a plot of land on which they had built a bungalow, all completed and ready to move into following their honeymoon. A while later Bob and Wendy even added a swimming pool to their des res although living on the outskirts of Stocksbridge under the shadows of the Pennines I think their logic in this added open air luxury was somewhat flawed.

Life went on and the superfast, eye-catching, limited edition RS2000 became Wendy's means of transport to and from work in the centre of Sheffield. Not only was the car eye-catching, Wendy was too, she was petite with long brown hair and a real looker. In the rush hour traffic she had a captive audience of wandering male eyes and she loved it. They bought a black Labrador puppy called Zoe and rather than leave the little mite at home Wendy would take Zoe to work every day. One morning Wendy was stuck in the rush hour traffic with Zoe loose in the back seat. Next thing Zoe jumped up onto the parcel shelf between the rear seat and the back window and started pacing from side to side. Wendy spotted her in the rear view mirror and smiled. Zoe's antics caught the attention of other commuters and Wendy lapped up the attention. Next thing Zoe's pacing stopped

as she then positioned herself fairly and squarely in the centre of the rear window and did a great big doggie dump!!
Poor Wendy, trapped in traffic with nowhere to go and no coal shovel either! She found a new route to work after that in the hope that any future embarrassment could be spared.

Almost the same, Bob's Cortina was white and his RS2000 was green

***

Spring Onions and a Summer Wedding

Records confirm that in 1976 a heat wave led to the hottest summer average temperature in the UK since records began. At the same time, the country suffered a severe drought. It was one of the driest, sunniest and warmest summers (June/July/August) in the 20th century. 1975 was hot too and during that year we made our wedding plans. When arranging such an event you hope that the sun will shine but with British weather, who knows? Because 1975 was having such good weather then the law of averages would surely mean that the following year would be wet, wet, wet, so to hedge our bets we plumped for the 3rd of July 1976. At least if it did rain then there was a reasonable chance that it would be warm. As things turned out it didn't rain, in fact it hardly rained from the day we started to plan our wedding right through to our wedding day the following year and beyond.

Records show that from mid-June to the end of August 1976 there were 15 consecutive days of 32c or more recorded somewhere around Britain resulting in the most prolonged period of heat in living memory.

We wanted a church wedding followed by a big reception and evening disco, a fancy wedding limo   too just for good measure! Weddings today with all the trimmings cost an absolute fortune and massive rip off businesses have grown very rich by putting out the idea that the more it costs then the better it will be. According to records from 2017 an average wedding now costs over £27,000!!

Well let me tell you that a fantastic wedding day can be had for a fraction of the cost if you put your mind to it.

We booked St Marks church in Mosborough, the village where Pamela was born and lived. We had to do the whole bit with a visit to the vicarage for the vicar to decide if we were marriage worthy for his church and have the wedding banns announced in the church "and of course you will be coming to the church service to hear your banns being read?", I think we were doing something else that day!

With the date set Pamela got to work with all the arrangements while I worked away on renovating our house in Killamarsh knowing that I now had a deadline to meet, which was also a great way of escaping all things wedding'y.

We booked Killamarsh Village hall for the reception at their standard fee of £20 which also included all kitchen facilities of fridges, ovens, crockery, knives, forks, spoons and all manner of cooking equipment but, we had to provide our own catering.

The Vine pub in Mosborough had a good reputation for outside catering and they were duly booked to provide the food for the reception and my mother in law to be showed her prowess in home baking by providing all kinds of pastries cakes and tarts for the evening do and what a spread they both put on for us. They even did the kitchen clear up at the end of the night!

Flowers, that was an easy choice, Powis's of course. C & A Powis was the type of shop that many local villages were lucky enough to have and none more so than Kiveton Park. Powis's was the kind of shop that should be your first port of call for any type of non food item. More often as not a day's shopping in Sheffield or Worksop would still not find that "specific something" which you felt sure would be available in a large town centre as no one locally could possibly sell such a thing but they did. At the end of the day when you were still empty handed the stock phrase to answer your frustrations was "I bet Powis's will have it", and they did or, if not they would order it for you. Powis's was an Aladdin's cave of hardware, software-pre computer software that is, fancy goods-a name given to items for a gift, and so much more. If that was not enough to keep Mr & Mrs Powis busy they also owned and ran a funeral business from behind the shop. Mr Powis was the funeral director while Mrs Powis was the company's florist, busily preparing wreaths and such fit for a grand funeral send off for folk from Kiveton and roundabout.

As a florist Mrs Powis was much in demand for weddings too. She had already done the flowers for my sister's wedding 3 years earlier so we had no hesitation in booking her for ours. The theme was red roses and she did us proud. Mr Powis was just as versatile, the black limousine that accompanied his hearse at funerals was also available for weddings. One day it would be full of mourners dressed in black and the next it would take on a new identity with the blushing bride dressed in white and two white ribbons stretching across the cars gleaming black bonnet to each side of the windscreen and a colourful floral display in the rear window courtesy of Mrs Powis.

We didn't need Mr Powis and his limousine. Gary Snowden, an old school friend of Pamela's had gone on to work for the family business, Snowdon's garage, based in Mosborough. His father owned a beautiful white Jaguar with interior red leather upholstery and was known to occasionally use it for family and friends weddings. Gary was happy to ask a favour of his dad who was only too pleased to offer the car for our wedding transport. Gary drove Pamela and her bridesmaids to the church and the newly married couple to the wedding reception and to add the perfect touch Gary wore a chauffeur's suit complete with peaked hat. Thanks Gary.

Our Classic Wedding Limousine

A 4pm wedding is the ideal time for the bride, it allows plenty of time to sort out all those last minute hiccups and of course to visit the hairdresser and do all the other bride things that have to be done.

A 4pm wedding for the groom is not ideal as it makes for a very long day of hanging around waiting for the hour and the Alter. What is there to do? Everything is arranged and if there are any last minute hitches how will the groom know? This was 1976, no mobile phones and the public phone in the pub was not much use as which pub has the best man taken the groom?

It wasn't quite like that you will be pleased to hear, Bob got me to the church on time and sober too, no alcohol breath neither, But!

It was 70 degrees Fahrenheit by 10am on the big day. Mrs Powis delivered our button holes mid morning telling us to keep them cool until the last minute or they wouldn't survive. I had spent my last night at Wallingfield and a new life with Pamela beckoned. There were nine of us around the dining table for our pre wedding lunch that mum had prepared. Mum, dad, my sisters Jane and Diane, my brother Andrew, brother in law Steve and my aunt and uncle sat down to a feast of cooked ham, cold beef, tongue and corned beef (the grooms favourite), with a fresh salad of lettuce, tomato, eggs, cucumber, watercress, spring onions, cucumber and onions soaked in vinegar, salad dressings and jars of assorted pickle that mum was so fond of making and so much more. It was the perfect lunch for a hot summer's day and so many of my favourite foods. Cold sliced beef with spring onion, lovely.

We ate at 12 and my best man Bob arrived at 1. With time to spare in abundance Bob took me for a drink. We sat outside the Roland Arms on a wall by the car park drinking shandy and soaking up yet another day of scorching, wall to wall sunshine, and to think that a year earlier we had worried that the hot weather of 1975 would be long gone and rain would spoil our big day!

We returned to Wallingfield in good time to change into our wedding attire complete with fresh cool button holes and we arrived at the church in good time.

Everything went without a hitch, the bride and broom stood together at the front of the congregation and looked into each other's eyes as we said our vows. Without a trace of stale alcohol on my breath I repeated the few short words required to make things legal when prompted to do so by the vicar, Pamela did too and following a visit to the vestry the marriage certificate was completed and we were man and wife, together. As we left the church, Pamela turned to me and spoke the words that every groom longs to hear.

How many spring onions have you eaten today??

The happy couple

The wedding reception was a great occasion with a grand finale of cutting the three tier wedding cake and of course a toast of champagne to the happy couple. The cake then disappeared into the kitchen where the remains were equally cut into fish finger size segments with each piece wrapped in a paper serviette and presented to all the guests as a memento of the day and to eat now, later, or not atall!

The hiatus between the wedding and the evening entertainment is always a problem, guests feel at a loose end, not knowing if there is time to rush home and change into something more comfortable or perhaps the more canny of the guests have brought a change of clothes but wondering where and when should they make the transformation, perhaps the toilets at the reception venue, a fellow guests house that lives close by or even the back of a car! Then there is the added problem of finding a suitable mirror where makeup and hairstyles can be touched up or, if the mirror is not big enough to take stock of the transformation another problem arises. Does my new outfit look good? Is it creased? Is my hair in place? Is my mascara ok? Does my bum look big in this?? You look gorgeous darling is always our response. Us men know which side our bread is buttered! Our 4pm wedding had been chosen to hopefully avoid the break between reception and evening festivities but it did provide Pamela and me the time to slip away and make a pre planned visit to Nether Edge Hospital.

Sadly Pamela's dad, Wilf, was too ill to attend our wedding. He was suffering from Parkinson's disease and had been hospitalised as a result. The hospital wing at Nether Edge was his home and what a depressing place it was, it did nothing to lift the spirit of its residents or their visitors. We drove to Nether Edge still both dressed in our wedding outfits and took ourselves onto the hospital wing. The sight of the bride and groom in such a depressing environment did wonders in lifting the spirits of all those present and it was oh so touching to see Wilf embrace the sight of his daughter looking beautiful and radiant before him. Even though he now looked out on the world before him through the mask of Parkinson's which, to the untrained eye suggested a look of disinterest and even boredom, we knew that he could see happiness before him in the both of us and we too could see in his eyes just a trace of his former self and the happiness our presence had brought him.

In subsequent visits to Nether Edge it was pleasing to see just how much our wedding day visit had lifted the spirits of one particular patient that shared the hospital wing with Wilf. Each time we visited his face would light up and he would continually tell Pamela how lovely she had looked in her wedding dress.

Sadly Wilf lost his fight with Parkinson's disease the following year.

Back at Killamarsh Village Hall the venue had now been transformed with the tables that had been carefully set across the room for our wedding reception earlier now neatly placed around the perimeter exposing the large shiny woodblock floor where the youngest of our wedding party were already chasing back and forth and dancing with each other even though the disco we had booked for the evening was still to arrive.

It had been such a hot day (again) and the July sun had still a way to go before it set on what had been a fantastic wedding day. By 8pm the disco was up and running and the hall began to fill with many of the younger of our afternoon guests together with new arrivals from our circle of close friends and of course our work colleagues. Sisters and Brothers from both sides filled the hall too, some of which now held the younger ones sleeping in their arms, over exhausted from a long day and their antics of chasing and dancing around the room. Our parents, grandma, great aunts, aunts, uncles and other elders were conspicuous in their absence but had already been forgiven as the afternoon had been their time and the evening was for us. A great time was had by all.

Since completing my apprenticeship 2 years earlier I had moved on from my job with Sheffield Public Works Department and taken up employment with local builder Geoff Woodward (read more in Bricks and Mortar). It had been a great career move and had advanced my knowledge of building so far beyond anything that the Public Works could have ever done. We had bought our first house in Killamarsh from Geoff's wife Pam and Geoff had been generous in his help in so many ways to turn the house from a wreck to a home. It will now come as no surprise to you that we had been drawn to our reception venue in Killamarsh as our new home was just a 5 minute walk away!

I had worked on the house for 18 months along with help from many of my work mates at Woodward's and they all came to our evening do together with the entire workforce, and of course Geoff and Pam. You will understand from references to Geoff that back then he was one of my heroes and has remained so ever since. I cannot overstate enough the impression he made on me back then and throughout my working life.

Looking back now the bombshell that Geoff was to reveal just two weeks later to 75% of his workforce, including me, was obviously well known to him a while before our wedding but I feel sure that he had withheld the news until after our wedding in order to avoid a grey cloud over the happy day as that's the kind of good hearted man Geoff was. Ok, so within 2 weeks of starting out in married life we were faced with me having no job and Pamela having to support the both of us but our team effort won through with Pamela providing a steady income while I parted company with Woodward's Builders just 6 weeks into our married life and at the tender age of 22 became my own boss, and 42 years later I still am or, at least I like to think so. As I said Pamela and me are a team and every team has a captain and in this team it isn't me.

We made our way home around midnight with hands full of bags of food that had avoided consumption which we stacked them away in the fridge for another day. I mentioned earlier that the village hall had provided all their facilities within the hire cost and this included the crockery which was a sensible robust set of green plates, cups, saucers and such. In addition to the bags of food there was a full jug of cream that had been forgotten and left in the village hall fridge so we carefully carried the jug home with the full intention of returning the jug to the village hall when empty. It remained on the kitchen worktop, washed and cleaned for a week or two but somehow we did not get round to returning it. Then it joined our selection of crockery in the cupboard as we feared it might get knocked from the worktop and it even got used occasionally. Each time it made an appearance we would say in unison "we must take that jug back". We moved house 4 years later and the jug went with us. As we wrapped it in newspaper ready for our move we looked at each other saying "we must take that jug back". It has now followed us for 42 years through 8 houses and we still use it regularly but one day "we must take that jug back" although I doubt that the green crockery set that it belonged too has stood the test of time as for as long as our jug has. So Killamarsh Village Hall, it has always been our intention to return the jug but after all this time perhaps you will excuse us if "we don't take that jug back".

Our Jug

It's often customary for friends of the bride and groom to set up a "surprise" on their first night together as man and wife in their new home. We had not given this probability a thought as we made our way home with our food rations that were to last us most of the following week. We had forgotten that we were not the only ones with a door key as while renovating the house I had given spares out to some of our helpers, oh dear. We didn't encounter and tricks or mischief as we looked around and made our way to bed and then the thought came to us that our "friends" might have made an apple pie bed, but no all was as it should be. About 3 hours later we both woke with start. Our bed was now leaning at an acute angle where the bed legs had completely collapsed. The "surprise" had worked but not at the time they had planned it too!

An apple pie bed :- a bed which, as a practical joke, has been made with one of the sheets folded back on itself so that a person's legs cannot be stretched out.

***

I Was There

I started my story in 1954, arriving into this world as a baby boomer; the world had started to go through a massive transformation of the likes no one had seen before. With WWII over there was a fresh optimism and a wind of change gathering strength. I have lived my life to date entirely with the reign of Queen Elizabeth II and my life so far has spanned the period when today's popular music came of age. There are so many different styles of music but all have a common thread in that they have their origin in the words written and sung within my lifetime. Music can make you feel happy or sad, infuse energy or relaxation, express feelings and emotions, create memorable moments, sooth pain, promote euphoria and so much more. It is all around us every day, sometimes as a conscious presence other times not but it is always there associating memory's to times and places.

I am not a fan of the many more recent and current genres in music but without the influences of song writers, singer song writers and performing artists of the 50's and 60's there would be no today's music. Equally, classical and many other early forms of music have played their part and still resurface in various ways. Words and music are a miracle of our world. Our western alphabet contains just 26 letters which create the almost endless combinations of words that we speak and write. Western music contains 12 unique named tones and all pitches are one of these 12 tones. There are only twelve starting notes for a key, and with major and minor scales there are 24 tonally unique notes. Just like the words we speak and write then these 24 unique notes are the basis for the almost endless tunes that we listen too.

With using just 50 combined letters and notes the lyrics and music just keeps on coming.

The Beatles and their music was a milestone in the early 60's with words and music that have stood the test of time and I embraced all that they produced but my real taste in music was fired in the summer of 69 (que for song!). A group of us would meet up at a friend's house whose parents were at work all day and we would "hang out" listening to music and drinking cider. This was my introduction to a music genre that was new to me and destined to set my musical preference from that summer onwards.

Singer song writers, Bob Dylan with Blowin' in the Wind, Mr Tambourine Man, Just Like a woman and The Times They Are A-Changin', Simon & Garfunkel singing Homeward Bound, April Come She Will, Blessed, Scarborough Fair, I Am a Rock and the 59th Bridge Street Song and our very own Donavan with Catch the Wind, Colours, and the Universal Soldier to name but a few.

This was easy listening music with a story to tell, this was my music epiphany.

I continued to explore similar artists and gravitated to a hippy style of dress with my hair getting longer and even wearing an Afghan coat. Flower power was my thing; I just loved everything associated with it. Starting work in 1970 tamed my dress sense at work but outside of work I was a hippie, at least as far as it was possible.

My sister Diane was also a fan of my type of music and in the summer of 71 we went to a concert near Lincoln. Generally referred to as The Bardney Folk Festival, it was a one day open air concert held in parkland around Tupholme Manor Park. The concert organisers had provided coaches to ferry the fans arriving at Lincoln train station on to the concert venue and all went smoothly. I remember arriving at the concert into fields packed with tents, cars, and people. Some concert goers had obviously arrived in good time and had camped overnight or longer. I had never seen such a large congregation of hippies all in one place and it felt like coming home. There were all forms of transport parked in no particular sense of order around the park, some of which had also served as overnight accommodation. Battered vans and buses long overdue for the scrap yard looked resplendent in their brightly painted bodywork and served as a base for more people than could have possibly arrived in it. Most of all I remember a hearse, still in black but no longer with shining paintwork that its former owner would have meticulously maintained. As we walked past the back door opened to reveal double decker sleeping accommodation. There had been little or no conversion of the hearse as it had been designed in every detail to fit bodies, but in this case, alive not dead!

Barney Folk Festival, Saturday 24th July 1971.

This poster of the event has become something of a rarity over the years as it seems that very few were printed and then only issued to record shops which were the point of sale for tickets (no online, postal or ticket touts back then!).

Most of the artists appearing at the Festival were new to me but their talents quickly won me over.

James Taylor, Tom Paxton, The Byrds, Tim Harden and Ralph McTell, just to mention a few who have withstood the test of time either through continuing to perform the words and music they wrote or for others to do so. Even back then in the early stages of their careers they were known to perform other songs as well as their own. James Taylor being a typical example with his version of You've Got a Friend making him a household name but being written by Carol King, however the true James Taylor follower knows that his own material is even better. The Byrds, perhaps best known for their version of Mr Tambourine man, borrowed the song from Bob Dylan who sings his original song and lyrics with depth and feeling rather than the Byrds poppy version however hearing either version makes me burst into song. Ralph McTell will always be remembered for "Streets of London" and why not, and Tim Harden, who? Perhaps you have never heard of him but you will know and sing along to the words of two songs that he wrote, "If I Were a Carpenter" and "Reason to Believe".

Tom Paxton, who in my view wrote only one memorable song, an amusing ditty about a wino's love of the bottle which I remember every word of:-

Ramblin' around this dirty old town
Singin' for nickels and dimes
Times getting rough I ain't got enough
To buy me a bottle of wine
Bottle of wine, fruit of the vine
When you gonna let me get sober
Leave me along, let me go home
I wann'a go back and start over
Little hotel, older than Hell
Cold and as dark as a mine
Blanket so thin, I lie there and grin
Buy me little bottle of wine

Bottle of wine, fruit of the vine
When you gonna let me get sober
Leave me along, let me go home
I wann'a go back and start over
Aches in my head, bugs in my bed
Pants so old that they shine
Out on the street, tell the people I meet
Won'ch buy me a bottle of wine
Bottle of wine, fruit of the vine
When you gonna let me get sober
Leave me along, let me go home
I wann'a go back and start over
Teacher must teach, and the preacher must preach
Miner must dig in the mine
I ride the rods, trusting in God
And hugging my bottle of wine
Bottle of wine, fruit of the vine
When you gonna let me get sober
Leave me along, let me go home
I wann'a go back and start over

While the journey to the Festival went without a hitch the journey back was not so smooth. Eventually we got a coach back to Lincoln Station but it was well after midnight and the last train home was long gone. We were in the height of summer but spending a night on the platform at Lincoln Station was not that warm or pleasant. We did eventually get the 6am early Sunday train.

Following the festival the local press wrote:-

On a bright and sunny Saturday, 24th July 1971, Frederick Bannister Productions Ltd, staged a very successful concert of

'Contemporary and Traditional Folk Music', at Tupholme Manor Park. Trains and coaches were overwhelmed with travellers attending this one-day festival. Hudson's Bus Company and Pilgrim Tours were operating a shuttle service from Lincoln station.
The crowd was estimated at 60,000, by Bill Hardy, the local farmer on whose land the event was held, with visitors from as far as Australia and New Zealand.
The organisers described it as a very successful, trouble-free event.
Tickets for the day were £2-00p.

32 years later Pamela and me went to Sheffield Arena to see James Taylor in Concert. His mellow tones floated out across the many thousands of his fans that sat spellbound at his seamless performance. His voice sounded just the same as on his many recordings which surely is the mark of a true genius. Rockabye Sweet Baby James Taylor.

Elton John released "Your Song" in 1970 which certainly got him noticed but was it to be a one hit wonder?
On a cold December evening I queued outside The Sheffield City Hall with ticket in hand to find out.
Following on from Bardney where we sat in a grass field looking at a stage of scaffolding in the distance, Sheffield City Hall was the height of luxury.

Elton John in Concert

At Sheffield City Hall

We had tickets for the balcony which was the tier above the circle and the cheapest seats. It was a case of first in, best seats and we managed to sit high above but close to the stage and below us was Elton's Grand Piano. I say Elton's piano but I suspect that unlike in his later years when his very own piano follows him to every concert the piano back then was the property of the City Hall, never the less he made it talk.

He was as zany back then in 1971 as he is now. As he came out on stage two of his band members followed carrying plates of sandwiches and cans of Coca Cola which they dutifully placed on top of the grand piano. The show started and 2 songs in I knew that Elton was going to be much more than a one hit wonder. He and his band munched through the sandwiches and drank the Coke when time allowed and then Elton took a break from his performance to address his fans. He was far more reserved back then but still a bit wacky and after asking if anyone would like a sandwich or a coke he climbed onto the grand piano and from his elevated position proceeded to throw sandwiches and coke to the audience.

33 years later in 2004 my two daughters took me to see Elton in concert at The Sheffield Arena for my 50th Birthday. He had his own grand piano then and at no point in the show did he climb on to it but his performance was just as exciting after 33 years, and of course he had a much larger back catalogue of material to choose from. I have been fortunate to have watched and listened to his live rendition of "Your Song" twice and both are still as memorable now as the day I first sat in ore of such a great talent, Thanks Elton.

The following year me and Andy, one of my college friends, went to the Buxton Pop Festival. The artists appearing were not turning out my favoured choice of music but it was still worth listening too. Andy also worked for Sheffield Public works and was one of our group who "hit the town" on a Friday night. Back then we got paid on a Thursday and rather than have a bad head from a drink or two that night it was far better to save our big night out until Friday. That said, our mutual employer had a policy that as soon as you reached the age of 18 you could do a

Saturday morning shift and 4 hours overtime at time and a half made a big difference to your pay packet so we had to box clever with Saturday morning shifts. During the week we would be issued with job tickets for various jobs around the Manor housing estate and while there was no written rule as to how long each job would take there was an understanding between all the tradesman as to how much work should be booked in for a complete day. The more job tickets that you asked for the better as it was impossible for our foreman to find us in one of the hundreds of houses on the Manor that we may, or may not, have been working in at any one time, also by working that little bit faster we could "bank" completed jobs and keep them in our back pocket until we needed to cash them.

Saturdays rarely saw physical work done on the estate but there was never a shortage of completed jobs to book in on the following Monday morning to claim our 6 hours for a our 4 hour shift that in many cases had not been worked but instead had been spent sleeping off a hangover in a vacant estate house before returning to the depot to sign out at 12 noon.

Andy lived close by so I would drive to his parent's house and then we would both take the bus into Sheffield as driving into town and then doing the rounds of various pubs was obviously a stupid idea! We all meet up at the Old number 12, a small quite pub and the only one where we could actually speak to each other without having to shout over blaring music! There were plenty of pub stops on out Friday night tour, The Claymore, Black Swan (Mucky Duck), Dove and Rainbow, Stone House, Red Lion, Nelson, Wapentake and the Albert to name just a few which all played different kinds of music but one thing was for sure, by 10pm we had to be in the Buccaneer. The Buccaneer was a cellar bar in the basement of the Grand Hotel in the centre of town and boy did it rock!

It was the first pub in Sheffield to use plastic glasses and it was standing room only. There were no tables or chairs which made even more room for customers. We crammed ourselves in, shoulder to shoulder and sang at the top of our voices to every record that was played. There were so many fantastic hit songs back then but beyond any doubt my everlasting memory of this iconic place was standing shoulder to shoulder with my fellow Buccaneers' and belting out our rendition of Jeff Becks Hi Ho Silver Lining with arms aloft while gripping half full plastic pint glasses of Trophy bitter, great days indeed.

Our pub crawl was over by the time we had spilled out onto Leopold Street at around 11pm and then it was a race to the bus station for the last bus home. Another reason for leaving my car at Andy's was that last bus to Wales Bar left at 11pm whereas Andy's left at 11.30 and the last hour at the Buc was not to be missed! As I mentioned earlier, driving into town for a Friday night pub crawl was a stupid idea hence my car was sensibly left at Andy's and just as sensible was to get a later bus home so that we got the most out of our Friday night. What was not sensible was to have my car waiting at Andy's to get me home in the early hours!

The Buccaneer was closed the following year (1973) to make way for the demolition of the Grand Hotel, it may be long gone but will always remain in the memory of those lucky enough to have experienced its truly unique atmosphere. The Buccaneer holds a very special place in the heart for both Pamela and me for another reason, Its where we met in the Summer of 1972, and 46 years on life is still a Hi Ho Silver Lining.

Actually to say we first met in the summer of 1972 is not strictly true. Around 6 months earlier me and Andy had planned a night out and Andy suggested that we go to a dance that was being held at his old school, Westfield Comp, Mosborough, which seemed like a good idea. We had been there a while and made our move on two girls that seemed to be sitting it out rather than dancing. One of the girls was wearing knee length yellow leather boots in which were a pair of exceptionally nice legs. Anyway, we got talking and I was quickly told that the reason yellow boots was not dancing was that her boot heal had broken. I immediately offered to try and fix it but my offer was politely turned down and soon after Andy and me took our leave which was rather a shame as yellow boots was a stunner.

Many years later Pamela and me were talking about old times and the subject of dances at her old school came up in conversation. I recalled the time when Andy and me had been there and the meeting with yellow boots. Pamela listened to my story and said "are you sure?" " yes I'm sure" I replied. Pamela looked at me and said "that girl in the yellow boots was me!" Anyway, I digress.

Let me take you back to the weekend of 21st July 1972. We got a train out of Sheffield early on Saturday morning having spent the night at Andy's following our usual Friday night drinking session around the city.

We arrived in Buxton by 10 am expecting to connect with the free bus service that the organisers has advertised would be running continuously to the festival site some 3 miles outside of Buxton.

It quickly became apparent that the organisers had got it wrong with the number of buses needed for the thousands that had descended on Buxton which did not go down well with the waiting crowds, us included. Eventually we joined the snake of festival goers making their way on foot to the site which took us about an hour in which time only one bus passed us!

The festival was good and I can say that I have been in the presence of the late great Chuck Berry whose contribution to music during his lifetime is insurmountable.

We planned to get a late train back to Sheffield that night which we had been assured had been laid on specially but it never arrived. I have had many highlights in my life but sleeping in a shop doorway in Buxton town centre is not one of them. We made it home the following day, grateful and wiser for the experience.

Buxton Pop Festival 21st July 1972.

In hindsight, which we all know is a wonderful thing, but sadly is not part of our genetic makeup, we should have instead returned to Bardney two months earlier where the previous year's one day festival had been extended to an entire weekend, and what a line up there was there.

Hindsight is a wonderful thing!

I have many more stories to tell of life as a youngster Bred in a Yorkshire village.
Playing childhood games like husky fusky, stretch and releavio, of climbing trees, nesting, digging tunnels, lighting fires and all things dangerous, eating crisp sandwiches, tomato ketchup or salad cream sandwiches or better still banana sandwiches.
Buying 2 ounces of spice (sweets) from the shop because a

quarter (4 ounces) was too expensive for the few pennies in our pockets. Sweets chosen from an enormous sweet jar on display in the shop window to entice you through the door, sherbet lemons, pear drops, sherbet dips, fruit salads, black jacks, penny bubbly and so many more.

Scrumping in orchards or bull roaring on mischievous night (Halloween and all its commercialism didn't exist back then, for us it was mischievous night and believe me we certainly got up to some but completely harmless of course!) Christmas morning and action toys, train sets, forts, cowboy outfits, football kit and a football or as we knew it then a case ball which if headed on the lacing left an imprint on your forehead. Stamp collecting, remember Stanley Gibbons?

Boring winter evenings, what can I do? Read a book or does a puzzle or, better still get your homework done!

All that and more will have to keep for another day.

If you are reading this then you have reached the end of my book and I hope that Yorkshire Bred has been an enjoyable read, if not then please pass it on to someone else to enjoy.

In Yorkshire Bred I set out to write about my early years and feel content that I have achieved my goal yet Yorkshire Bred has turned out to be so much more than an autobiography. It contains Humour and History, Facts and Family, Thrills and Spills, Sadness and Joy, and above all the Spirit of adventure that life offers in bucket loads. Life's adventure is the only one on offer so grasp it with both hands and enjoy it.

I think I may have mentioned somewhere in these pages that Yorkshire Bred is the prequel to my first book "Bricks and Mortar" which I wrote 10 years ago, I find it hard to believe just how fast those 10 years have gone. If you have already read Bricks and Mortar then you know what happens next but if not then please indulge yourself and buy a copy now to see where life goes from here.

Even more exciting news is that book 3, as yet untitled, is already in my head and ready to be told!

With Bricks and Mortar I was forced to take time out from a busy life for a few months which gave me the time to write. Now 10 years on, my retirement has given me the opportunity to do what I want to do rather than what I have to do so I'm able to write again, and what a pleasure it's been.

Rest assured that you will not have to wait another 10 years for book 3 as writing has been a great joy for me over these winter months and next winter is already set aside for more of the same. There are already signs of spring in our garden and the days are getting longer. Here in our corner of France spring comes early and autumn stays late, I can already feel the draw of the garden and can't wait to get out there and while I revel in the joys of nature that we fight to tame each year, in my head I shall be putting the finishing touches to book 3, ready to transfer into print next winter.

This is not the end but just a pause before my next book !

L - #0225 - 200420 - C0 - 210/148/22 - PB - DID2816868